CICERO
ON MORAL OBLIGATION

A new translation
of Cicero's 'De Officiis'
with Introduction and Notes
 by

JOHN HIGGINBOTHAM

FABER AND FABER LTD
24 Russell Square, London

*First published in mcmlxvii
by Faber and Faber Limited
24 Russell Square London WC1
Printed in Great Britain by
Latimer Trend & Co Ltd Plymouth*

To Martin Wight,
whose suggestion inspired
and whose encouragement sustained
the writing of this book

Acknowledgements

The brief survey of influences on Cicero's thought and of Cicero's influence on others involved consulting more books and works of reference than could possibly be mentioned here. I am mainly indebted to the introduction and notes to Holden's text, the excellent collection of source material in C. J. de Vogel, *Greek Philosophy—a selection of Texts* (Leiden, 1950), R. R. Bolgar, *The Classical Heritage and its Beneficiaries* (Cambridge University Press, 1954), *Cicero* in the *Studies in Latin Literature series*, edited by T. A. Dorey (Routledge and Kegan Paul, 1965), Michael Grant, *Cicero—Selected Works* (Penguin, 1960) and the *Oxford Classical Dictionary*, whose firm scholarship piloted me through many troubled waters. The errors that remain are my own.

J.E.H.

Contents

Preface   *page* 11

Introduction   13

Synopses   31

Text
  BOOK I   39
  BOOK II   99
  BOOK III   137

Notes   185

List of Cicero's Works   206

Index of Proper Names   209

Preface

The *De Officiis* of Cicero is one of the great watersheds of European thought. It gathers together the philosophy of the post-Aristotelians, Stoics, Academics, Cyrenaics and Epicureans, selects much that is valuable and discards much that is not. This selection and transmission of ideas had an enormous influence on subsequent European thought from the early fathers down to modern times.

It is for these two reasons rather than the intrinsic merits of the work as a piece of thinking that the need for an up-to-date translation has long been felt. The work was originally intended, ostensibly, by Cicero for the instruction of his son, Marcus. It is a handbook of good conduct rather than a cogently-argued philosophical discourse. This has been borne in mind in the translation, which has been kept as non-technical as possible. Free use has been made of synonyms—reflecting Cicero's own variety in his use of terms—and much of what is purely rhetorical or pleonastic has been rigorously pruned. Two examples may perhaps suffice to illustrate the translator's approach. In Chapter 2 of the first book *tradita* and *praecepta* mean no more than *teaching*; *ibidem*, the phrase *neque forensibus neque domesticis* is a mere repetition of *neque publicis neque privatis*, and therefore the point has not been laboured. This may help to explain the freedom of translation and apparent omissions which occur at some points, and which have been found necessary to produce a readable twentieth-century version.

The text used is that of Holden (Cambridge University Press, 1869) except where otherwise stated. The main doubts about the state of the text centre not so much round *variae lectiones* as round the numerous glosses and marginal notes. These seem to reflect the haste in which the work was produced and the almost-certain fact that Cicero left it unrevised. There is no good reason for believing them to be later interpolations and they have therefore all been included in the translation.

11

Introduction

1. *Cicero the Philosopher*

Cicero's work *On Moral Obligation* (*De Officiis*) represents both the culmination of his ideals as a statesman and his failure as a politician. His retirement from Rome took place towards the end of March 44 B.C., soon after his undisguised jubilation at Caesar's murder had given way to disillusionment at the failure of Brutus and Cassius to restore the former dignity of the Republic, and disgust at being debarred by Antony from public life.

It was not an accident that he should have turned to philosophy after the collapse of his ideals as a politican. The inclination had long been there:[a] the *De Re Publica* of 51 contained one of the finest summaries ever written of the concept of eternal, immutable law of which all tyrants are violators.[b] In fact, the most interesting facet of Cicero is that he is the only statesman of the Roman world to have left us a comprehensive account of his political ideals. He explains at the beginning of the second book of *De Officiis* the reasons for his enforced political inactivity, and makes it quite clear that although the political life was his first calling, he was unable to lead a life of idleness when debarred from it, and so felt himself obliged to turn to philosophy. Thus, in the course of the summer of 44 B.C. he completed the *Tusculanae Disputationes*, on which he had been working for some time, and the *De Natura Deorum*. The same period also saw the writing of essays *De Amicitia*, *De Senectute*, *De Divinatione*, *De Fato* (of which only fragments remain), *De Gloria* (not extant) and, finally, the most comprehensive and influential of his philosophical works, *De Officiis*.

It is a work redolent with the spirit of disillusionment with the times—which was not new to Cicero. 'O Tempora, O Mores,' had been his battle-cry in 63, the high watermark of his self-appointed role as saviour of the Republic, and almost every schoolboy who has

---

[a] *Vd. De Divinatione*, II, 7.   [b] *De Re Publica*, III, 33.

ever learned Latin knows that most unbeautiful line of verse with which he celebrated his achievement. But now he speaks of the ruin of the state,[a] of the pernicious influence of Caesar still remaining after his death,[b] and of Antony's reign of terror which has driven him from both politics and the bar.[c] Thus it is clear that to Cicero philosophical writing is a second-best pastime for a man whose taste is by nature for the active life of politics.

Herein lies the clue to the understanding of Cicero the Philosopher, who was not so much concerned with metaphysics, logic and the theory of knowledge, as with living the good life. It has often been fashionable to deride him for this, as though ethics were the only suitable study for the down-to-earth, practical Roman, who knew his place and left the other and higher branches of philosophy to the Greeks. Nothing could be further from the truth. Cicero himself paid tribute to Socrates for his down-to-earth approach to philosophy in a famous passage in the *Tusculanae Disputationes*: 'Socrates was the first', he says, 'to bring philosophy down to earth, to establish it in cities, to bring it into the home and to make it the study of life and morals, of good and evil.'[d] In his *Academica Posteriora* he defines his aim *qua* philosopher as 'to introduce to Latin literature that branch of philosophy which started with Socrates'.[e] Ethics with him always comes first, and he is as quick to condemn the philosophical study of difficult and abstruse subjects which yield little practical result[f] as he is to praise the study of moral obligation as the richest and most fruitful field for thought.[g]

Although it is true that Socrates was the inspirer of his quest, it was to the Hellenistic schools that he owed his material. Cicero was not a thinker of great originality, and his works are primarily valuable as a commentary on and a critique of the values current in the ancient world. Not that he was solely an eclectic: he makes it quite clear in the *De Officiis*[h] that he is not going to follow Panaetius slavishly as mere translator; moreover, as he explains in a letter to Atticus, although he accepts Panaetius' framework as a beginning he is sufficiently critical of it to modify it to suit the needs of his own thought.[i] For example, Panaetius discussed moral goodness and expediency independently, but did not consider the conflict which often arises, or appears to arise, between them. Cicero addresses

[a] *De Officiis*, II. 1. [b] Ibid., II, 7. [c] Ibid., III, 1.
[d] *Tusc. Disp.*, V, 4, 10. [e] *Acad. Post.*, 3. [f] *De Officiis*, I, 6.
[g] Ibid., III, 2. [h] Ibid., I, 13. [i] *Ad Att.*, XVI, 11, 4.

himself to this in Book III of *De Officiis*, citing *inter alia* the example of Regulus. The famous general had gained release from captivity in Carthage to go to Rome and discuss the return of certain leading Carthaginian prisoners, promising that he would himself return if he did not secure their release. In Rome he advised against the return of the prisoners and chose instead to go back himself, on the grounds that the prisoners were more valuable to Rome than he was.

I have quoted this example, as Cicero did, because it illustrates what lies at the root of his thought: should we act according to moral principle, or expediency, or regard them as one and the same? It is important to note Cicero's approach to such a problem, as the method is very much the man. His life and training were that of a barrister. In this, the culmination of his political philosophy, he rejects the dialogue form of his earlier works, and, with it, any claim to inquire into a subject impartially; he is pleading a case, not acting as judge. He does so under the guise of a father instructing his son. 'I am addressing Cicero,' he says in a letter to Atticus. 'After all, on what better subject could a father instruct his son?'[a] The form, then, is an indication of serious intention; after a number of 'composition pieces' written in the style of a Platonic dialogue, he sheds the form, in which he had never been happy, and which, as most modern commentators agree, he had never succeeded in bringing to life, and expresses his meaning in the form of advocacy of which he has always been an acknowledged master.

2. *Sources*

So much for form. Any consideration of Cicero's matter requires some knowledge of the philosophical schools whose teachings he attacked or accepted. Let us start with Cicero's own summary of the beliefs of the two main philosophical schools to which he was attracted and between which he wavers. At the beginning of Chapter 3 of Book III he says that the Stoics believed that to do what is right is the *only* good, whereas the Peripatetics believed that it is the *highest* good.

Right action was to the Stoic the sole aim of life, because it is good, not because of what it produces, be it wealth, pleasure or the like, but good in itself. How was this perfect good to be attained? The teaching of Zeno of Citium (335–263 B.C.), the founder of Stoicism, and his successors, Cleanthes and Chrysippus, was concerned

[a] Ibid., XV, 13, 6.

with the pursuit of virtue, by which alone the perfect good was to be attained. Man, alone of all creatures, was endowed with reason, the purpose of which was to lead him to virtue, the logical goal of his own nature. Hence the equation formulated by Diogenes Laertius that living according to the demands of virtue meant living according to nature.[a] The concept of natural law is found in Greek thought long before Zeno. Heraclitus[b] regarded all human laws as 'nurtured by' divine law. Plato[c] speaks of a transcendent divine reason which can only be apprehended by man through participation. Cicero probably had this in mind when he speaks of law as being 'that supreme reason (ratio summa), embedded in nature, which orders what must be done and forbids the reverse'.[d] The authority of empirical law is attacked in Tusculanae Disputationes[e] where Chrysippus' examples of immoral laws are quoted.

Cicero's reference to the need to keep the more violent emotions (πάθη) and the appetites (ὁρμαί) in check[f] and the fact that he regarded restraint generally as an aspect of Virtue owed a good deal to Stoicism. Diogenes Laertus[g] defines πρώτη ὁρμή (primary impulse) as self-preservation. To look after oneself is natural, but what of parents, children, friends etcetera? Are they not to be seen as an extension of one's own being? Hence the Brotherhood-of-Man concept found a dominant place in the thought of later Stoics such as Epictetus and Marcus Aurelius. We see the practical application of the doctrine, known as oikeiosis, in De Officiis.[h] In De Finibus[i] Cicero applies it to the human race as a whole, but excludes animals as they do not possess reason. He does not, however, mention slaves. It was left to Seneca[j] to point out that no one was a slave by nature.

The whole of human society, then, is to be seen as a unit. Moreover it is a natural, not an artificial unit. Cicero argues this point at some length at the end of Book I of De Officiis.[k] There are two complementary results of this: not only is each man by nature dependent on others around him,[l] but also he must be aware of the dependence of others on himself and act accordingly.[m] This includes regarding all things produced by nature for man's use as to be shared for the

[a] D.L., VII, 87.
[b] Fragment, 114 (Diels).
[c] Laws, 716c.
[d] De Legibus, I, 6, 18.
[e] Tusc. Disp., I, 45, 108.
[f] De Officiis, II, 5 ,18.
[g] D.L., VII, 85.
[h] De Officiis, I, 7, 22, I, 16, 50
[i] De Finibus, III, 19, 62 et seqq.
[j] De Beneficiis, III, 28.
[k] De Officiis, I, 44, 157 et seqq.
[l] De Officiis, II, 4, 13.
[m] Loc. cit. (h.)

general good. Thus nature lay at the root of Stoic belief. What was according to nature was good, what was contrary to nature was bad. Virtue was by definition *living according to nature.*

The results of this creed were twofold: first, as right action was to be pursued for its own sake and not for pleasure, as the Epicureans thought, a great stress was placed on political activity; secondly, it led to that indifference to every worldly condition, whether pleasurable or painful, which has ever since been described by the word '*Stoic*'. Thus not only was pleasure not regarded as good, but pain was not regarded as evil; in fact the only things to be regarded as good were those which were morally good, and *vice versa.* Moreover Stoicism did not admit of degrees: all good men were equally good and all wise men equally wise. Naturally this rather austere doctrine in time underwent modification, and it was Panaetius of Rhodes (185–109), founder of what is generally known as the 'Middle Stoa', who led the way. He pointed out the rigidity of the 'Stoic Paradox' which led to the absurd conclusion that only the perfectly good could live the good life, or even do a single good action. This led to a distinction between absolute or perfect obligation (*officium perfectum*), which could only be fulfilled by the man who was wholly good and wholly wise, and secondary or middle obligation (*officium medium*), which could be fulfilled by other men when acting in conformity with law and reason. Moreover absolute obligation is to be obeyed at all times, whereas secondary obligation admits of variation according to circumstances. Cicero recognizes this distinction when he points out that the fulfilment of a promise is normally obligatory,[a] but not invariably, for example when the fulfilment of a promise is to the detriment of the promiser or promisee.

Cicero based his work on the *three categories* of Panaetius. These were: first, the division of actions into those which are morally good and their opposites; secondly the division of the expedient from the non-expedient; and thirdly the discussion of conflicts arising between goodness and expediency and how to resolve them. But he goes a good deal further than Panaetius in three ways: first, whereas Panaetius only actually dealt with the first two categories and neglected (for reasons about which even Cicero can only speculate) the third, Cicero makes the third the nub of his whole work; secondly Cicero expands Panaetius' *three categories* into *five* by subdividing the first two as follows: the first is subdivided into (*a*) the study

[a] *De Officiis,* III, 31.

of what is morally good and what is not, (*b*) a comparative study of different goods, while the second is subdivided into (*a*) the study of what is expedient and what is not, and (*b*) a comparative study of different expedients; thirdly, Cicero claims in his third book to resolve the conflict between moral good and expediency by showing any such conflict to be illusory. The idea that Panaetius' categories needed expanding was sound enough, but Cicero does less than justice to the two new categories he creates, especially that dealing with the conflicts between expedients which he dismisses very superficially in one short chapter at the end of Book II.

Panaetius' successor, Posidonius of Apamea (*c.* 135–50 B.C.), further developed and 'Romanized' the Stoic concept of Natural Law. He argued that if this law exists by nature in every human being and is identified with Divine Providence, of which each man possesses a spark within him, then it unites all men in a universal brotherhood or world state (*cosmopolis*) which Posidonius equated with the Roman Empire. It is clear from at least one passage in the *De Officiis*[a] that Cicero had read Posidonius' work, but in view of the fact that he appears to have done so only in order to solve the problem of why Panaetius omitted his third category, it does not seem likely that he borrowed much from him. Besides, it is clear that he regarded Panaetius as the master in this field, since he quotes with approval a remark of Publius Rutilius Rufus, a pupil of Panaetius, that just as no one had been able to complete the unfinished painting of Venus of Cos by Apelles because of the beauty of the face, so no one could complete Panaetius' work because what he had written was so outstanding.

In Book III Cicero draws on an essay of Hecato of Rhodes, a pupil of Panaetius, for examples of the clash between right and expediency, but although he approves of Hecato's questions, he does not always agree with the answers.[b] Above all he rebuts as less than just the idea that a wise man is justified in consulting his own interests provided that this involves no contravention of law, morality or established institutions.

Cicero owed a great deal to the successors of Panaetius as heads of the Middle Stoa—practical, down-to-earth men like Diogenes of Babylon and his pupil, Antipater of Tarsus, who applied the Stoic ethic to everyday problems of commercial conduct. The striking contrast between the thorough-going morality of Antipater and the

[a] *De Officiis*, III, 2, 8, *et seqq.*   [b] Ibid., III, 23, 89.

rather negative, legalistic approach of Diogenes introduces a lively element of dialogue into what might have descended to rather flat moralizing (as it is, the multiplicity of examples becomes rather tedious); moreover, Cicero presents their arguments in such a way that the shining principle of Antipater stands out against the murkier background of apparent expediency which is invariably Diogenes' approach, so that he merely causes us to smile when he comes to the point of recording his own opinion. We are again reminded that we are hearing no judge's summing-up, but the voice of Cicero the advocate.

The main lines of Cicero's treatment of his Stoic sources are now apparent. Hardly any of his material is original, yet he does not follow his predecessors naïvely or uncritically. The shortcomings of Panaetius, Hecato and Diogenes are all pin-pointed. Only Antipater wins consistent approval for views which invariably reflect the more austere Stoic approach. His degree of reliance on the Stoics and his own independence are brought into focus in his own statement in Book I: 'I have particularly followed the Stoics, not as a mere translator, but using them as a source by selecting from them in whatever quantity and manner I thought fit.' Nor do we rely on Cicero's own testimony to his independence; Aulus Gellius[a] speaks of him as a rival to Panaetius, while Pliny the Elder in the preface to his *Natural History* refers to his work as one worth not just possession, but thorough study[b] for its own sake.

Whereas the Stoics believed virtue to be the only good and therefore to be pursued for its own sake, the Peripatetics merely defined it as the highest good. Cicero mentions this fact *en passant*[c] and does not appear to have laid great store by the distinction. In fact, although he took the Stoic Panaetius as his model, he says that his own theories 'are not much different from those of the Peripatetics, since we are both followers of Socrates and Plato'.[d] It may be, of course, that Cicero was fully aware of the differences between the Stoics and the successors of Aristotle, but wanted to play them down, so that his own primarily Stoic views should not seem to his son to be at variance with those of his Peripatetic teacher, Cratippus, on whom he bestows lavish praise.[e]

Much more likely, however, Cicero was pursuing a deliberately

---

[a] *Noct. Att.*, XIII, 287. [b] *Nat. Hist.*, 22.
[c] *De Officiis*, III, 3, 11. [d] Ibid., I, 1, 2.
[e] Ibid., II, 2, 8.

Academic line in welding together the good points of both schools into a single coherent whole. To understand the thought of the so-called 'New Academy' it is necessary to look back to the original Academy and its founder, Plato. Plato lived in an age of scepticism when traditional morality was under attack. His primary concern was to establish morality on a firm rational basis, and he saw that this could only spring from a firm knowledge of the universe itself. To this there were two obstacles: first, he accepted Heraclitus' dictum that everthing is in a constant state of flux, and saw that because of this it was difficult to make any statements about this world which are permanently valid; secondly, even if there were any truths that are permanently valid, how could they be known? Plato thus founded epistemology as a distinct branch of philosophy, and it was in an attempt to solve the first of these problems that Plato put forward the idea of the existence of a world of forms, which would be the source of all concepts such as mathematical axioms, which we be-lieve to be eternally true, as well as of physical objects which he regarded as copies of eternal prototypes.

Practically all Plato's successors found it easier to accept Plato's views about mathematics than his concept of eternal 'forms'. Hence the concentration upon mathematics, accompanied by a sceptical approach to any dogmatism about ethics, which characterized the Middle Academy under Arcesilaus of Pitane (315–241 B.C.) and Carneades of Cyrene (214–129 B.C.). Scepticism, however, should not be confused with nihilism. The aim of a sceptic is not to destroy ethical hypotheses, but to undermine the certainty with which they are held, and substitute probability in its place. The main attacks of Carneades were therefore against the *other-worldly* certainty of Plato and the *this-worldly* certainty of the Stoics and Epicureans, resulting in an ethical code based on probability and common sense. Cicero was much influenced by this undogmatic approach, of which we see a definitive statement in Book II of *De Officiis*.[a] We also see a full account of the Academic position in the *Academica*, a work which was originally drafted in two books (*Academica Priora*), but was subsequently revised and divided into four (*Academica Posteriora*). Unfortunately we do not possess both works *in toto*; all that survives is the second book of the first edition, which deals with the Stoic arguments in favour of certain knowledge about the world based on the reliability of sense-perception and the Academic refuta-

[a] Ibid. II, 2, 7–8.

tions of them, and a part of the first book of the second edition, which is of considerably less interest because the account of the views of Arcesilaus and Carneades themselves is lost. An interesting passage in *Academica Priora*[a] explains Carneades' teaching on the need to accept probability as a guide to moral conduct. Cicero uses a similar argument in the *De Officiis* to refute the criticisms of those who claimed that as a sceptic he had no right to lay down moral rules.[b]

Cicero's position, then, is essentially that of an eclectic. The doctrines of Epicurus, as I shall show later, were the only ones which he rejected out of hand. His opposition to Stoic metaphysics did not preclude him from accepting much of its ethics, which he did not regard as being significantly different from Peripatetic teaching; he admired the concentration of Plato and Socrates on ethics and their abandonment of the rather arid study of physics which had exercised their predecessors; but above all, he is a reconciler of different schools even to the point of blurring their differences. In this he was influenced by two successive heads of the 'New Academy', Philo of Larissa (160–80 B.C.) and Antiochus of Ascalon (130–68 B.C.) under both of whom he had studied. Antiochus was the more dominant influence; on taking over the Academy after Philo's death in 80 B.C. he rejected the sceptical approach of his predecessors up to Philo, and proclaimed a return to the teachings of the original Academy which he regarded as the source of all the various rival doctrines. The claim was bogus enough: it was in fact simply a cloak for an eclecticism which embraced the epistemology of the Stoics and the ethics of the Peripatetics; this he attempted to justify by claiming that there had never been any difference between Aristotle and Plato on ethics, while the Stoics had borrowed from both, their only innovations being those of nomenclature.[c]

The influence of Antiochus on Cicero is apparent in the ability of the latter to support the austere ethic of Stoics like Antipater, to commend to his son the teaching of a Peripatetic, Cratippus, and still to regard himself as an Academic. This intellectual contortion leads to a number of serious flaws in his work, notably the inconsistency of accepting Stoic ethics while rejecting the metaphysics on which they were based, and an inconsistency in his attitude to the Peripatetics; for at the very outset of *De Officiis* he says that there

[a] *Acad. Pri.*, II, 31, 99.   [b] *De Off.*, II, 2, 7.
[c] *Vd. De Finibus*, V, 8.

are no significant differences between their views and his, and yet his identification of expediency with moral good in Book III is a Stoic rather than Peripatetic judgement. His claim to identification with the Peripatetics is further belied by a passage in the *Tusculanae Disputationes* in which he says, 'The same Peripatetics say that those emotions which we think are to be rooted out are not only natural, but are conferred upon us by nature for our advantage.'[a]

Having examined some of the tangled cross-threads of Cicero's thought, let us now turn to those threads which were altogether excluded from the tapestry, and in particular the thought of 'The Garden', founded by Epicurus of Samos (341–270 B.C.). Like the Stoics, the Epicureans accepted the validity of sense-perception, but they were alike in very little else. Epicurus taught that the world was composed of material atoms and nothing else; the gods, if they existed at all, lived a life utterly remote from any concern for humanity, while for man himself the only world was that of the here and now. Hence to the Epicurean the only goal worth seeking was pleasure, which was to be identified not with abandoned self-indulgence (which was just as abhorrent to the Epicurean as to the Stoic), but with the absence of pain and trouble. The Epicurean therefore believed in non-involvement in public life and in all forms of cultural activity. Cicero's close friend Atticus obeyed the former, but not the latter. Cicero himself had in his youth admired the Epicurean philosopher Phaedrus, but The Garden never held out any real temptations simply because there was so little in its teachings that he found acceptable. In the *De Natura Deorum* he states the arguments for and against belief in Divine Providence, but his eloquent pleading of the oft-since-repeated argument from design leaves no room for doubt about his own convictions. Moreover, the closing sentence with its contrast between religion and superstition is clearly an implied criticism of the case for Epicureanism as presented by Lucretius. The '*Somnium Scipionis*' contains a Platonic 'proof' of the immortality of the soul with all the moral injunctions which it involved. Above all Cicero's high ideals of public service (summarized in *De Divinatione* as 'service to the largest number possible')[b] were diametrically opposed to that freedom from care which was the ideal of Epicurus.

Thus it is clear that Cicero was a discriminating adopter and critic

[a] *Tusc. Disp.*, IV, 19, 43.
[b] '*Prodesse quam plurimis*', *De Div.*, II, 1.

of other philosophies rather than an original thinker of any depth. His importance lies in the fact that by his power of words he was able to popularize ideas which but for him might not have gained such wide currency. About the latter point one can, of course, only speculate; what cannot be challenged is the enormous influence of Cicero on later thought—and it is to this that I shall now turn.

3. *Cicero's Influence*

Cicero's immediate influence was in the sphere of style rather than of ideas. Livy remarked that it would require a second Cicero to give him due praise. Quintilian commended him as a model for the young orator.[a] But to the young thinker Cicero's cautious wisdom sounded too much like the staid voice of a previous generation, and he lost favour first to the prevalent Epicureanism propagated by Lucretius, and, under the early empire, to the cynicism which greeted any well-thought-out philosophical system. One has only to read the satirical writings of Lucian to see the 'old philosophies', particularly the thought of Socrates, Plato, Aristotle and Chrysippus, mercilessly pilloried.

It is one of the surprises of history that Cicero had a greater influence on Christian thinkers than on pagans in the following centuries. Lactantius, dubbed the *Christian Cicero*, and Minucius Felix both admitted that their treatises owed much to him in both form and content. The former, in particular, drew on *De Officiis*, which he adapted to the needs of the Church, and he was closely followed by St. Ambrose in his treatise *On the Obligations of Ministers*.

St. Jerome and St. Augustine both found themselves in a dilemma. They were fascinated by Cicero, and yet saw his work as a pagan temptation which was to be resisted. St. Jerome tells in one of his letters how as a result of his over-zealous study of Cicero he saw himself in a dream arraigned before the judgement seat of God with the words, 'You are a liar; you are no Christian, but a Ciceronian; where your heart is, there is your treasure also.'[b] St. Augustine in the *City of God* was primarily concerned with refuting Cicero's idea that there is a supreme good which can be attained in this life. One by one Augustine examines the *Four Cardinal Virtues* as expounded in Book I of the *De Officiis*, and argues that as long as each is a purely mortal virtue unhallowed by the grace of God, it falls short of the supreme good. On the other hand the Stoic concept of Virtue as

[a] *Institutiones Oratoriae*, X, 1, 102.   [b] *Epist.*, XXII, 30.

'Living according to Nature' (very probably gleaned from Cicero) is found in *De Lib. Art.*, III, 13, 38.

It can be argued that the most important feature of the writings of the Fathers as regards Cicero is not that they were influenced by or rejected his ideas, but that they preserved and transmitted the philosophy of Natural Law which was to form such an important part of the doctrine of the Church. The Church's resistance to Cicero which we saw in Jerome and Augustine reached its climax with Pope Gregory the Great, who wanted to destroy his works because he saw in them formidable rivals to Holy Writ, a judgement probably as much a compliment as a condemnation. It was mainly due to such ecclesiastical resistance that Cicero's influence came under partial eclipse until restored by the Carolingian Renaissance in the ninth century. Einhard in his introduction to his *Life of Charles the Great* refers to Cicero *qua* philosopher and quotes from the *Disputationes Tusculanae*, a work in which there seems to have been a great deal of interest, if one can judge from an extensive collection of manuscripts made at this period by Servatus Lupus. Moreover, Carolingian manuscripts of all Cicero's extant works survive.

It was from the eleventh century that Cicero's influence started to rise to the zenith which it ultimately reached with its remarkable contribution to the Renaissance Ideal. His common-sense, undogmatic approach to philosophical problems appealed to the rising professional classes, who sought not the subtleties of metaphysics, but a practical code for daily living. But it was just as much, if not more, as an orator and master of Latin style that Cicero was cultivated. His handbook of rhetoric, *De Inventione*, took its place in the rhetorical curriculum of schools during their great period of expansion in the twelfth century. Another handbook, the rhetorical treatise *Ad Herennium*, then mistakenly attributed to Cicero, shared its prestige. It is significant that in spite of the interest in rhetoric at this period Cicero's speeches seem hardly to have been read at all. What evidence we have points to the wide currency of the two works mentioned above as well as the *Disputationes Tusculanae*, *De Officiis* and the two short essays, *De Senectute* and *De Amicitia*. The Tusculans were recommended by Meinhard of Bamberg in the eleventh century, while the ethical code of *De Officiis* is to be found in the works of William of Conche of the School of Chartres in the early twelfth century. His pupil, John of Salisbury, followed *De Officiis* in accepting the 'probable' as a basis for ethics rather than claiming any

24

means of intellectual certitude. Hildebert of Lavardin, living at the turn of the century, shows in his treatise *On Moral Goodness and Expediency* a substantial debt to the same source, while Marbord of Rennes and Conrad of Hirschau show familiarity with the two essays.

In an age abounding with literary figures of note John of Salisbury stands out as the greatest. On him the influence of Cicero was a strong and lasting one. He declared that Cicero was his favourite Latin author, and as a politician would have been the greatest of the great had his conduct matched his thought. Clearly he found in Cicero a style on which to base the pure Latinity for which he himself became famous, a fount of humanistic ideals, and a protagonist in his own opposition to philosophical dogmatism. It is significant that *De Officiis* was among the books which he bequeathed to the School of Chartres on his death in 1180.

Towards the end of the twelfth century Alexander Neckham included among his recommended reading the *Tusculans*, the *Stoic Paradoxes* and the two essays as well as *De Officiis*. One is left to speculate on how far this means that they were read, or whether it was merely a plea that they ought to be read. Certainly the two essays were largely responsible for Cicero's great reputation as a humanist in the thirteenth century. They were the principal sources for the love romance *Roman de la Rose* which also shows borrowings from the '*Somnium Scipionis*' in the *De Re Publica*. They also exercised an influence on Dante whose references to Cicero are invariably *qua* philosopher rather than *qua* orator or politician. We find him in Limbo where the unbaptized but virtuous pagans dwell,[a] but his most important memorial comes later when the classification of sins is based on the violation of the Four Cardinal Virtues as laid down in Book I of *De Officiis*.[b] Aquinas quotes Cicero in the *De Regno*, and his account of natural law in the *Summa Theologica*[c] probably owes something to Cicero, although he makes it quite clear that he regarded natural law as transcendent rather than immanent.

That remarkable resurgence of Classical art and learning which is usually known as the Renaissance is generally regarded as a watershed in the history of ideas, a period of transition from 'medieval' to 'modern', from superstition to rationalism, from a way of life in which this world was regarded as merely a preparation for the next to a dynamic emphasis on human achievement and potentiality. Cicero's undoubted vanity would have been flattered by the thought

[a] *Inferno*, Canto IV.   [b] Ibid., Canto XI.   [c] *S. Th.*, II, 1, qu. 91.

25

that he was a dominant influence on the chief figure in this movement
—Petrarch. Petrarch was a humanist, and in this he personified the
Renaissance; he was a humanist not in the modern, atheistic sense,
but in that, though a devout Catholic, he was much more concerned
with actions than beliefs. Thus Cicero appealed to him in two ways:
first, his down-to-earth pragmatic philosophy and the forceful eloquence with which it was expressed was much more relevant to
human life than the rigid metaphysics of scholasticism; secondly,
Cicero's efforts to put his ideals into practice commended themselves
to a man of action much more than definitions of virtue, however
admirable, of a pure teacher like Aristotle. In 1333 Petrarch discovered two of Cicero's speeches at Liège, and with great delight read
and transcribed them. Twelve years later he discovered the *Letters to
Atticus, to Brutus* and *to Quintus Cicero* at Verona, and was fascinated by their revelation of the politician as well as the thinker who
was by now well-known to him. It was largely due to Petrarch that
Cicero became accepted as a guide to the active life. It was Petrarch
who said that in Cicero's works one might imagine that it is not a
pagan philosopher but a Christian apostle who is speaking. What is
more important is that he became accepted in his own right. No
longer was it considered necessary to do with Cicero what Aquinas
had done with Aristotle, namely to baptize the intellectual gropings
of a pagan by showing them to be confirmed by revelation. No
longer was ancient thought to be relegated to the status of an *ancilla
fidei*, but to be accepted as rational moral teaching with its own
validity as such. This was probably the most important change in
thinking which marked the post-scholastic period.

Cicero's influence in this period was many-sided. The *De Oratore*
became a standard textbook of rhetoric in the schools of Guarina at
Ferrara and Vittorino da Feltre at Mantua; the letters were studied
for their political content, the philosophical works (especially the
two essays, the *Tusculans* and *De Officiis*) as guides to the good life.
Evidence of this is to be found in the writings of men like Coluccio
Salutati, Chancellor of Florence during its last days as a free state,
who not only discovered the *Epistulae ad Familiares* in a library
at Verona, but claimed that they had influenced his political career.
Perhaps he saw himself as a latter-day Cicero in a city which was the
heir of the Roman Republic and the sole champion of its ideals, a
conception of Florence shared by Guicciardini and Machiavelli in
the following century.

26

The influence of Cicero in England was greatly promoted in the fifteenth century by the great patron of letters, Duke Humphrey of Gloucester, who invited Leonardo Bruni, a Florentine contemporary of Salutati and a leading Ciceronian scholar, to England in about 1430. Guarino was another Italian scholar who had a very great influence on Humphrey as well as on William Grey, Bishop of Ely, who had sat at his feet at Mantua about the middle of the fifteenth century, and John Free who provides us with an eloquent testimony to the quality of Guarino's lectures on Cicero. The main works of Cicero to receive mention in this period are the oratorical treatises, especially *De Oratore*, the two essays and *De Officiis*; the latter had commanded extensive study by Robert Flemmyng during his stay at Padua and greatly influenced Free and Chaundler, the leading Oxford humanists.

The advent of printing also contributed to the widespread dissemination of Ciceronian ideals in this period. The two editions of *De Officiis*, published at Subiaco (1465) and Mainz (1466) were among the earliest printings of classical authors. By the end of the fifteenth century two hundred printed editions of Cicero had appeared, while in England Caxton published translations of the two essays in 1481. Editions continued unabated throughout the sixteenth and seventeenth centuries, ten of *De Officiis* alone between 1553 and 1610. The regulations for Wittenberg University in 1546 prescribe the main works of Cicero for detailed study, especially *De Officiis* and the letters of '*Ad Familiares*'. Melanchthon followed Erasmus in advocating intensive rather than extensive reading; in fact, so concentrated was his approach, that nine-tenths of his Latin courses during the forty-eight years of his teaching life were devoted to Cicero, and he described *De Officiis* as the perfect philosophical work. Erasmus, notwithstanding his attacks on pedantic adherence to Ciceronian style in the '*Ciceronianus*', had a great admiration for him and in particular for his philosophical works whose moral teaching he considered more essentially Christian than that of many theologians.[a]

The Elizabethan age was perhaps only second to the Jacobean as a high-water mark of Ciceronian studies in England. That the Queen

[a] *Vd. Epistula ad Ioannem Ulattenum:* 'I do not know what others feel, but when I read Cicero, particularly his dissertations on how to live the good life, I am so affected that I become incapable of doubting that some divine power possessed the heart which gave birth to such thoughts.'

27

herself read Cicero extensively was no doubt due to the influence of her tutor, a noted Ciceronian scholar, Roger Ascham, who was perhaps only rivalled by the theologian Hooker as an exponent of the Ciceronian style. It is difficult to stress too highly the influence of the fifteenth- and sixteenth-century humanists who impressed the ideas and values of the ancients on so many minds. The fact that Cicero's works were more widely produced than those of any other classical author meant that he was the dominant contributor to this influence. Nor was that influence confined to England; Montaigne was largely prompted by the first book of *De Officiis* when he emphasized the need to be true to one's character in all deeds and actions.

The Jacobean age was perhaps even more seduced by Cicero the stylist than Cicero the thinker. Ciceronian rhythms are the basis of much of the finest prose of the time. Milton, a Latinist in prose as well as in verse, reflects the general trend, although its finest flower is probably the dedication to the Authorized version of King James' Bible. Cicero's style was not lost on the eighteenth century either; the rolling periods of Gibbon and Samuel Johnson bear witness to this. But on Gibbon the influence of Cicero was a deeper and more lasting one; he greatly respected Cicero as a thinker, and in spite of his scepticism enumerates him among those 'who always inculcated decent reverence for the religion of their own country and mankind'. As an expounder of philosophical ideas Gibbon says of him, 'He represents with candour and confutes with subtlety the opinions of the philosophers.' Of the politicians of the period Burke probably owed most to Cicero for his rhetorical training. Not only are all the distinguishing marks of Ciceronian rhetoric to be found in his work, but he refers to Cicero's attacks on Verres in his famous invective against Warren Hastings.

Of the philosophers Hume pays tribute to *De Officiis*: 'I desire to take my catalogue of virtues from Cicero's Offices, not from the Whole Duty of Man.' Voltaire produced an even warmer tribute when he said in 1771: 'No-one will ever write anything more wise, more true or more useful. From henceforth those whose ambition it is to give men instruction, to provide them with precepts, will be charlatans if they want to rise above you, or will all be your imitators.' Frederick the Great agreed; he said of *De Officiis* that no better book on morals had ever been or could ever be written, and always had his Cicero with him on his campaigns.

Natural Law philosophy as expressed in *De Officiis* was particularly dominant among the late eighteenth-century philosophers. Kant and Schiller both knew the work well and were influenced by it. Adams in his *Preface on Government* makes numerous references to it and specifically states that as philosopher and statesman in one Cicero was *sanspareil*. He was also taken up by the leaders of the French and American Revolutions as a champion of the rights of man. Mirabeau copied his rhetoric, while Desmoulins admired his philosophy as the epitome of common sense. Thomas Jefferson did not wholly admire Cicero as a politician, but quoted him extensively in his work; his greatest tribute was contained in the *Declaration of Independence* with its reference to 'certain inalienable rights', based firmly on a concept of Natural Law.

The nineteenth century saw the eclipse of Cicero as a thinker. The fact is plain enough; he is less quoted as an authority and little recommended for the edification of the young; true, Macaulay advised Sir George Trevelyan, his nephew, to take *De Officiis* to Cambridge with him as suitable matter for whiling away tedious mathematics lectures, but he was the exception rather than the rule. It was probably Mommsen more than anyone who was responsible for the decline of Cicero's reputation generally; he attacked his republicanism and compared his political ideals unfavourably with the *dyarchy* as established by Augustus. He also attacked his integrity, refering to him as 'a notorious trimmer'. Even so, it is doubtful whether even Mommsen can be held solely responsible. In an age of technical advance and discovery originality was admired more than any other factor in thought as in other spheres. Cicero was dubbed 'eclectic' and immediately damned. Perhaps also the latter half of the nineteenth and the first half of the twentieth centuries have been characterized by being increasingly the age of the specialist, and have therefore proved sceptical of the many-sidedness which is an outstanding feature of Cicero's genius. Moreover the growth of technical education has led to a much more 'functional' use of language as a means simply for expressing scientific facts; this, combined with a lack of leisure for composition for its own sake, has led to a rejection of the periodic style of which Cicero was the prime exponent and which was for long, as we have seen, a dominant influence on English thought and letters.

Perhaps the most important reason, however, for Cicero's decline is none of these. The nineteenth century saw the sacrifice of many hitherto-sacred cows. The growth of experimental science saw the rejection of many purely theoretical hypotheses: Darwinism sparked off the need to re-examine Biblical truths in the light of scientific discovery. The same spirit of criticism made itself felt on the Classics: the authority which had been attributed to them since the Renaissance as the equivalent of the Bible in matters secular began to crumble.

If Cicero has returned slightly to favour since the end of the nineteenth century, he has certainly not come near to achieving his former influence, nor does it seem likely in an age which is increasingly iconoclastic about the past that he will in the years that lie immediately ahead. That his reputation has recovered is not, I think, a matter for doubt, when one considers the number of new editions of his works and critical assessments of many aspects of his genius which have appeared in recent years. It may be that he has to some extent shared in the increasing popularization of classical literature, which the many cheaper editions in translation have made available to a wider public than ever before; but there are other and deeper reasons. The first is political. An age which has seen the freedom of the civilized world threatened by a succession of dictators has become less sympathetic to Caesar and correspondingly more appreciative of Cicero as the propounder *par excellence* of the republican ideal; the second is philosophical: an age which is, probably more than any other, hostile to dogmatism has found a sympathetic echo in this voice of common-sense liberalism and humanism. H. J. Blackham, in his introduction to *Objections to Humanism*, restates Cicero's denial of an ultimate *summum bonum* and accepts his second-best, the *probabile*. He goes on to illustrate the lack of an overall pattern for the good life by a reference to the distinction Cicero makes in *De Officiis* between what was right for Cato in a particular circumstance and what was right for others.[a] He goes on to point out that, when praising Hume for his advocacy of 'public spirit, or a regard for the community,' he is praising Cicero too for advocating involvement in a community in which not to prevent injustice when we are able is equal to committing it.

It is only when Cicero is seen in the light of his enormous influence, that we see the full stature of the man and realize that the study of ancient thought is not just an archaeological pursuit, but the study of part of the organic unity of European culture, of which we today are merely the latest inheritors.

[a] *De Officiis*, I, 31, 112.

SYNOPSES

Book I

Chapter
1. Introduction
2. Cicero's reasons for writing on moral philosophy
   Moral obligation defined
3. Outline of the scope of the work as a whole
   Panaetius' *three categories* found to need expanding into *five*
   as follows:
   - I. Absolute morality (I, 4–42)
   - II. Comparative morality (I, 43–5)
   - III. Absolute expediency (II, 1–24)
   - IV. Comparative expediency (II, 25)
   - V. The conflict between morality and expediency (III)
4. The basic nature of man
5. Morality divided under four headings—the cardinal virtues:
   - I. The search for truth
   - II. Justice and generosity
   - III. Courage and magnanimity
   - IV. Moderation and reasonableness
6.   I. The search for truth
7–13. II. Justice
14–18. II. Generosity
18–26. III. Courage and magnanimity
27–42. IV. Moderation and reasonableness, subdivided into two parts:
27–34.   (*a*) Living according to nature
35–42.   (*b*)Living according to reason
43–45. A comparative survey of the four headings of morality

31

Book II

Chapter

1–2. Cicero's defence of his position as a philosopher

3–5. The necessity of human society

6. Digression on fortune. Ways in which men's favour and esteem are to be cultivated and held:

7–8.   I. *Affection*, which is as reliable as fear is unreliable

9–14.   II. *Glory*, which is based on:
       (*a*) General popularity
       (*b*) Confidence (9)
       (*c*) Admiration (10–12)
       Ways in which glory is to be obtained (13–14)

15–24.   III. *Generosity* and the benefits it produces.
       Two kinds of generosity:
       (*a*) Through money (15–18)
       (*b*) Through services (19–24)
       The latter is further subdivided into:
         (i) Services to individuals (19–21)
         (ii) Services to the state (22–4)

25. A Comparison of differing expedients

Book III

Chapter
1. Cicero contrasts his own approach to philosophy with that of Scipio Africanus Major

2. Exhortation to his son

3–33. The conflict between apparent expediency and the four cardinal virtues:

3–9.   I. *Conflict with Truth* (3–9)

3–4. Any real conflict between Morality and Expediency is impossible. The two are to be identified

5–6. To do wrong is contrary to nature

7. Moral good is the only, or at any rate the highest, good

8. What is morally wrong cannot be expedient

9. The story of Gyges' Ring, and its moral

10–25.   II. *Conflict with Justice* (10–25)

10–11. A warning against apparent expediency and its capacity for seduction from what is morally right

12–14. Application of the above to specific cases in commerce

15–16. Some test-cases in law

17. Moral obligation goes beyond civil law

18–26. Examples of immorality not subject to civil law

22. Three instances of apparent conflict between morality and expediency

23. Some points raised by Hecato

24–25. Are promises always binding?

26–32. III. *Conflict with Courage* (26–32)

    26. Examples of courage: Ulysses and Regulus

27–28. Objections to Regulus' conduct

29–31. Answers to the objections

    32. Further examples

       IV. *Conflict with Moderation*

    33. An attack on Epicureanism on the grounds that it conflicts with all four cardinal virtues. Conclusion

Book I

BOOK I

Chapter 1

1. My dear Marcus,

The fact that you have been studying under Cratippus[1] for a year now—and at Athens too—means that your mind should be overflowing with philosophical rules and doctrines. Indeed, both your teacher and the city enjoy such an unrivalled prestige that you can benefit both from the knowledge of the former and the examples of the latter. Even so, may I give you a piece of advice? It is to keep a fair balance between Latin and Greek in your rhetorical and philosophical studies, a thing which I have always done and found greatly to my advantage. In fact, I have contributed a great deal, I think, to my countrymen in this sphere. For not only those with no Greek but even those with a good knowledge of it are prepared to admit that they have improved their style and judgement by reading my works.

2. I am happy, therefore, that you should study under our leading contemporary philosopher for as long as you wish, and I think that you ought to be prepared to continue as long as you are satisfied with your progress. But you should also read my writings, which are very close to the Peripatetics in spirit, since both they and I claim to be followers of Socrates and Plato. As for the subject matter, use your own judgement. I place no restrictions upon you. Simply reading my works will improve your Latin. I would not like you to think that I said this out of sheer vanity. It is simply that, although not claiming pre-eminence as a philosopher, I have spent my whole life in the study of oratory, and think that I may reasonably lay claim to that skill which is germane to it, namely, clear, stylish and appropriate diction.

3. For this reason I am very anxious, Marcus, that you should give careful attention not only to my speeches, but also to those philosophical works which now almost equal them in quantity. For whereas the speeches excel in forceful eloquence, the even and

restrained style of the other works deserves equal attention. Indeed, I do not know of any Greek yet who has achieved as much in both *genres*, pursuing the oratory of the bar as well as this more reflective kind of disputation, unless perhaps Demetrius of Phalerum[2] may be counted as such. But he was a clever essayist and an elegant rather than a forceful speaker, in whom one can clearly recognize a pupil of Theophrastus.[3] However, it is for others to decide how far I have been successful in each *genre*. At least I have attempted both.

4.   I myself believe that Plato would have been a powerful and resourceful speaker had he wished to attempt the rhetoric of the law-court, and that Demosthenes[4] would have expressed what he had learned from Plato stylishly and with great distinction had he wished. The same is true of Aristotle and Isocrates,[5] had not each been so caught up with his own field that he scorned the other.

Chapter 2

Having decided, then, to give you just a little advice now and keep the bulk of it until later, I have been particularly anxious to begin with what is most appropriate to your youth and my position as a father. For there are many serious and profitable subjects which philosophers have discussed with fine logic and at great length; but it is their teaching on moral obligation that seems to have the widest relevance. Obligation embraces every aspect of life, public and private. It covers personal matters as well as those affecting others. In fact, all morally good behaviour is the fulfilment of obligation, just as all morally bad behaviour is the result of its neglect.

5.   Ethics is a field of study common to all philosophers. Indeed, who would have the temerity to assume the name unless he had justified it by writing on this subject? Yet there are some sects who undermine the whole concept of obligation in their definitions of good and evil. For whoever defines the highest good in such a way that he divorces it from moral excellence, is measuring it by utilitarian rather than by absolute criteria. Moreover, if a man follows his own subjective principles and never allows himself to be over-

ruled by natural goodness, he can neither cultivate friendship nor embrace justice or generosity. The man, for example, who considers pain the greatest evil can never be brave, nor can someone who considers pleasure the greatest good ever show self-control.

6.   This is so obvious that it should be beyond all argument, and yet I have argued it elsewhere.[a] These sects, therefore, if they are to be consistent, are in no position to pronounce on moral obligation, since any rules which are to be reliable, lasting and in accordance with the natural law, can only be laid down by those who consider that moral excellence should be sought solely, or at any rate primarily, for its own sake. Thus moral teaching is the prerogative of the Stoics, Academics and Peripatetics, because the ideas of Aristo,[6] Herillus[7] and Pyrrho[8] have long been exploded. Yet even they might have had some grounds for arguing about moral obligation had they left any scope for choice between good and evil which might have opened the way to a discovery of what moral obligation is. This is why I now adhere to the Stoics generally, and in this discussion in particular. I shall not act merely as translator, but shall use my own judgement, as I normally do, in deciding the extent and manner of my borrowings from that source.

7.   As my work as a whole is going to be about moral obligation, I have decided to start with a definition. I am surprised to find that Panaetius omits this, as any logical analysis, whatever the subject, ought to start with a definition, so that the subject of the discussion may be intelligible.

Chapter 3

In discussing obligations, questions of two kinds are involved; one kind concerns the definition of what is morally good; the other the principles by which our whole life is to be governed. The first category includes questions such as whether all obligations are absolute, or whether one can take precedence over another, and so on. The second concerns the principles behind such obligations. Although such principles are relevant to the definition of what is

[a] *Vd. De Officiis*, III, 33, 117; *De Finibus*, II, *passim*; *Tusculanae Disputationes*, IV & V, *passim*.

good, they are less obviously so, because they seem to be more concerned with the ordering of everyday life. It is the latter with which I am to be primarily concerned in this work.

8.   There is a further subdivision into 'absolute' and 'secondary' obligations. I suggest we call the former 'what is right'. The Greeks[9] call it '*κατόρθωμα*', while referring to the latter as 'general obligations'. Their definition is such that whatever is right is an *absolute* obligation, while *secondary* obligations are those which can merely be backed by strong argument.

9.   Panaetius confines the discussion to three main headings: first come the criteria of good or evil for any subject under discussion (which often give rise to considerable disagreement); second, the criteria by which men judge whether or no a particular action contributes to their advantage or pleasure, to their possessions or wealth, to the power or resources by which they can help themselves and their families (all of which comes under the heading of expediency); third, the apparent clashes between the good and the expedient, for when expediency seems to pull in one direction and good in the other, the mind is divided and reduced to an anxious dilemma.

10.   To attempt to categorize and to omit categories is a serious fault, and Panaetius is guilty of this in two cases: first, it is usual to consider not only whether a course of action is right or wrong, but also, in cases where two right courses are open to us, which is the more right; secondly, two actions may be expedient, and yet one more expedient. So, you see, Panaetius' three categories are found to need expanding into five. First, then, we must discuss right action under two headings,[a] then expediency likewise,[b] and, finally, resolve the clash between the two.[c]

Chapter 4

11.   First we must remember that self-preservation is a universal instinct in living creatures. This includes the avoidance of all that seems hurtful as well as the acquisition of the necessities of life such as food, shelter and the like. Common also to living creatures

[a] Book I.   [b] Book II.   [c] Book III.

is the desire for intercourse for the purpose of procreation, and some concern for their young. But the great difference between man and beast lies in the fact that the latter is motivated purely by its senses and adapts itself only to what obtrudes and affects it at the moment, having little sense of the past or the future; while the former, being endowed with reason, by which he can discern a sequence of events, sees their causes, and so is aware of their forward course as well as what one might call their backward course. He compares similar events and links the present with the future, so that he can quite easily conceive a complete picture of life ahead and take necessary measures to meet it.

12. It is through reason that nature also unites man with man and joins them in bonds of speech and common life. Moreover, it breeds in them a particular affection for their own offspring and spurs them on to take part in meetings and assemblies, to strive to attain the things which contribute to their livelihood and well-being—not for themselves alone, but for their wives, children and all others a man holds dear and is obliged to protect. This concern arouses their better feelings and steels them for the task ahead.

13. But the principal function of human reason is the search for truth until it is finally tracked down. Therefore, when we are free from the necessary concerns of business, we have an urge to see, hear and learn something new, and to seek knowledge of things marvellous or obscure, a necessary ingredient of the happy life. From this it is clear that nothing is more consistent with human nature than what is truly straightforward and sincere. To this desire for seeing the truth is linked the quest of excellence; for the mind truly moulded by nature will never willingly submit to any man, unless he be someone capable of instruction and advice, or invested with right and proper authority in the general interest. Such an attitude breeds moral courage and a disdain for the ephemeral.

14. Another important natural capacity, to which man alone is heir, is that of discerning order, decency and a sense of proportion in words and deeds. Indeed in objects of perception no other creature can discern beauty, grace and symmetry. It is our natural reason which extends the comparison from the eye to the mind, so that beauty, consistency and order are thought even more worthy of observance in intentions and actions as a precaution that nothing dishonourable, unmanly or lustful be done or even contemplated.

I

It is from such components that the good conduct which we seek is compounded. Even if its goodness were not recognized, it would still be good; for whatever we can say in all truth is commended by its own good nature, even if not approved by any man living.

Chapter 5

15. You now see, My dear Marcus, at any rate the outline and as it were the 'look' of goodness, which, 'if it could be seen with the eye, would excite' according to Plato,[a] 'a great love of wisdom'. But goodness as a whole arises from any one of four sources: it is to be found, first, in wisdom, which is the perception and know- ledge of truth; secondly in justice, which consists in preserving a fair relationship between men, giving to each his due and keeping one's word; thirdly in the greatness and strength of a courageous and invincible mind; and fourthly in observing that due order and sense of proportion in all words and actions which makes for moderation and reasonableness. However closely these four are interwoven, each has its own particular duties to perform. For example, from the first source, in which we included all wisdom and shrewd judgement, arises the search for truth and its discovery, which is an appropriate function of goodness.

16. It is only when a man is expert at extracting the maximum truth from a given statement, and when he can spot and explain the reason behind an occurrence with great speed and shrewdness, that he is rightly considered a man of wisdom and judgement. There- fore truth lies at the root of wisdom, and is as it were the stuff of which it is moulded, and with which it is concerned.

17. The other three virtues are concerned with the necessity of acquiring and retaining those conditions necessary for the progress of life, such as the preservation of human society and relation- ships, and the promotion of those high principles and strength of mind which are not only exercised in increasing one's own wealth and advantage and that of one's family, but which shine through all the more, when we rise above these needs. A sense of order, consistency, proportion and qualities similar to these belong not

[a] *Phaedrus*, 250d.

only to the intellectual sphere, but to the active life as well. It is by imposing upon these practical aspects of life some moderation and order that we shall preserve our honour and respect.

Chapter 6

18. Of the four categories into which we have divided the nature and influence of the good it is the first, namely the perception of truth, with which man is most concerned. For we are all attracted by a desire for knowledge and discovery, in which we consider it a fine thing to excel, but a bad and disgraceful thing to falter, to stray, to be ignorant or deceived. In this natural and honourable activity two faults are to be avoided: the first is hastiness of judgement and the rash assumptions that go with it (whoever is anxious to avoid this fault—as indeed all ought to be—will take time and care be-
19. before coming to a decision); the second is the waste of great enthusiasm and effort on matters which are abstruse, problematical and at the same time unworthy of consideration. If you avoid these faults, you will receive just recognition for your pains in whatever good and worthy study you undertake. Consider, for example, how Caius Sulpicius[10] was renowned for his skill in astronomy, Sextus Pompeius[11] in geometry, many others in logic and more still in jurisprudence; for all these subjects are concerned with the discovery of truth. It would be wrong, however, to be so carried away by our eagerness for the truth that we neglected our daily tasks; for the active life is of the highest merit, and contemplation is merely a relaxation from it when the occasion allows. Then our intellectual quest, which is never dormant, can hold us to the pursuit without any conscious effort on our part. The whole of our mental activity, then, will be devoted either to the active attainment of the good which crowns a noble and happy life, or the pursuit of knowledge and discovery. So much for the first source of obligation.

I

Chapter 7

20.   Of the three remaining categories the one which covers the widest field is that which concerns human relations and social harmony. It can be divided into two parts: justice, which stands out above all virtues and is our criterion of the good man, and generosity, which is closely allied to it and is sometimes referred to under the heading of goodwill or liberality. Now the prime requirements of justice are that no man should harm another unless provoked by injustice, and that he should use common possessions for the common good and only his own possessions for his own good.

21.   Now no man has a natural right to private property, but merely possesses, either by virtue of ancient acquisition, like those who first landed in unoccupied territory, or by conquest, like those who have won land by the sword, or by some law, covenant, agreement or lot. Hence the land of the Arpenates becomes Arpenatian and that of the Tusculani Tusculan. A fair analogy may be drawn between such acquisition and private estates. Since, therefore, each man has acquired a share of what was common to all, it is right that he should retain what has become his; and if anyone seeks to rob him of this he will be violating the law of human rights.

22.   But, as Plato has admirably put it,[a] 'We were not born merely for our own good, but our country and friends can both lay claim to some part of us.' Moreover, according to the Stoics, all the fruits of the earth are for man's use and all men are born for mutual help and advantage. Hence we ought to accept nature as our leader in this and pool all our natural advantages, so that by an exchange of duties on a give-and-take basis we strengthen the bonds of society by contributing our efforts, skills and resources to it.

23.   Justice is founded on mutual trust, by which I mean being steadfastly true to words and agreements. If we are bold enough to follow the Stoics, those avid researchers into the derivation of words, we may believe that *fides* is derived from *fiat*, meaning 'it

[a] *Letters*, 358a.

must be done'—although this may seem to some rather far-fetched. There are, however, two kinds of injustice: one is the actual committing of a crime; the other is the refusal to prevent injustice being done to the innocent as far as one can. For the man who unjustly attacks another, motivated by anger or some other passion, seems as it were to lay hands on a comrade; and if one does not defend him or resist the injustice to the best of one's ability, one is just as guilty as if one were to desert one's parents, friends or country.

24.   Injustices of the first kind which are inflicted on purpose with the intention of hurting are often motivated by fear, since the man who plans another's harm is afraid that if he does not do it he may find himself at a disadvantage. But for the most part men turn to crime to attain some object of passionate desire. The commonest motive is therefore greed.

Chapter 8

25.   Men seek riches either to attain the necessities of life or to enjoy its pleasures. Those who have higher ambitions desire money because of the patronage that it wields; for example, M. Crassus[a] recently said that no one who had designs on the highest offices of state should be satisfied with any sum of money, however large, unless he could maintain an army on its annual yield. Others delight in the splendour and extravagance of surroundings which display their taste and wealth. This has often resulted in an inordinate desire for riches. Not that the innocent increase of one's estate is to be deplored, but it is only innocent as long as it is free from injustice.

26.   Another reason which induces a great many to forget the claims of justice is ambition for political power, high position and distinction. As Ennius[12] has put it:

        'Nor bond nor faith within a kingdom is.'

This is applicable on a much wider scale than he intended. For in those spheres in which not more than one can succeed there is such great competition that to keep such a sacred bond is practically

---

[a] Marcus Licinius Crassus, the Triumvir.

impossible. We have seen a recent example of this in the unscrupulous behaviour of Caius Caesar,[a] who has ridden roughshod over
all laws both human and divine to attain that dominion which he
had dreamed of in the depraved perversion of his own mind. This
prompts one to reflect how in the greatest personalities and most
gifted intellects there exists the desire for high office, command,
power and prestige. Thus all those who are in this position have
all the greater need to beware of injustice.

27.   But in all cases of injustice it is of the highest importance to
gauge whether the crime is prompted by some temporary and
short-lived gust of passion, or whether it is coolly planned and
premeditated; for the former are not nearly so serious as the latter.
So much for injustice.

Chapter 9

28.   The reasons for neglecting our duty by not defending the innocent are more numerous: men are either loth to bring upon themselves enmity, trouble or expense, or they allow themselves to be
held back by negligence, idleness, inactivity or preoccupation with
their own affairs. It is clear therefore that we cannot accept Plato's
dictum about philosophers—that because they are absorbed
in the pursuit of truth and scorn and neglect the things that the
majority seek and are prepared to cut each other's throats for,
they are therefore just.[b] It is true that they conform to our first
criterion of justice, which concerns the avoidance of injustice to
another, but they fall down on the second by neglecting their duty
to protect others because of their academic preoccupations. He
also thinks that the philosopher would never take part in public
life except under compulsion. It would however be preferable that
it should be undertaken voluntarily; for an action good in itself
can only be considered truly just if done voluntarily.

29.   There are some who, through a desire to protect their own interests or because of their morose nature, say that they mind their
own business and seem to commit no injustice. These, while avoiding the one kind of injustice, rush headlong into the other; they

[a] Caius Julius Caesar, the Dictator.   [b] *Republic*, 485 f.

neglect the common interest by refusing to contribute any of their energies, efforts or resources to it. I have now explained the two kinds of injustice and the causes of each. I have also illustrated the kind of action which exemplifies justice. We shall therefore easily be able to decide, unless we are too self-indulgent, where our obligations lie on any given occasion.

30.   Concern for other people's interests is an irksome thing; yet that famous character in Terence,[13] Chremes, thought that no human affair was beyond his concern.[a] Nevertheless it is because we are more conscious and perceptive of those things which concern our own success and failure than those which concern others, which we only regard as though on a distant horizon, that we treat others differently from ourselves. Hence some teach the very good rule not to do anything if we have doubts about its justice; for fair-dealing is apparent by its very nature, whereas doubt indicates a suspicion of injustice.

Chapter 10

31.   There are, however, circumstances in which what would normally be the action of a just man becomes quite the reverse; and it becomes right to omit or neglect duties such as returning another's possession, fulfilling a promise, or any other action, which is concerned with adherence to truth or good faith. We must always observe the two basic principles of justice which I laid down at the beginning, namely that no man should be injured, and that the common good be served. As these things change according to circumstances, our obligations cannot always be expected to remain the same.

32.   It is possible to imagine a promise or agreement of which the fulfilment would be detrimental either to the person to whom it was made or to the one who made it. For example, if Neptune had not done what, according to the legend, he promised Theseus,[14] the latter would not have lost his son Hippolytus. The story goes that Theseus was granted the fulfilment of three wishes; the third was the wish, expressed in a moment of anger, that Hippolytus

[a] *Heautontimorumenos*, I, 1, 25.

should die. This was duly fulfilled, but caused Theseus lasting grief. Promises therefore, which are to the detriment of those to whom they have been made, are not to be kept, any more than those which are more to the detriment of the promiser than they are to the advantage of the man to whom they were made. In such a case it is right to put the greater good before the lesser, so that if, say, you have promised to defend a man in an impending legal case, but find in the meantime that your son has become dangerously ill, it is not a violation of duty if you do not defend him, but rather is it he who is to blame, if he complains that he has been let down. Moreover it is obvious to anyone that obligations are not binding, if incurred under compulsion, threats or deceptions. They are generally rendered void by the praetors's edicts and often by the laws themselves.

33.   Cases of injustice are often due to the sort of trickery that results from over-subtle or even fraudulent interpretations of the law. Hence the well-worn saying, '*The greatest justice is the greatest wrong*'. Frequent examples of this kind of thing are to be found even in the highest affairs of state as in the case of the man who agreed to a thirty-day truce with his enemy and then plundered his territory by night on the grounds that he had agreed to thirty days, but not to thirty nights. Nor can we approve the story of Q. Fabius Labeo,[a] or whoever it was (for I have the story on hearsay), who was commissioned by the senate to arbitrate in a territorial dispute between the people of Nola and the Neapolitans; when they came to discuss the matter he took each party aside in turn and advised them not to be too greedy or ambitious in their demands, but to be prepared to concede rather than be anxious to extend their dominions. This they did, and as a result a certain amount of land was left unclaimed. This he awarded to the Romans, leaving each side merely in possession of what it had modestly claimed. This kind of travesty of justice should be seen for the chicanery that it is, and avoided in all our dealings.

[a] Colleague of Marcus Claudius Marcellus in the consulship, 183 B.C.

I

Chapter 11

You should recognize that there are certain standards of conduct to be maintained even towards those who have done you wrong. There is a mean to be observed in exacting vengeance and punishment; for repentance on the part of the miscreant may perhaps suffice to prevent a recurrence of his offence, and also serve as a deterrent to others.

34. There are certain laws of war which the state should particularly see enforced; for there are two ways of contending an issue—one is by force, and the other is by reason. The former is the prerogative of beasts, the latter of men, so that we should only have recourse to the former when the latter is of no avail.

35. Therefore the only justification for war is that peace and justice should afterwards prevail. When we have won a victory, we should respect our enemies, provided that they have not been the agents of cruelty and barbarity. Acting on this principle, our forebears accepted the Tusculans,[15] Aequians, Volscians, Sabines and Hernicians into their state, but utterly destroyed Carthage and Numantia. I should prefer not to have to add Corinth to this list, but believe that in this case we had a sound motive in the convenient position of the place, which itself might have been an incitement to aggression. I am convinced that our goal must always be a stable and secure peace; moreover, if due regard had been paid to these words, our state, even if it had not flourished greatly, would at least have not reached its present parlous state. Furthermore, in addition to showing compassion for those actually defeated, we should welcome those who lay down their arms and throw themselves upon the general's mercy, even though their walls are actually being breached. Our leaders have always been punctilious in this respect, so that those who received states or tribes into the Roman allegiance had the traditional title of *patroni* conferred upon them.

36. All the rights and duties of war have been rigorously established by the Roman Fetial Laws, from which it is abundantly clear that no war is just unless preceded by an absolute or conditional declaration. Our scrupulousness in observing the rules of war will be

51

apparent from the following example: once Cato's son was serving as a recruit in the army of Popilius Laenas, who was a provincial commander at the time. Popilius decided to disband one legion, which happened to be the one in which Cato's son was serving; but so great was the young man's enthusiasm for fighting that he remained in the army, and Cato wrote to tell Popilius that if he allowed his son to remain he should put him under military oath again, for as he had been legally disbanded he could not lawfully fight an enemy.

37.   A letter from Marcus Cato to his son is exant in which he writes that he has heard of his demobilization while fighting in the war[a] against Perseus in Macedonia, and he advises him not to take any part in a battle, as it is illegal for one who is no longer strictly a soldier to fight.

Chapter 12

I should like to bring to your notice at this point the fact that they used to call a man who was really a '*perduellis*' or 'stubborn foe' a '*hostis*', a name which mitigated the harshness of his situation; for our ancestors used the word '*hostis*' just as we now use the word '*peregrinus*' (stranger). The Twelve Tables[b] contain the words, 'or a day fixed for a trial with a stranger (*hostis*)' and again 'right of ownership can never be usurped by a stranger'. What could be gentler than calling an enemy by such an inoffensive name? And yet usage has given the name a harsher ring, for it has ceased to mean merely a stranger and taken on the meaning of an aggressor.

38.   When a war is undertaken for the glory of conquest, there must nonetheless exist the same causes which I mentioned previously as the sole justification for a war. Wars, however, fought merely for the glory of conquest should be fought with less acrimony; for just as in our political differences we draw a distinction between a personal enemy and a rival, for competition with the latter merely concerns the honour of office, while that with the former our lives

---

[a] The Third Macedonian War, 171–168 B.C.
[b] From Ennius, *Annales*, VI. *Vd.* Note 12.

and reputations; so in the military sphere our ancestors treated the
Cimbri and Celtiberi as personal enemies, as the war was not a
fight for mastery but a fight for existence, whereas their conflicts
with the Latins, Sabines, Samnites, Carthaginians and Pyrrhus
were struggles for dominion. The Carthaginians, it is true, were
treacherous and Hannibal ruthless, but the rest were more reasonable. Look, for example, at those famous words of Pyrrhus about
restoring captives:

> 'Nor gold do I demand, nor seek a price;
> For war's for waging, not for trafficking.
> Let us decide the issue not by gold, but steel;
> Whether Dame Fortune will that you or I
> Should reign, let courage try. And hear too this:
> That those who for their courage have been spared
> By war, by me also shall find their liberty;
> Freely I give; freely take in Heaven's name.'

A truly regal speech and worthy of the family of the Aeacidae!

Chapter 13

39.   Moreover if people are ever forced by circumstances into making
a promise to an enemy, they are bound to keep that too; for example, in the First Punic War Regulus was captured by the Carthaginians and sent to Rome (on solemn oath that he would
return) to discuss an exchange of prisoners. On arrival, he advised
the senate against such an exchange; then, though implored to stay
by friends and relations, he chose to undergo certain punishment
rather than break even an oath sworn to an enemy.

40.   In the Second Punic War, however, we read a different story.
After the battle of Cannae Hannibal sent ten men to Rome, bound
by oath to return if they did not succeed in restoring his captives.
They were permanently deprived of their privileges by the censors
for their perjury; this ruling included one who had been found
guilty of trying to avoid the consequences of his oath by a trick.
For when he had been allowed by Hannibal to leave camp, he
returned a short while after with the excuse that he had forgotten
something; then he made a second exit from the camp, thinking

that he had absolved himself from his oath. He had nominally done so, but in fact his action was not valid; for in oaths one is always under an obligation to act in the spirit rather than in the letter of the bargain. But the finest example of justice to an enemy was that shown by our ancestors when a refugee from Pyrrhus promised the Senate that he would poison the king. Caius Fabricius and the Senate, however, handed the traitor over to Pyrrhus, for they did not approve of such dishonest dealing, even if it would procure the death of a powerful enemy who was engaged in quite unprovoked aggression.

41. So much for obligations in war. But let us not forget that justice is to be observed even towards men of the lowest kind. The lowest estate is in fact that of slaves, and it is a good rule to treat them as hired labourers by setting them tasks in return for a just reward.

There are two ways in which one man may wrong another, by force or by fraud. A man may be as violent as a lion or as crafty as a fox. Both are quite inhuman kinds of behaviour, but fraud is the more odious. Particularly to be deplored is the hypocrisy of those who under the guise of respectability practise the worst acts of deception. So much for justice.

Chapter 14

42. Having completed our study of justice let us now go on in accordance with our scheme to discuss generosity and kindness, for there is nothing more suited to the essential nature of man, provided that one accepts the following *caveats*: first, we should see that acts of kindness are not prejudicial to those we would wish to benefit or to others; second, we should not allow our generosity to exceed our means; and third, it should be proportionate to the merits of the recipient.

The first point lies at the root of all justice, and all actions should be performed in accordance with it; for the man who seems to do a kindness, but in fact does something prejudicial to another, is not to be considered kind or generous, but an insidious flatterer; and those who hurt some in order to be generous to others are guilty of the same injustice as those who appropriate the property of others for their own ends.

43.   It is those—and there are many of them—who seek honour and glory who are particularly prone to steal from some to bestow upon others; for they think that they will give an impression of beneficience to their friends if they enrich them by any means at their command. Nothing could be more diametrically opposed to the true spirit of obligation than practices such as these.

    We must ensure then, that the generosity with which we treat our friends harms no one. Nor should we approve the actions of Sulla and Caesar in transferring estates from their rightful owners to others who had no claim on them; for no action can be at the same time generous and unjust.

44.   The second *caveat* was that we should not allow our generosity to exceed our means. Those who try to be more generous than their means allow are wrong on two counts: first, they are wronging their relations in that they are giving away wealth which could be more fairly used in supporting their families, especially after their death; second, their extravagance may well contain the seeds of avarice and wrongful appropriation, which becomes necessary if such generosity is to be sustained. There are indeed many who are not so much induced by their natural generosity, as by ambition, to be particularly liberal with their gifts; thus many of their actions are motivated by exhibitionism rather than goodwill, and such hypocrisy is more akin to self-seeking pride than to honest generosity.

45.   The third *caveat* was that we should ensure that our generosity is proportionate to the merits of the recipient. In assessing these we should consider his character, his attitude towards us, his position as a relation or friend, and any services previously performed on our behalf. It is desirable that all these qualities should be combined in one man; failing that, the number of qualities and the relative strength of each should be the deciding factor.

Chapter 15

46.   Since, then, our dealings are not with men who are perfect and all-wise, but with men in whom we congratulate ourselves if we see but shadows of true worth, I would lay it down as a principle that

no one should be altogether neglected, if there is at least some semblance of quality in him; but this is not to say that we should not particularly cultivate those who are especially gifted with the gentler virtues of moderation, self-control and—the subject of much of our discussion—justice itself. These are the virtues which are the distinguishing mark of the good man; others, such as great courage, which, untempered by wisdom, often leads to rashness, often lead to an imbalance of character.

47.   To pass from character to my second point, let us consider his goodwill towards us. It is clearly a moral obligation to do most for the man by whom we are best treated. But we should be careful to judge goodwill not by the rather naïve criterion of superficial warmth, but from the more mature standpoint of stability and reliability. If, however, an act of kindness has been done to us and our duty is not so much to take the initiative in being kind, but to pay a debt, then we must take greater care; for there is no greater obligation than repaying a kindness.

48.   If we accept Hesiod's rule[16] and return that which was no more than borrowed, with interest if possible, what ought we to do when prompted by an act of goodwill? Surely we should follow the example of fertile fields, which produce far more than they have received. Moreover, if we do not hesitate to confer benefits on those whom we hope will be of use to us, what benefits should we confer on those who have already served our interests? There are, then, two kinds of generous behaviour, the one consisting in conferring benefits, the other in repaying them. It is a matter of choice whether we undertake the former, but the latter is an inescapable duty for any right-thinking person, provided that he can do it without injustice.

49.   We must discriminate between the quality of the benefits we have received. Of course, where most has been received, most is due. But it is important to consider whether the benefit was conferred deliberately, eagerly and generously; for men often act rashly and injudiciously as though spurred on to indiscriminate benefactions by some infectious urge or by a sudden blast of goodwill. Clearly such benefits are not to be valued as highly as those which are motivated by stable judgement and careful thought. But in conferring as well as in repaying kindnesses, our greatest obligation, other things being equal, is to fulfil the need where it is greatest. Usually it is the reverse that happens; men are quick to

56

shower their favours not on those who need their help, but on those from whom they have the greatest expectations.

Chapter 16

50. As for man's position as friend or relation, this will be best served if we proportion our benefits to his closeness to us. But here we must trace from the fountain-head the natural principles on which human society rests. We must recognize that the whole human race should coexist as a single fellowship, cemented by reason and common speech, which unites men in teaching and learning, in communication, discussion and judgement, and binds them together in a natural society. This is the main factor which distinguishes us from the animal kingdom; for whereas we often speak of courage in horses and lions, we do not mention justice, equity and moral goodness. The reason is that animals are beyond the reach of reason and speech.

51. Human society is the most comprehensive of all societies, embracing men of all kinds and conditions, and it is their common duty to share all those things which nature has produced for man's use, to confirm in its *status quo* all that is established by laws and civil rights, as has been laid down by the laws themselves, and that all other things should be regarded as subject to the words of the Greek proverb, '*all things in common amongst friends*'.[a] This would appear to apply to the sort of thing which Ennius had in mind when he wrote:[b]

> 'The man who kindly guides a stranger on his way,
> Lights as it were another's lantern from his own,
> Nor is his light the less for kindling the other.'

This example could be applied well outside its own particular context. Its lesson is clear enough: whatever kindness can be done without personal loss should be done even for a stranger.

52. From this arise fundamental principles of humanity, such as not denying anyone running water, or allowing a man to light his

---

[a] Attributed by Plutarch to Diogenes; also quoted by Aristotle, *Nicomachean Ethics*, VIII, 11.
[b] Ennius, Fragment 140. *Vd*. Note 12.

fire from ours, if he wishes, or giving a man impartial advice when he is in doubt; for such things are to the advantage of those who receive them without being any trouble to the giver. Just as we should all be able to take advantage of such things, so we should always be prepared to contribute to the common weal. The problem is that each man's individual resources are small, whereas the number of those in need is legion. Therefore we must limit our general generosity to the bounds which Ennius implies in the words, 'Nor is his light the less', so that we may still be able to be generous to our own.

Chapter 17

53.   Let us now leave our duties to humanity as a whole, and consider how human society exists on many different levels. Among man's closest bonds are those of race, nation and language, but closest of all is that of city, for fellow-citizens have many things in common: not only do they share markets, temples, porticoes and roads, but laws, civil rights, courts of justice and the power of the vote; in addition there are close friendships, personal relations, business and commercial dealings. But above all these it is between members of the same family that the greatest bonds are to be found. For in the family the broad expanse of human society is compressed into a compact, tightly-knit unit.

54.   All living creatures have a common desire to reproduce their kind, and human beings are no exception; the closest bond is therefore between man and wife, the next closest between parents and children, and thirdly that of the whole household which shares a common life. This lies at the root of every city and is as it were the seedbed of the state. Next comes the relationship of brother to brother, then that of cousins and second cousins, who sometimes become too numerous to inhabit the same house and so found other homes like colonists expanding their empire. Marital relationships come next, resulting in the extension of the family. It is from the offspring of these unions that states are formed. Blood relationship then is the prime factor in uniting men in bonds of love and goodwill.

I

55.   The sharing of common ancestors, religious rites and burial places is the hallmark of family relationships. But of all the ties which exist among men the finest and most stable is the alliance in a common purpose of men of the highest moral character; for moral goodness, as I have often observed, always has a profound effect on us wherever we see it and attracts us to those who possess it.

56.   It is true that all moral qualities attract us and inspire our love for those who possess them, and yet justice and generosity have a greater influence than the rest. No society can be more harmonious or more closely cemented than that in which men of equally high character are to be found; for they share the same aims and desires; each takes as much delight in the other as in himself with the result that Pythagoras' ultimate goal in friendship, 'unity in plurality',[17] is achieved. Good relations can also be forged out of kindnesses freely given and accepted on both sides, where mutual gratitude binds the participants in lasting harmony.

57.   But when all is considered, there is no relationship more important or worthy of our devotion than that of each one of us to our country. It is true that we love our parents, children, relatives and friends. But it is a love which is transcended by that which we feel for our country, for there cannot be any good man who would hesitate to give his life in its service. How detestable is the barbarity of those who have wounded their country with every conceivable crime, and have made it their business, and still do, to destroy it!

58.   If, however, there should be any conflict of priorities, our duty to our country and our parents should come first, for we are bound to them by great debts of gratitude. Next come our children and our whole household, which is entirely dependent on us, and finally those who are near to us and bound by ties of sympathy and common interest. Therefore we owe to those whom I have just mentioned all that is necessary for their protection; but then friendship is the most fertile basis for living together, sharing meals, advice, conversation, encouragement, consolation and sometimes even rebuke; but the pleasantest of friendships is that based on sympathy of personalities.

Chapter 18

59. As we look at our obligations further we shall have to consider the needs of each in the light of what he can or cannot do without our help. For close ties will not always coincide with circumstances and certain obligations will be due more to some than others; for example, one should be prepared to help a neighbour in getting in his corn before a brother or close friend; whereas if the question of legal defence arises, the reverse should apply. These and similar examples should be considered when reflecting on our obligations. Moreover we must become trained and practised in them so that we may become able to calculate our duties, and, by adding and subtracting, to see what the answer is in terms of our debt to others.

60. Just as no doctor, general or orator can achieve anything praiseworthy, however skilled in his art, without experience and training, so it is easy enough to lay down rules of behaviour as I am doing, but it is a more formidable task to acquire the requisite training and experience. I have merely deduced from all the principles on which human society is based the origin of honourable conduct and have shown how our obligations are based on it.

61. It is important to notice that although we laid down four general headings of conduct from which goodness and obligation were to be derived, the most spectacular is that, which, proceeding from a great and exalted spirit looks down on all merely human resources. Thus, how often do we hear in reproaches words like:

    'You men assume a woman's spirit, but she a man's.'[a]
or something like this:

    'A coward's spoils, by neither sweat nor blood procured.'
The converse is true. We praise brave and noble deeds in more enthusiastic strains than anything else. Hence Marathon, Salamis, Plataea, Thermopylae and Leuctra are such a fruitful field for orators. So also Horatius, the Decii, the Scipios, Cnaeus and Publius, Marcus Marcellus and countless others, above all the people of Rome itself, all are renowned for their great courage.[18]

    [a] The source of these lines is unknown.

I

It is a tribute to our high regard for military glory that practically all our statues are clothed in military uniform.

Chapter 19

62.   There is however no credit in the sort of courage which appears in dangers and crises, unless it is allied to justice and fights for the common cause rather than its own advantage; for selfish courage is not only lacking in virtue, but is barbarously inhumane. Stoic philosophers define true courage most accurately when they call it 'virtue fighting for justice'. This is why no one has ever become renowned for courage by trickery and deceit; for no action lacking in justice can ever be considered honourable.

63.   Plato has an excellent remark on this subject when he says, 'Knowledge unallied to justice should be called cunning rather than wisdom. Moreover when the human spirit is prepared to undergo danger from a desire for its own gain rather than the common good, this is not to be considered courage so much as unscrupulous boldness.'[a] Truly brave and noble men are those whom we would also expect to be good and straightforward, loving truth and hating deceit; for these are the principal characteristics of justice.

64.   The unpleasant truth is, however, that men of such great spirit often tend to be dominated by innate stubbornness and excessive ambition. Plato observes that the Spartans were dedicated to the sole aim of military glory;[b] similarly there are men today, who, because of their outstanding qualities of daring, see themselves as one of a group of leaders, or, preferably, the only one. But it is difficult to maintain that sense of fair dealing which is particularly germane to justice, if one is constantly trying to stand out above the rest. The result is that such men never allow themselves to be defeated in argument or by any legal right or statute, but maintain their position in the state by means of factions and corruption. This induces them to acquire great wealth so that they may be superior in power rather than equal in justice. But the steeper the

[a] *Menexenus*, 246e, and *Laches*, 197b.
[b] *Laches*, 182e.

way to justice, the greater the glory. Injustice can never be justified by circumstances.

65.   It is those who protect others from injustice rather than those who commit it who are the truly great and valiant spirits. True courage governed by wisdom results in honourable action, which is our instinctive aim and which is to be seen not in the trappings of triumphal pomp, but in deeds, and prefers to show its pre-eminence in fact rather than in appearance. The man who depends on the mistaken plaudits of an ignorant populace is not to be numbered among the great. There is nothing that drives a man of high courage to injustice so much as ambition. It is a slippery slope, and there are few who undertake difficult and dangerous tasks without expecting glory as the reward for their achievements.

Chapter 20

66.   All true courage and greatness of spirit is comprised for the most part of two factors: one is a disdain for externals which arises from the conviction that a man should never admire, wish for or seek anything that is not honourable or decent, or be a slave to another man, to his own impulses or to the caprices of fortune; the other is this: that when one is in the state of mind I have described above, one should perform actions which are not only great and good in themselves, but also particularly difficult, wearisome and dangerous to life itself as well as the many things which are a necessary part of it.

67.   Of these two factors the latter brings the greater glory, dignity and advantage, but it is the former which contains the seeds of true greatness; for it contains that principle which raises the spirit of man to its true height and induces a contempt of all things worldly. It contains two elements, first that honourable conduct should be seen to be the only good, and second the insulation of a man from his baser emotions. What could, in fact, be a finer hallmark of the courageous and truly great spirit than to make little of those things which seem dazzlingly attractive to the majority, and to scorn them from sound and stable principles? Moreover, to bear the many divers misfortunes which can happen to a man in the course of his

62

life in such a way as never to depart from basic principles or from the dignity of true wisdom is the mark of a man of real integrity and unswerving constancy.

68.   We must, in short, be consistently virtuous. It would be quite incongruous for a man not to buckle under fear and yet give way to desire, or for one who has shown that he cannot be broken by pain to be conquered by pleasure. These temptations are to be avoided at all costs; but above all one must beware of avarice, for there is no more certain sign of a narrow and petty mind than the love of riches, and nothing more indicative of a fine and honourable spirit than contempt for money not possessed or generosity with money possessed. Similarly, as I have already pointed out, we should avoid any craving for glory, for it robs a man of his freedom—the one thing for which any great man would fight to the death. Positions of power should never be sought; on the contrary they should sometimes be refused and sometimes resigned.

69.   We should free ourselves from all spiritual disorders, not only desire and fear, but worry, excessive pleasure and anger, so that our disposition may be placid and free from care, and our whole life maintain a steady and dignified course. There have been many —and there still are—who have retired from public life to a life of leisure in search of that serenity which I have been advocating. Among them have been some of the finest and most eminent philosophers as well as men of serious purpose and rigid self-discipline, who could not bear the moral decline of people and leaders alike, and so in many cases took pleasure in retiring to the management of their own private estates.

70.   Their aim was to be like kings, having no wants, being subject to none, but enjoying absolute freedom which consists in living to suit one's own tastes.

Chapter 21

Thus the power-seekers and the lovers of leisure whom I have mentioned just now, have one aim in common. The difference is that the former think that they can attain it by amassing wealth, the latter by being content with their own humble means. Neither life is to be altogether despised: the life of the leisured is easier, safer, and causes less concern and trouble for others; the life of those dedicated to great matters of state is more fruitful for mankind as a whole as well as bringing the advantage of public recognition.

71.   Some people are to be excused for not taking an active part in public life: there are those who have the ability, but prefer to devote themselves to study; there are also those who decline office through ill health or for some other good reason, and so leave to others the power and recognition it would bring. Those, however, who have no good reason, but merely affect to despise those offices, whether military or civil, which carry prestige, deserve not only to forfeit all credit but to incur disrepute. One would not criticize their judgement in despising glory and not setting any store by it: what one would criticize is their true motive for refusing, in that they do not care to suffer trouble or fatigue or the shame and dishonour of failures and rebuffs. Some men are extremely inconsistent in their attitudes; for they are most stern in their strictures against pleasure, and yet quite effeminate when facing pain. They scorn recognition, and yet are distressed by disrepute.

72.   Those, then, who possess the required ability should not hesitate to obtain office and manage the affairs of state. How otherwise can the state be governed or true greatness be given scope for action? Moral greatness and contempt for worldly things are, as I am constantly stressing, just as essential for the statesman as for the philosopher—perhaps even more essential. Moreover serenity of mind and freedom from care are equally important, if the statesman is not to be plagued by perplexity but is to live a steady, sober life.

73.   All this is much easier for the philosopher in that his life is less vulnerable to the attacks of fortune and his needs are smaller. Furthermore, if disaster does strike, his fall is not so great. It is quite understandable, therefore, that men in public life are subject to greater emotional stress and greater anxiety about success than those who live a contemplative life. Hence their greater need of moral courage and freedom from the tendency to worry. Let the man who enters public life see that he not only considers whether his aim is an honourable one, but whether he is capable of achieving it. He should also be on his guard against groundless despondency due to faint-heartedness or over-confidence born of

64

greed. Moreover in all his affairs he should prepare the ground thoroughly before embarking on any task.

Chapter 22

74.   Most people believe that military affairs are more important than civil, a view which I shall do my best to discourage. There are many who have often sought wars because of their yearning for military glory. Such desires have possessed the most gifted minds and imaginations, especially if they have a particular bent towards the military life. On mature reflection, however, we shall see that there are many civil achievements which have been of greater value and have conferred greater distinction than military ex-
75. ploits. For however justly Themistocles may be praised and his name thought more illustrious than that of Solon, Salamis, the scene of his famous victory being quoted as evidence on the grounds that it was a greater exploit than the founding of the Areopagus, the latter should not be regarded as in any way inferior; for Themistocles' achievement was a single event, whereas Solon's was one which conferred lasting benefits on the community, in that it was due to his policies that Athenian legal practice and traditional institutions were safeguarded. Moreover Themistocles could not claim to have benefited the Areopagus in any way, whereas Solon could justly claim that he benefited Themistocles inasmuch as the war was undertaken by the very council which he himself had in-
76. stituted. One could say the same of Pausanias and Lysander, who may be thought to have built up Spartan hegemony by their own achievements, and yet their achievements are not to be compared with the laws and training laid down by Lycurgus, to which they owed the superior courage and discipline of their armies.

For my part, I never in my childhood days thought Marcus Scaurus inferior to Caius Marius, nor since I entered politics, have I ever considered Quintus Catulus[a] to lag behind Cnaeus Pompeius. Foreign conquests are of little value unless there is wise government at home. Nor did Africanus, equally outstanding as a man and as a leader, do more for the state by his destruction of Numantia

[a] The Younger, consul 78 B.C.

I

than Publius Nasica,[a] his contemporary, who, though holding no
public office, secured the death of Tiberius Gracchus.[b] It is true
that this was something approaching a military achievement as it
entailed the use of physical force, and so does not strictly come
under the heading of civil action, but it was done without an army

77. as a matter of domestic policy. This is all very well summed up in
that line which I believe has been the object of much abuse by
those who lack both principle and goodwill:

'Let arms to toga yield, and milit'ry to civil praise.'[c]

When I was at the helm, not to mention others, did not arms give
way to the toga? Never was the state in more dire peril, and yet
there was never found a more peaceful solution. It was through my
careful planning that those very arms were wrested from the grip
of some of our most dangerous citizens.[d] What military achieve-

78. ment could ever rival this? What triumph could be compared to it?
I think that I can boast to you, my son, who will inherit the glory
of my achievements and emulate them. For even Cnaeus Pompeius,
who was particularly renowned for his military exploits, paid me
this tribute before a large audience, when he said that his return
home for his third triumph would have been of no avail, had I not
by my services to the state preserved a city in which to triumph!
Civil courage, then, is in no way inferior to military courage. In
fact, it requires much more effort and application than the latter.

Chapter 23

79. It is clear, then, that the virtue which we look for in a great
man is the product of moral rather than physical forces. We should
not, however, neglect the exercise of the body or the training of it
to obey the instructions of reason in performing its duties and in
undergoing difficulties. The virtue we are looking for consists entirely in qualities of mind and intellect. In this sphere the politician
has just as great a contribution to make as the general; for he by

[a] For the Scipios *Vd.* Note 18.
[b] For the Gracchi *Vd.* Note 39.
[c] Cicero, *De Suis Temporibus*, III (frag. X in Orelli's edition).
[d] The Second Catiliniaran Conspiracy was put down by Cicero in 63 B.C.

66

his policies has often been responsible for preventing wars or securing their speedy conclusion, or sometimes for initiating them, just as Marcus Cato[a] was responsible for the Third Punic War, even though his influence was only effective after his death.

80.　In affairs of state political judgement is more important than military courage, but it is important to ensure that one's motive is the common good rather than a desire to avoid fighting. War should only be undertaken with the aim of securing peace. The main characteristic of the brave and determined man is not to panic when in difficulty, nor to be ruffled or put off his stroke, but maintain presence of mind and not depart from reason or good sense.

81.　What I have just mentioned pertains to moral courage; what I am now going on to say concerns natural ability, namely the capacity to anticipate future events and possibilities well in advance, to decide on the appropriate course of action, and never to find one's self in the position where one has to admit, 'I hadn't thought of that.' This is the duty, not only of a great and courageous spirit, but of a wise and judicious mind. To join battle and engage in physical combat with an enemy without due cause is an inhuman and bestial act; but there is an occasion for physical combat when necessity demands, and then death is to be preferred to the disgrace of slavery.

Chapter 24

82.　It is particularly important when razing and plundering cities to see that nothing is done without careful thought and humanity. A great general should take everything into consideration and punish only the guilty while sparing the great mass of the people. Whatever the circumstances, he should observe the canons of right and honourable conduct. Just as there are those, as I mentioned above, who prefer military to civil affairs, so there are many who think that plans involving danger and cunning are of a higher order than calm and well-considered policies.

83.　We should never acquire the reputation for cowardice by avoid-

[a] Marcus Porcius Cato, the Censor. *Vd.* Note 47.

I

ing dangers which should be faced, but we should particularly
avoid that most stupid of all courses of action in committing ourselves unnecessarily to a dangerous position. Our approach to
dangers should be modelled on the practice of doctors, who prescribe mild remedies for those who are only slightly afflicted, and
reserve desperate and doubtful means of treatment for their more
difficult cases. It is therefore madness when all is calm to look for
a storm, but prudence to seek all ways of avoiding the storm when
it does come. This is all the more true if one can derive greater
benefit from success than harm from failure. Some actions only
bring danger to those who perform them, while others harm the
state as a whole. Some risk their lives, others merely their reputation and the goodwill of their fellows. It is our duty therefore to
be more ready to jeopardize our own safety than that of the state,
and to fight for honour and glory rather than other advantages.

84.   I have known of many men who were prepared to sacrifice their
money as well as their lives for their country, and yet would not
lose one iota of the glory involved, even though the interests of the
country demanded it. For example, Callicratidas, who had distinguished himself on many occasions as Spartan admiral in the
Peloponnesian War, finally ruined everything by not obeying the
advice of those who urged him to withdraw from Arginusae and
not risk facing the Athenians in battle. He justified his action by
saying that the Spartans could fit out another navy if that one were
lost, but he could not withdraw without damaging his reputation.
It was not, however, a crushing defeat for the Spartans: the really
disastrous example which brought about Sparta's downfall was
when Cleombrotus allowed himself to be goaded by taunts into an
ill-advised attack on Epaminondas. How much wiser was Quintus
Fabius Maximus, about whom Ennius says:[a]

'One man alone has saved the republic by constant delaying,
Refusing to put men's pleas before the demands of its safety.
Thus as the years go by, the more his glory increases.'[19]

This kind of mistake should also be avoided in civil affairs. There
are those who do not dare to voice their opinion through fear of
giving offence, even when it might be for the best.

[a] Ennius, *Annales*, XII. *Vd.* Note 12.

68

I

Chapter 25

85.   Those who intend to be statesmen should have a firm grasp of those two principles laid down by Plato: first, that they should so value the well-being of their fellow-citizens that whatever they do is directed to that end regardless of their own advantage;[a] secondly, that their concern should be for the state as a whole, lest their concern for any one section of the community should lead them to neglect the rest.[b] The guardianship of the state is a kind of trusteeship which should always be managed to the advantage of the person entrusted rather than of those to whom he is entrusted. Those who act in the interests of one section of the community against those of another cause revolt and disunity, which can most disrupt the life of the state. The result is a division into factions, popular and aristocratic, with little support left for the common interest.

86.   This was the cause of great disunity at Athens;[c] while at Rome we have seen not only revolution, but civil wars bringing destruction in their wake. These are things which any serious, courageous man, who deserves high office in the state, will avoid and hate, so dedicating himself to the service of the whole community, that he not only acts in the interests of all, but refuses the quest for personal power and wealth. He will not bring any man into disgrace or disrepute by false accusations, but will be so dedicated to just and honourable conduct that he will be prepared for any loss, however heavy, and would even prefer to die sooner than abandon his principles.

87.   Canvassing, and the competition for public office generally, is to be deplored. Plato again has apt words on the subject: 'Those who compete with each other for the honour of governing the state are analogous to sailors struggling for mastery of a ship.'[d] And again: 'We should consider only those who bear arms against the state its true enemies, not those who would govern it according to their

[a] *Republic*, 342e.
[b] *Republic*, 420b.
[c] Due largely to the rise of demagogues after the death of Pericles, 429 B.C.
[d] *Republic*, 488b.

69

own policies.'[a] Publius Africanus and Quintus Metellus provide a good example of this rivalry without animosity.

88.   We must disregard the words of those who think that bitter anger with personal enemies is the correct attitude for a man of greatness and spirit; for in a great and distinguished man there is no more admirable or commendable quality than meekness and gentleness. Indeed in free cities, where all are equal before the law, we should cultivate an imperturbability and generosity of spirit so that we do not succumb to a pointless and detestable sourness when irked by inopportune callers or those who make impertinent requests. And yet civility and gentleness are only to be commended in so far as they leave room for firmness when public duty demands it and efficient administration requires it. All correction and reproof, however, should be free from insult, and not administered for the advantage of the man who punishes or reprimands, but for the good of the state.

89.   One should also ensure that the penalty is not out of proportion to the crime, and that corporal punishment is not awarded in some cases and complete remission in others for the same offence. Above all, one should not give vent to anger when inflicting punishment. For the man who inflicts punishment in the heat of anger will not observe the mean between excess and insufficiency which the Peripatetics teach, and teach with justification. I cannot, however, agree with their teaching that anger is a good thing, given by nature for a good purpose, since those who are in positions of authority in the state should be like the laws they represent, whose function it is to punish fairly rather than in anger.

Chapter 26

90.   We should also be at great pains to avoid pride, disdain and haughtiness in times of success. For in success as well as in failure to be emotionally affected is a mark of weakness. Evenness of temper and expression throughout one's life are the marks of greatness, as is apparent from what we have heard of Socrates and Caius Laelius.[20] I find Philip of Macedon inferior to his son

[a] *Republic*, 567c.

in the glory of his achievements, but superior in civility and generosity.[21] The former always acted like the great man that he was, while the latter was often very mean in his behaviour. Thus it is a good rule which someone laid down, that, the higher our position in life, the more modest should our behaviour be. Panaetius, for example, says that his pupil and great friend, Africanus, used to say: 'Just as horses after many races become fierce and unruly and have to be tamed, so as to be fit for riding again, so men who have become uncontrollable and over-confident need to be confined within the barriers of reason and discipline to learn the uncertainty and vicissitudes of human fortune.'[a]

91.   In times of success we should particularly take advantage of our friends' advice, and value their words even more than before. At the same time we should beware of opening our ears to flatterers and succumbing to their deceptive praises. It is human nature to think that the praises we receive are justified. This results in countless delusions when men allow their ego to be so inflated by false notions, that they become objects of ridicule and are very often led astray. But I shall not labour the point any further.

92.   We can, then, draw this conclusion, that the greatest and most courageous achievements belong to those who are in charge of the affairs of state, for their activity covers the widest field and affects the largest number of people; but there have been, and still are, men of the highest calibre, who live a life of leisure in the search for truth and the practice of virtue within the limits of their own private affairs, or else, leading a life midway between that of the philosopher and the statesman, take pleasure in their own estates, not amassing wealth by every possible means and hoarding it, but sharing it with their friends and their country whenever the occasion demands. Now an estate should in the first place be honestly acquired; next, it should be put at the disposal of as many people as possible, provided that they are worthy of it; and, finally, it should be increased by reasonable care and economy and serve the interests of kindness and generosity rather than of self-indulgence and riotous living. The man who observes these rules can combine fine, dignified and vigorous with honest, faithful and generous living.

[a] For the intimacy of Panaetius and Scipio Africanus Major *Vd.* Aulus Gellius, *Noctes Atticae*, XVII, 21; *Velleius Paterculus*, I, 3, 13.

I

Chapter 27

93.　One component of honourable conduct now remains to be discussed: it includes modesty and, what is an ornament to any life, self-control, as well as reasonableness, the calming of the passions and observation of the happy mean. Under this heading is contained what in Latin is called '*decorum*', the Greek equivalent being

94.　πρέπον. Its properties are such that it cannot be separated from moral goodness. For what is fitting is morally good, and what is morally good is fitting. The difference between them is more easily conceived than explained; for whatever there is in any action that is fitting, is apparent in that it has true goodness as its prerequisite. Thus what is fitting is apparent not only under our present heading of moral conduct, but in the three previous ones as well. For the use of reason and moderate speech, due consideration before taking action, and in all things perception of and regard for what is true are all fitting; on the other hand what is not fitting includes mistakes of fact, judgement and action, as well as delusions, which are a kind of mental derangement. Similarly, just action is fitting, just as injustice is unfitting as well as disgraceful. The same analogy may be drawn with courage. Whatever is done in a spirit of manly courage is seen to be worthy of a man and therefore fitting. The reverse is unworthy and therefore unfitting.

95.　Thus it is apparent that what I have called 'decorum' is relevant to every good action and is relevant in such a way that it should be obvious rather than requiring any abstruse processes of reason for its discovery. What is right and proper can be conceived at the very root of all virtue; but the distinction between 'decorum' and virtue is theoretical rather than empirical. Just as physical attraction and good appearance cannot be separated from bodily health, so this 'decorum' which I am expounding is inextricably bound up with virtue so as to be only conceptually distinguishable.

96.　'Decorum' can be divided into two parts. There is the general 'decorum' which is apparent in every good action, and, subordinate to this is the particular 'decorum' appropriate to a particular action. The definition of the former is this: it is that which is in

72

harmony with the general quality of man which distinguishes him from the rest of the animal kingdom. The latter is defined as the particular 'decorum' which is so much in harmony with man's nature that it gives rise to particular qualities such as reasonableness and self-control combined with good breeding.

Chapter 28

97.   We may infer that this is so from that 'decorum' to which poets aspire, but that is not a theme relevant to my present work. We do admit, however, that poets observe what we call 'decorum', when the actions and words are appropriate to each particular character, so that if Aeacus or Minos were to say, 'Let them hate, as long as they fear,' or 'The father is his children's sepulchre,'[a] this would not strike us as fitting, as we have always taken them to be just men. But if Atreus were to say these words, there would be an outburst of applause; for the speech fits the character.[22] Poets, then, will judge what is fitting for each person from the standpoint of character; but Nature herself has given us our character by en-
98. dowing us with a nobility high above all other living creatures. Poets are faced with such a wide variety of characters that they can see what is right and proper for each, even the most depraved. But our role is allotted to us by Nature herself; it is one requiring steadiness, reasonableness, self-control and consideration for others, and as it is Nature again who teaches us circumspection in our behaviour towards our fellow-men, we begin to realize what a wide field is covered by that 'decorum' which is at the root of every good action, and the other kind which is apparent in individual qualities. For just as physical beauty attracts our attention because of the perfect harmony of its component parts and is a source of great delight because of their matching charm, so this 'decorum' which shines forth in life, stirs the admiration of all around us because of its logical consistency and reasonableness in all its words and deeds.
99.   Hence we should have a respect for all men, the judgement of

[a] Probably from the Atreus of Accius, also quoted by Seneca, *De Ira.*, I, 20, 4.

the many just as much as that of the leading few; for to disregard what men think of us is not just arrogant, but utterly depraved. There is, however, a difference between justice and consideration which we must take into account in making our assessment of men. The chief characteristic of justice is not to wrong any man; that of consideration not to offend him. It is in this latter that the force of 'decorum' is particularly apparent. I think it should now be clear from these examples what we mean by 'decorum'.

100. As for the obligation derived from it, the first path on which it leads us is that towards harmony with nature and observance of its principles. If we take her as our guide, we shall never go wrong, but will pursue what is by nature wise and true, what is in harmony with the principles of human society, and what is vigorous and brave. The force of 'decorum' is to be seen at its greatest in this section which we are now discussing. For we not only commend the motions of the body when they are in accordance with nature, but those of the mind as well.

101. Now the natural composition of the mind is twofold: the first component consists of the appetites, which the Greeks call ὁρμή, and which provide the spur and constantly changing direction of the passions; the second consists of reason, which teaches and explains what should be done and what avoided. It is clear that reason should govern, and the appetites should be subject to it.

Chapter 29

Every action should be free from rashness and negligence. One should not do anything unless one can give reasonable justification for it; this could almost be given as a definition of moral obliga-
102. tion. One should therefore ensure that the appetites are subject to reason and neither anticipate it, nor lag behind it through idleness or apathy; they should be kept calm so as never to disturb the activity of the mind, for it is from this calmness that emotional control and stability will be apparent. Appetites which get out of hand, and, rejoicing in their freedom, as it were, reject the controlling hand of reason in their desires and aversions, will run riot beyond all reasonable bounds: for they abandon that very alle-

giance to reason to which they are subject by natural law. This leads not only to mental, but also physical disturbance. One has only to look at the faces of those who are angry or consumed by fear, passionate desire or extravagant pleasure to see how their expressions, voices, gestures and bearing are changed.

103.   To return now to our definition of duty, it is apparent from what I have said above that the appetites are to be restrained and calmed, while care and attention are to be cultivated, so that none of our actions is rash or haphazard, inconsiderate or careless. We were not created by nature to spend our time in frivolous jesting, but rather for serious matters and the more important pursuits of life. Frivolity of course has its place, but it is to be used, like sleep, as a means of recreation when serious and important matters are finished. Even then, the way in which we enjoy ourselves should not be too lavish or immoderate but gentle and discreet; for just as we do not allow children complete freedom in their play, but only permit the most inoffensive pursuits, so our enjoyment should be illuminated by the light of good taste.

104.   There are two kinds of merriment; one is ungenerous, rude, offensive and in a bad taste; the other is refined, witty, clever and polished. The latter category includes our own Plautus as well as the old Attic comedians and the works of the Socratic philosophers. There is, besides, the collective wit of many writers to be found in compendia like that of old Cato, known as ἀπόφθέγματα .[23] The distinction, then, between good and bad taste is a fairly clear-cut one. The former, provided the moment is opportune, for example during relaxation, is reasonably civilized; the latter, if accompanied by tasteless words as well as improper subject-matter is unworthy of any free-born man. Our enjoyment should be kept within reasonable bounds, so that we do not entirely let ourselves go, and allow ourselves to be carried away by pleasure into misbehaviour. Hunting and taking exercise in the Campus Martius can serve as examples of innocent enjoyment.

Chapter 30

105.   We should never forget, in any discussion on moral obligation, how much the nature of man transcends that of the rest of the

animal kingdom. Animals are motivated solely by physical pleasure, and all their impulses tend to that end; man on the other hand has a rational mind which is fed by thought and learning, so that he is always searching for and discovering something new, and is led on by the joys of seeing and hearing. But if a man is too prone to succumb to sensual pleasures, he should beware of becoming an animal. There are in fact those who are human in name only. If, indeed, he finds pleasure irresistible, then his instincts are only a little above the animal level, and he will conceal and disguise his appetite for pleasure, if only for modesty's sake.

106.　　It is thus apparent that physical pleasure is quite unworthy of human dignity and should be scorned and rejected. But if any man is to be found who sets any value upon it, he should ensure that his enjoyment is kept within reasonable limits. Moreover, the way we live and look after our bodies should be dictated by considerations of health rather than pleasure. And does not the same reflection on the quality of human dignity lead us to realize how disgraceful it is to indulge in luxurious, voluptuous and soft living, rather than the good life, which consists of frugality, self-restraint, strictness and sobriety?

107.　　It is important too to realize that each of us is endowed by nature with two characters: the first is common to all, in that we share that reason and dignity which is the mark of our superiority over the animal kingdom, and from which is derived all that is good and fitting as well as the capacity for discovering our duty; the second is particular to each individual, for just as bodies differ enormously, some being able to move quickly, others being strong in combat, some having an impressive presence, others possessing an endearing charm, so in characters there are just as many, or rather even more, differences.

108.　　For example, Lucius Crassus[a] and Lucius Philippus[b] both had a great deal of charm. Caius Caesar,[c] the son of Lucius, had more than either, but it was more cultivated. Their contemporaries, the young Marcus Drusus[d] and Marcus Scaurus,[e] were exceptionally

[a] Lucius Licinius Crassus, the orator (consul 95 B.C.).
[b] Lucius Marcius Philippus (consul 91 B.C.).
[c] Caius Julius Caesar Strabo Vopiscus (aedile 90 B.C.).
[d] Marcus Livius Drusus the Younger, son of the colleague of Caius Gracchus in his second tribunate (122 B.C.), tribune in 91 B.C.
[e] Marcus Aemilius Scaurus (consul 115 B.C. with Marcus Caecilius Metellus).

earnest, while Caius Laelius[a] was particularly gay in contrast to his friend,[b] who had more ambition and led a much more austere life. Of the Greeks, they say that Socrates[c] was a good-humoured man who was cheerful in conversation and a great dissembler (or εἴρων, as the Greeks called him) in all his speeches; but that Pythagoras[d] and Pericles[e] achieved their great prestige without any humour at all. We are told that of the Carthaginian leaders Hannibal[f] and of our own Quintus Maximus[g] were crafty, good at disguising their intentions and keeping their counsel, at pretence, plotting and anticipating the enemy's plans. In this field the Greeks put Themistocles[h] and Jason of Pherae[i] ahead of the rest, but they award the prize for that ingenious stratagem of Solon, who pretended to be mad so as to ensure the safety of his own life and his continued services to the state.[j]

109.   Some, however, are of quite the reverse temperament, simple and straightforward, who think that nothing should be done by cunning or intrigue. They are lovers of truth and enemies to deceit. But there are some who will submit to any indignity, or fawn on anyone, in order to fulfil their ambitions, men like Sulla[k] or Marcus Crassus.[l] We are told that the Spartan Lysander[m] was an exponent of artful diplomacy, in marked contrast to the straightforward Callicratidas[n] who succeeded him as admiral. Men can be just as artful in their manner of speaking, so that a man who may be pre-eminent in this field can adopt the pose of being one of the many. We have seen this in the Catuli, father and son,[o] and in

[a] *Vd.* Note 20.
[b] Scipio Aemilianus, *Vd.* Note 20.
[c] For the irony of the Socratic dialogues, *Vd.* Note 23.
[d] *Vd.* Note 17.
[e] For Pericles's lack of humour, *Vd.* Plutarch, Pericles, 5.
[f] *Vd.* Note 19.
[g] Quintus Fabius Maximus Cunctator, *Vd.* Note 19.
[h] The victor over Xerxes at Salamis in 480 B.C.
[i] For Jason's character, *Vd.* Note 33.
[j] During the war between Athens and Megara over Salamis.
[k] Sulla, the Dictator, called *The Fox* by Plutarch, *Sulla*, 5, 6, 28.
[l] Marcus Licinius Crassus, the Triumvir. For his flattery *Vd.* Plutarch, *Crassus*, 6.
[m] Lysander won victories over the Athenians at Notium (407 B.C.) and Aegospotami (405).
[n] *Vd.* Note 19.
[o] Quintus Lutatius Catulus the Younger (consul 78 B.C.) was a judge at the trial of Verres in 70. His father, Quintus Lutatius Catulus the Elder (consul 102), with Marius, defeated the Cimbri at Vercellae in 101.

Quintus Mucius Mancia,[a] and I have heard my older contemporaries say the name of Publius Scipio Nasica.[b] His father,[c] on the other hand, who put an end to the nefarious plans of Tiberius Gracchus,[d] had no charm of speech, but seems to have achieved greatness and eminence for that very reason. There are countless other variations in human character and behaviour, but none of them is in itself blameworthy.

Chapter 31

110. In order, then, to achieve that 'decorum' which we are seeking the more easily, each man should stick to what is natural for his own character, provided that it is not harmful. For we should always act in such a way that we do not conflict with the universal nature of man, and yet follow the dictates of our own nature as far as it is consistent with that; hence we should regulate our aims in life by the yardstick of our own character, even though other aims may be higher and preferable. It is useless to fight against your own character or to pursue what you cannot attain. Hence a clearer idea of 'decorum' now emerges, for nothing can be fitting which is contrary to the will of Minerva, that is against a man's natural genius.

111. One general conclusion can be drawn from this, that nothing is more fitting than complete consistency of life and individual actions, and this cannot be achieved if we neglect our own natural inclinations and follow those which belong more properly to others. For just as we ought to use the language which we know, and not, as some people do, rightly incur derision by dragging in Graecisms, so we ought not to spoil our actions and our life in general by introducing inconsistencies into them.

112. Such is the effect of this difference of character, that there are occasions when it may be right for one man to accept death, while

---

[a] Completely unknown. He is mentioned nowhere else.
[b] Publius Cornelius Scipio Nasica (consul 112 B.C.), son of below.
[c] Publius Cornelius Scipio Nasica Serapio (consul 138), *Vd.* Notes 18 and 39.
[d] For the Gracchi, *Vd.* Note 39.

I

for another it may be wrong. For example Marcus Cato[a] refused to surrender to Caesar, while his companions in Africa did, and yet were not their circumstances the same? Perhaps it would have been wrong for them to commit suicide as he did, because their life was less austere and their whole character less rigid; but Cato himself had been endowed by nature with incredible firmness reinforced by relentless consistency in carrying through anything to which he was committed, so that he had to die rather than look upon the face of a tyrant.

113.   Look at the enormous sufferings of Ulysses in the course of his long journey, which even involved submission to women (if Circe and Calypso can be called women),[b] and the need to curry favour and to commend himself to all his hearers. Even on his arrival home he had to put up with the abuse of slaves and maidservants,[c] if he was ever to achieve his hoped-for end. Ajax, from what we know of his character, would have faced death a thousand times rather than submit to such indignities. We should reflect on these examples and consider what are *our* essential points of character, and regulate our actions to them rather than testing the results of actions which are more appropriate to another. For the most fitting conduct for each man is conduct which is strictly in character.

114.   Each man, then, must know his own genius, and prove himself a critical judge of his own virtues and vices. Otherwise actors may seem to have more wisdom than ourselves; for they do not always chose the best roles, but those which are most suited to their abilities. Those who have the best voices choose the *Epigoni* or the *Medus*; those who excel in gestures the *Melanippe* or the *Clytemnestra*.[24] Rupilius, I recall, always played the part of Antiopa. Aesopus very rarely played Ajax. If an actor can observe this rule in choosing his role, cannot a wise man do the same in his way of life? We should therefore apply ourselves to those fields in which our greatest talent lies; but whenever we are driven by necessity to what is against our natural bent, the greatest care, thought and application will be required to carry it through, if not perfectly, then with the minimum of faults. In fact, we should not so much strive to reach unattainable excellence as to avoid the mistakes to which we are prone.

[a] Cato Uticensis, great-grandson of Marcus Porcius Cato the Censor.
[b] *Vd.* Homer, *Odyssey*, V and X.
[c] Melanthius, Melantho and Irus, *Vd.* op. cit., XVII and XVIII.

I

Chapter 32

115.   To the two characters which I have mentioned above must be added two more: one is allotted to us by time and chance; the other we choose for ourselves on our own initiative. The states which are subject to chance and change are these: positions of power, be it royal, military or civil, and power due to high birth, riches or influence, and also the opposites of these. The role we
116. choose in life, however, depends entirely on our own wishes. Thus some apply themselves to philosophy, others to jurisprudence, others to oratory. The same applies to virtues; different men like to excel in different ones. Those whose fathers or ancestors have attained distinction in one particular field are generally eager to excel in the same field, as, for example, Quintus, the son of Publius Mucius,[a] in jurisprudence and Africanus, the son of Paullus, as a soldier.[b] Some add to the distinction of their family by their own exploits; the Africanus whom I have just mentioned was noted for his feats of rhetoric as well as for his military achievements; so did Timotheus, the son of Conon, who not only equalled his father in military distinction, but won a reputation for scholarly genius as well. Some do not attempt to emulate their ancestors, but strike out on their own. This category includes particularly those who have no distinguished ancestors, but have great ambitions for themselves.
117.   All these factors should be taken into consideration when we are considering what is our proper course. We should first decide what sort of men we want to be and in what sphere of public life. It is a most hazardous decision, for it is in the first flush of youth, when his judgement is at its most immature, that a man chooses the particular course of life which most attracts him; and so he becomes firmly embarked on his future career before he is in any position to judge what is best.
118.   According to Xenophon, Prodicus tells this story about Her-

[a] Quintus Mucius Scaevola, consul 95 B.C., *Vd.* Note 56.
[b] Scipio Africanus Minor, son of Lucius Aemilius Paullus Macedonicus. *Vd.* Note 18, Appendix, Scipio (12).

cules: when he was in the first bloom of youth (which is the time appointed by nature to choose one's future course of life) he withdrew to a solitary place, and sat there, immersed in thought, pondering which of two ways he should take, the Way of Pleasure, or the Way of Virtue. This could perhaps happen to Hercules, the son of Jupiter, but it could hardly happen to us. We follow whatever examples we decide upon and, thus committed, accept their instruction. Most of us have our parents' standards firmly ingrained within us and so follow their way of life. Others allow themselves to be seduced by public opinion and set their sights on what seems best to the majority. Some, however, whether through good fortune or good character or parental discipline, have found the right course of life.

Chapter 33

119.   The rarest class of all consists of those who are distinguished by their great natural ability or fine education or both, and have enjoyed ample leisure to consider which career would suit them best. Such consideration must particularly take into account the character of the man himself. I have already explained how we should judge the correctness of every action from the standpoint of the man's own background. Moreover, by far the greatest attention should be given to that background in determining the way ahead, so that we can preserve an uninterrupted consistency in the course of our life and not falter in the performance of any one duty.

120.   In making this decision character is the most powerful determining factor; fortune takes second place. The former therefore must be given precedence, although both are to be taken into account; for character is much more stable and consistent, and for fortune to oppose it is akin to mortal competing with immortal power. The man, then, who has devised a whole plan of life to suit his own character, provided that character is a good one, should stick to it consistently. That is most important. But should he find that he has made a mistake in his plan of life, as sometimes happens, the whole established ethos of his life will have to be rethought. If the times favour such a radical change, it can be made

I

quite easily and conveniently; if not, it must be done cautiously step by step. It is like friendships which become irksome and lose their savour, where the only wise course is to loosen the knot gradually rather than to precipitate a sudden rupture.

121.   It is most important that any change in our course of life should be seen to have been made for a good reason. Having just said that we should follow the example of our ancestors, I must point out two exceptions to the rule: first, that we should not copy their faults; second, that we should not attempt to do what is out of character; for example, the son of Scipio Africanus the elder,[a] who adopted the son of Paulus, because of ill health could not follow his father's example as closely as he had followed his father's. If, then, a man cannot assume the role of a barrister, an orator or a general, he should undertake what is within his capabilities, so that he can display qualities such as justice, loyalty, generosity, moderation and self-control, and thus make up for his lack of ability in other directions. The finest inheritance that can be left by fathers to their sons, finer than any legacy, is the fame of their character and achievements; but to dishonour such an inheritance is the vilest and most culpable offence.

Chapter 34

122.   Since each age-group has its own particular obligations, some being appropriate to youth, others to older years, I should perhaps say something about their differing roles. A young man should respect his elders and choose the best and most tested of them so as to rely on their advice and judgement. Indeed, the inexperience of youth needs the wisdom of old age as its ruler and guide. It particularly needs to be protected from immorality, to be inured to hardship and steeled to mental and physical endurance so as to be able to perform military and civil duties with energy and vigour. Even when young men allow themselves to relax and succumb to pleasure, they should not forget the dangers of over-indulgence and the advantages of moderation. Their task in fact will be made easier, if their elders are willing to join them in such activities.

[a] Publius Cornelius Scipio (10); *Vd.* Note 18, Appendix.

123.   The duty of the old is to spare their physical efforts and to give increasing exercise to their minds. Their particular aim should be to give the maximum help to their friends, young people and the state by offering them wise advice. Above all they should avoid giving themselves up to a life of ease and idleness. Excessive comfort is a danger at every age; it is a particular snare for the old. If they find that they cannot control their desires, this is a bad thing in two ways, for not only does it bring disgrace upon them, but it encourages an increased lack of restraint among the young.

124.   I do not think it would be irrelevant to say something about the duties of magistrates, private persons, citizens and aliens. It is the proper function of a magistrate to realize that he is an official representative of the state and so bound to maintain its prestige and honour, to guard the laws, to administer justice, and to remember that all these things are entrusted to him. Private persons should be content to live on equal terms with their fellow-citizens, not seeking too low or too high a position, but pursuing what contributes to the peaceful and honourable government of

125.   the state. Such a man we should both consider and call a good citizen. The duty of aliens, whether visiting or resident, is to restrict themselves to their own affairs, not to pry into those of others, and certainly not to concern themselves with the affairs of a state which is not their own. Thus our duty will generally be found, when we consider what is fitting, and what is suited to individual character, time or age. But in all our plans and undertakings there is nothing so fitting as consistency.

Chapter 35

126.   This 'decorum' of which I have been speaking can be seen in all our deeds, words, and in physical movement and bearing. It is apparent in three ways: in natural beauty, in the due order of parts, and in outward embellishment suited to the appropriate function. These things are difficult to describe, but if their meaning is understood, that will suffice for my purpose. These three facts include the care that should be taken to commend ourselves to those with whom we live, and I think a few words should be said about each of them.

I

First we should consider the great care which Nature has lav-
ished on our bodies. The parts which are pleasant to see she has
made visible; but those parts which perform a necessary function
127. but are rather unsightly she has covered and hidden. Human
modesty has followed this careful workmanship of Nature; all
right-minded people keep out of sight those parts which Nature
herself thought best to hide, and they are careful to do what is
absolutely necessary with the utmost concealment, nor do they call
those parts or their functions by their real names, but recognize
that it is indelicate to speak of certain things which are not indecent in themselves provided they are done discreetly. Thus the
only things that are indecent are the open performance of these
functions or the indelicate mention of them.

128.   We should not, then, pay any attention to the Cynics,[25] or to
some of the Stoics who are little better, who scorn and deride us
for thinking it wrong to mention things which in fact contain no
wrong, and calling by their own names things which are wrong in
themselves. It is not, for example, considered indecent to mention
robbery, fraud or adultery, even though the actions themselves are
shameful, while the procreation of the species is a good thing, but
not to be mentioned. Many are their arguments against modesty
on these lines. Let us, however, take Nature as our guide, and avoid
everything which is offensive to the eyes and ears. Let our bearing
and step, the way we sit and the way we recline, our expressions
and the movements of our hands all preserve that essential
'decorum'.

129.   In all our gestures two extremes are to be avoided: on the one
hand preciosity and affectation, and on the other boorishness and
vulgarity. Nor should we give our actors and orators the impression that certain actions are fitting for them, but not for ourselves.
Modesty is preserved on the stage by such an ancient tradition of
discipline, that no one would appear on the stage indecently
dressed; for actors are afraid, that should certain parts of the body
be revealed by some misfortune, they would present an unedifying
spectacle. Indeed it is our custom that adolescent sons should not
wash in the company of their parents, nor should sons-in-law in
the presence of their fathers-in-law. These then are the particular
rules of modesty to be observed, if we accept nature herself as our
mistress and guide.

84

Chapter 36

130. There are two types of beauty, one gracious and the other dignified. The former is more appropriate to a woman, the latter to a
man. Thus a man should avoid any kind of adornment, gesture
or movement which is inappropriate. The studied movements of
the *palaestra* are often rather tiresome and many of the gestures
of actors are too affected. In both cases it is the simple and
straightforward that is most to be approved. Fine features are to
be preserved by keeping a good complexion, which in turn is produced by physical exercise. Not all adornment is to be considered
repugnant, provided that it is not overdone, but just sufficient to
combat any impression of boorish slovenliness. The same rule
applies to dress. As in most things, moderation is the best course.
131. We should be careful also to avoid that delicate slowness of
movement which is more appropriate to processional carriages,
nor should we in our haste try to go too fast, for this results in
panting spasms, reddening of the face and distortion of the features
—a strong indication that our lives are lacking in consistency. But
it is much more important to see that the mind be kept within its
natural limits. We shall achieve this, if we are careful to avoid fall-
ing into fits of passion and dejection and keep our minds alert to
the preservation of dignity.
132. The functions of the mind are twofold—reflective and desidera-
tive. The former is exercised in the search for truth, the latter provides a spur for action. We should be sure of using our reflective
powers on the most worthy objects and subjecting our desires to
the government of reason.

Chapter 37

The power of speech is great. It performs two functions, that of
public debate and that of private conversation. Debate should be
reserved for legal, public and political disputes; conversation finds

its place in small groups and private discussions, in the meetings of friends and at banquets. For debate there are rules of rhetoric, but for conversation there are none, although I think there might well be. Teachers would readily be found to satisfy eager pupils; but nobody studies conversation, whereas pupils come in crowds to the teachers of rhetoric. And yet the rules which they give for the use of words and sentences would also be relevant to conversation.

133.   Since the voice is a vehicle for communication, there are two things which we require of it: first, that it should be clear, and second, that it should be pleasant to the ear. Both these are natural gifts, but the former can be improved by practice and the latter by the imitation of those who speak with charm and precision. There was nothing about the Catuli which would lead you to suppose that they were men of fine literary taste. They were literary men, of course, but so were many others. And yet they were considered the finest exponents of Latin usage. The sound of their words was harmonious; they were neither careless nor over-emphatic in their pronunciation of every letter, so that they avoided both obscurity and affectation. They never strained their voices and avoided monotony as well as over-modulation. The speech of Lucius Crassus was no less polished, and had a richer quality, but his reputation as a speaker never surpassed that of the Catuli. Caesar,[a] who was the brother of the elder Catulus, excelled them all in wit and polish, with the result that in any legal wrangle he could with his conversational style surpass the debating speeches of his opponents. All these points should be noted, if we are to discover what is proper to each occasion.

134.   Our conversation, then, should be of the kind in which the Socratics excel—easy, gentle and charming. It should not exclude others as though the field were exclusively its own, but just as in other things we do not regard mutual participation as a disadvantage, neither should we in speech. We should particularly take our subject-matter into account. If it is serious, then let our conversation be grave, if jovial, then let it be gay. It is more important that our conversation should not reveal any fault of character. This can very easily happen when we are eager to abuse men in their absence whether seriously or by way of a joke, by misrepresenting or mocking them.

[a] Caius Julius Caesar Strabo Vopiscus (aedile 90 B.C.).

135.   Conversation often revolves round domestic affairs, or politics
or some cultural study or pursuit. We should take particular care
to stick to the subject, however tempted we may be to wander from
it. But we should also take the assembled company into account.
For we do not all derive the same degree of enjoyment from the
same things all the time. We should notice how far our conversation proves entertaining, and remember that just as there is an
appropriate point at which to begin, so there is a right place at
which to stop.

Chapter 38

136.   It is a good principle for our life as a whole to exercise strict
control over the emotions, by which I mean, those insistent urges
which are least subject to reason. Our conversation too should be
free from them, not marred by anger or desire on the one hand, or
feebleness and lack of spirit on the other. Above all we should
show kindness and respect for those with whom we converse.
Sometimes, of course, rebukes are called for; then we can perhaps
allow ourselves to raise our voices and be sharper in our use of
words. As long as we give the impression of being angry, that is all
that is needed. We should only rarely, and then unwillingly, have
recourse to rebukes of this kind, and even then, like doctors resort-
ing to cauterization or amputation, only when all other methods
have failed. Anger, however, should be kept at a distance, as it
does not provide the right climate for just and generous treatment.

137.   For the most part we should be content with a mild rebuke, provided it is reinforced by earnestness of purpose, so that our sternness may be balanced by lack of vindictiveness. What bitterness
there is in our rebuke should be seen to be present for the benefit
of the person being rebuked. In quarrels with our bitterest enemies
the only justifiable course is to maintain one's dignity and repress
one's anger, no matter how unmerited is the abuse with which one
is reviled. For whatever we do in a passion cannot be reconciled
with our normal standards of conduct or be approved by casual
observers. Boasting is always to be deprecated, particularly when

it is false, and to play the 'Braggart Soldier'[a] is to invite the derision of one's hearers.

Chapter 39

138.   As it is my aim at any rate to cover everything bearing on the subject, I must say something about the sort of house which is becoming for a man of eminent position. The construction plan should take into account the use to which it is to be put, but style should be considered just as much as function. Cnaeus Octavius,[b] the first member of his family to become consul, is said to have won himself a great reputation for the magnificent stately home which he had built on the Palatine Hill. People flocked to see it, and it was thought to have been worth many votes to its master, a *novus homo*,[c] in his quest for the consulship. Scaurus[d] later demolished it and used the materials for extending his own house. Octavius by building the house had made himself consul; Scaurus, although the son of a leading politician of great distinction, had by extending his house not only lost the consulship, but brought himself to disgrace and disaster.

139.   A man's position, then, may be enhanced by his house, but should not wholly depend on it. A man should bring honour to his house, not the reverse. As in everything else, one should not only consider one's own convenience, but that of others. This particularly applies to the house of a distinguished man, which needs to be fairly roomy, because of the number of guests to be entertained there. But if a house is spacious, but always wears a rather deserted air, although frequently visited under its previous master, it can become a source of reproach to its owner. It is a terrible state of affairs when passers-by are heard to comment:

> 'O ancient house, how different now,
> Thy master's mastery.'[e]

This can be said of many in our own times.

---

[a] Pyrgopolinices in Plautus' *Miles Gloriosus*.
[b] As praetor he defeated Perseus at Samothrace in 168 B.C.
[c] The first member of a family to reach curule office.
[d] The son of Marcus Aemilius Scaurus (consul 115 B.C.).
[e] The lines are also applied to Antony's occupation of Pompey's house: *Vd. Philippics*, II, 41. Their author is unknown.

140.   You must be particularly careful, especially if you build your own house, not to be too lavish or extravagant. This is a bad thing, if only because of the example that it sets. For in this sort of thing men are particularly prone to follow the lead of the most eminent. Who has ever taken the virtuous life of that great man, Lucius Lucullus, as his example? And yet men have not been slow to copy the magnificence of his villas. Bounds, then, must be set, and fixed within the rules of moderation, determined only by what is convenient and requisite for decent living. That sums up my whole argument on this question.

141.   Three precepts are to be observed, therefore, in every action: first, that our desires should be subject to reason, for there is nothing more relevant than this to the fulfilling of obligations; second, that we should assess correctly the importance of what we want to achieve, and see that our efforts are commensurate with it; and third, that all externals, designed to give an impression of good breeding and rank, should be kept within the bounds of good taste. The best rule to follow is to keep to that standard of what is fitting which we have already discussed and never to go beyond its limits. Of the three precepts here mentioned the first is the most important.

Chapter 40

142.   Next we must go on to discuss the correct order and timing of our actions. Both these elements are included in that branch of knowledge which the Greeks call εὐταξία. The word has two equivalents in Latin: one is *modestia* (moderation, from the root *modus* the mean); the other is *ordinis conservatio* (the preservation of due order). I shall use the word *modestia*, but with the sense of the latter—according to the definition of the Stoics, who explain it as the knowledge of how to put all our actions and words in their appropriate place. Thus it will be clear that ordering and correct placing are two terms identical in meaning; for the Stoics also define due order as the setting out of things in the positions most suited and fitted for them. Thus the right place for an action in time is called an opportunity; and the right period of time for an

action is called a εὐκαιρία in Greek, and an *occasio* in Latin. Hence *modestia*, in the sense in which I have explained it, is the capacity for good timing in all our actions.

143.   Judgement, which we discussed at the beginning of this book, can be defined in the same way. But at the moment we are considering moderation, self-control and kindred virtues. All that was relevant to a study of judgement was discussed in its proper place. I must now discuss all that is relevant to the virtues on which I have already spent some time, in particular humility and the other qualities which make us liked by our fellow-men.

144.   The order which we observe in our actions should be such that all the parts of our life fit together in a consistent pattern, just like the stages of an argument. For what could be more tiresome or infuriating than to introduce quips suited to feasting or polite conversation into a serious discussion? An apt remark of Pericles will illustrate the point. Once when he had met his fellow *strategos*, Sophocles, to discuss some matter of state, a particularly handsome boy happened to pass by. 'What a beautiful boy!' remarked Sophocles. To which Pericles retorted, 'Really, Sophocles! A *strategos* should keep his eyes as well as his hands chaste.' Now had Sophocles made this remark at some athletic contest, no one would have thought fit to rebuke him. Such is the importance of time and place. Similarly, if a barrister has some case in hand, no one would reproach him for taking a long walk by himself to rehearse his speech, or to give close attention to any other matter to do with the case. But if he were to do this at a banquet, his poor judgement of the occasion would brand him as a man of little breeding.

145.   Gross lapses from good taste, such as singing in the market-place or any other solecism one might imagine, are obvious enough, and do not need elaborate rules or *caveats* for their avoidance. Those which need to be more carefully guarded against are the minor mistakes which most people would not even recognize. But just as in a piece of music even a minor discord can be noticed by the expert, so in our lives we must see that there is no disharmony. In fact, it is much more important in life, as harmony of deeds has a far greater impact and is therefore preferable to harmony of sounds.

Chapter 41

146.   The sensitive ear of a musician can detect the slightest fault in a piece of music. Similarly, if we want to be astute and perceptive critics of what is wrong, we shall often learn a great deal by studying minutiae. From a glance of the eyes, from the knitting or relaxing of the brows, from an air of sadness or gaiety, from laughter, speech or silence, from the raising or lowering of the voice and so on, we may easily discover the propriety or otherwise of our actions. It is also useful to observe similar faults in others so that we can avoid them in ourselves. In fact it often happens that we are more perceptive in noting faults in others than in ourselves. Thus when we are learning, our faults are most easily put right when our teachers repeat them so as to impress them upon us.

147.   It is also right that whenever we are in doubt about what we should do, we should consult men of wisdom and experience, and ask their views on the matter in question; for most men when in doubt generally follow the dictates of their own character. In such consultations we should take note not only of the opinions expressed, but of those implied and the motives behind them. For just as painters, sculptors and poets value popular criticism so that they can put right what is criticized by the majority, and also consider the faults of their work with others as well as by themselves, so we must make use of the judgement of others in deciding what we should do or not do, or what needs to be altered or put right.

148.   Some issues will be settled by custom or national tradition. I will not lay down any rules here, for the customs and traditions are rules in themselves. No one should be misled into thinking that because Socrates or Aristippus[26] flouted both custom and tradition in their actions as well as their teaching, he is justified in doing the same. For they claimed this freedom by virtue of their great and almost superhuman personalities. The practice of the Cynics,[25] however, is to be entirely ruled out of court, as it precludes modesty, without which no action can be considered right or honourable.

149.   We should respect and consult those whose lives have been dis-

tinguished by great and honourable achievements, who are loyal to the state and have served or are serving her well, or who have attained high political office or military command. We should also pay great deference to old age, never challenge those in office, observe the distinction between citizens and aliens, and in the case of the latter distinguish between their functions as public representative and private citizen. Without labouring the point with further details, we may sum up by defining our obligation as the preservation, defence and advancement of the general unity and harmony of the human race.

Chapter 42

150.   I will now discuss trading and money-making; some methods we have been taught to consider gentlemanly, others sordid. The first to be condemned are those which make for unpopularity, such as tax-gathering and usury. Equally ungentlemanly and sordid are the earnings of hired hands who are paid for their physical efforts rather than their skill; for the very wages they receive are a token of slavery. Retail dealers are little better, for they have little to gain unless they are pretty dishonest, and deserve no credit if they are. The occupation of a craftsman is also to be scorned, for what well-born man could possibly spend his time in a workshop? Least of all to be commended are those trades which pander to our desires, the ones that Terence mentions,[a] butchers, cooks, sausage-makers, salt and fresh fishmongers. Add to these, if you wish, perfumers, stage-dancers and those who run games of chance.

151.   Those professions which require skilled training or fulfil a useful function, such as medicine, architecture or the teaching of the liberal arts, are reputable for those whose station in life they suit. The career of a merchant is only to be despised if pursued on a small scale, but if it includes large and valuable transactions and imports from all over the world resulting in a large clientèle from honest dealing, it is not so much to be condemned; in fact, if those who indulge in it become satisfied or at any rate are prepared to be content with their profits, and retire from the harbour to their

[a] *Eunuch*, II, 2, 26; *Vd.* also Note 26.

country estates just as they had frequently retired to the harbour from the sea, this seems to be entirely commendable. But of all the sources of income the life of a farmer is the best, pleasantest, most profitable and most befitting a gentleman. I have dealt at great length with this in the *Cato Major* and refer you to that for all that is relevant to the subject.[a]

Chapter 43

152.   I have now concluded the four categories of good conduct and my exposition of the way in which our duties are derived from them. But a conflict, or rivalry as it were, can often arise between two categories, so that it is difficult to choose between them. This is a point completely ignored by Panaetius. Virtue as a whole is built up of four components: wisdom, public spirit, courage and self-control. In choosing the right course of action some compara-

153. tive assessment of these categories is inevitable. For example, obligations motivated by public spirit are more consistent with our nature than those motivated by wisdom, as the following argument will prove: if a wise man found that he could live in great comfort and enjoy the leisure to reflect and ponder everything worthy of thought, he might welcome it; but if he found that it involved cutting himself off from all human company, life would become unbearable.

First of all the virtues is philosophical wisdom (*sapientia*, the Greek σοφία). Practical wisdom, the knowledge of what should be done and what should be avoided, is *prudentia* (the Greek φρόνησις). The former is the knowledge of all things, both human and divine, and includes understanding of the need for social unity and harmony. If that is the most important thing, and *it is*, then any obligation arising from that concept is also of supreme importance. All philosophical study and contemplation of nature is maimed and imperfect unless it has some practical outcome, that is, to preserve what is to the advantage of mankind as a whole. Such an action would be a contribution to social harmony, and is therefore preferable to pure contemplation.

[a] *Cato Major*, 15, 51, *et seqq.*

154. Indeed this is what all the best men judge and show to be right by their very actions. Is there anyone so devoted to study and contemplation of the universe that if some sudden danger or crisis came upon his country while he was engaged in some study thoroughly worth while in itself, he would not throw everything aside and do what he could to help? Surely he would, even if he thought he was about to number the stars or measure the size of the earth. And the same would apply in the case of any danger to a parent or friend. From this it is clear that the duty to search for truth must be put second to the duties of justice, which are concerned with our love for our fellow-men, the most ancient duty of mankind.

Chapter 44

155. Those whose whole life's work has been the search for truth have never shrunk from promoting the interests and good of mankind. As a result of their teaching many men have improved and given greater service to their countries. Look, for example, at the Theban Epaminondas, who owed his education to the Pythagorean Lysis,[27] or Dion of Syracuse, who was taught by Plato,[28] and many others. In fact, whatever I personally have contributed to the state, is due to the teachers and teaching from which I benefited.

156. Their instruction of all who are eager to learn is not restricted to their leaders' own lifetime, but is continued after their death by the literary memorials which they leave behind them. There is no theme that they have neglected relevant to the laws, customs or discipline of the state. It is clear that their leisure has been devoted to our advantage. Thus those very men, who have devoted themselves to the pursuit of learning and wisdom, have by their judgement and understanding contributed to the general good. For this reason eloquence, provided that it is backed by judgement, is far better than the most penetrative thought, if there is no eloquence to express it; for reflection by itself is entirely introvert, whereas eloquence embraces those with whom we are communally linked.

157. In the case of bees the making of hives is the result rather than the cause of their swarming together. Similarly men are by nature

gregarious, but to a far greater degree, and so apply their minds to the problems of thinking and acting together. Thus it is apparent that unless that virtue which consists in protecting men, that is the maintenance of human society, accompanies the search for truth, then it will be an arid and fruitless pursuit. Even courage, unless it is directed towards the advantage of human fellowship and society, will seem little more than savage blood lust. Thus it is that the unity and harmony of the human race must come before the pursuit of knowledge.

158.   I must here reject that common heresy that human society was dictated by the necessities of life, simply because man was not able to obtain his natural requirements without the help of his fellows, and that if all that is necessary to our life and comfort could be supplied, as they say, by the stroke of a wand, then all the ablest men would abandon all public duties and devote themselves entirely to the pursuit of truth. This is not true. For in his desire to avoid being alone he would seek some companion in his studies, so as to profit from teaching, learning, and discussion. And so it is clear that every duty which is relevant to the maintenance of human society is to be put before any duties involved in the pursuit of truth.

Chapter 45

159.   Perhaps we ought now to consider whether our social duties, which are particularly in accordance with nature, are always to be put before the demands of justice and moderation. I think not. For there are some actions so disgraceful and so criminal that no wise man could perform them even to save his country. Posidonius[29] has collected many examples, but they are so disgusting and offensive, that it would be shocking even to mention them. They are such that a wise man would not undertake them for the state, nor would the state wish them to be undertaken on its behalf. Indeed it is perhaps as well that the occasion can never arise in which such actions could be in the interests of the state.

160.   This, then, is our general conclusion, that in determining our duties the kind which should have pride of place are those which

I

are of vital importance to the maintenance of human society. Well-considered action is the goal of all thought and learning, and therefore reasoned action is to be more highly valued than careful thought. That in fact sums it up. I think that I have now clearly shown the way, so that in the pursuit of our obligations it should be quite easy to see an order of priorities. Social duties can be divided into grades so that the priority of any given duty is apparent. The order would be as follows: first our duty to the immortal gods, secondly to our country, thirdly to our parents, and lastly to the rest of society in due order.

161.   From this argument it will be clear that not only do men have doubts about the morality or immorality of an action, but about the comparative merits of two equally moral actions. This is a point, which, as I mentioned before, was omitted by Panaetius. But let us now pass on to the questions that still remain.

Book II

BOOK II

Chapter 1

1. My dear Marcus,

I think I have given an adequate explanation in my first book of the way in which our obligations are derived from goodness as well as from every individual moral quality. It now remains for me to discuss the kinds of obligation which are relevant to our way of life and to the acquisition of those things from which men derive advantage, namely power and riches. In my former book I said that we should consider what was expedient and what was not; and under the heading of expediency I mentioned that we should consider not only expediency itself, but in its relative and absolute terms. But first I want to make a few observations about the work itself and the judgements expressed in it.

2. My books have inspired a number of people with a desire to write as well as read; and yet I am afraid that some good men may hate the name of philosophy and express surprise that I devote so much time and effort to it. I would reply that as long as the state was ruled by its own elected representatives, I devoted all my thought and attention to its interests. But when it became wholly subject to the domination of one man and there was no longer any place for my leadership and advice, when, above all, I had been deprived of those eminent men who had been my colleagues in governing the affairs of state, I neither abandoned myself to despair, which would have been my undoing had I given in to it, nor gave myself up to the sort of pleasures which ill befit a man of learning.

3. I cannot but wish that the state had continued in its former constitution and had not fallen into the hands of men whose aim was not so much to change as to destroy its institutions. This, then, is my first point, that I would prefer to put my efforts into politics rather than into literary composition, as I did when the republic

still survived. Then of course writing would be confined to my public speeches, as it often has been, rather than these discourses which I now undertake. But now that the state, which absorbed all my thoughts, attentions and efforts, has now been utterly ruined, my legal and political speeches no longer make themselves heard.

4. But I cannot allow my mind to be inactive, and, as it has always been inclined to such pursuits from my earliest days, I thought that I could best keep depression at bay by having recourse to philosophy once again. I had spent a good deal of time on it as a young man in the course of my education, but when I began to serve in the highest offices of state and devoted all my energies in that direction, the only opportunity for philosophy was the time that remained over and above that devoted to my friends and the state. This was spent entirely in reading so that I did not have the leisure which one needs for writing.

Chapter 2

5. Our greatest disasters, then, seem to have brought us this advantage, namely the opportunity to write about subjects which are worth consideration and about which too little is known. What indeed is there, in heaven's name, more to be desired than philosophy? What has a more outstanding claim? What is more becoming to a man or more worth his attention? Those who pursue the subject are known as *philosophers*, and philosophy itself is by definition *the love of wisdom*. The ancient philosophers call it the knowledge of all things human and divine and the causes which lie behind them. I cannot imagine what kind of study any man would commend were he to object to this.

6. If we seek mental satisfaction or freedom from care, what can compare with the pursuits of those who are engaged in a constant search for what affects and is relevant to the good and happy life? If on the other hand we are concerned with moral fibre, either this is the means by which it is attained, or else none exists. To say that there is no skill involved in attaining the greatest things when even the smallest are not achieved without it, is the mark of those who speak before they think and so fall into great error. No! If there

100

II

is any means of teaching goodness, where is it to be sought if this method of approach is abandoned? But when I encourage others in the study of philosophy, these are the questions which they usually discuss in some detail, as indeed I have done myself in another book. My only aim at the present time, now that I have been debarred from all public duties, is to explain why I particularly devoted myself to this study.

7.　　There are those—and they are men of learning—who object that I do not show the consistency that I ought to, when, in spite of declaring that nothing can be known, I discourse on many matters including my present theme—obligations. I wish that they had a better grasp of my intentions; for I do not include myself among those whose mind flounders in uncertainty and has no fixed goal. Can you imagine the sort of mind a man would have, or rather the sort of life he would lead, if he were completely debarred from rational discussion and a rational way of life? There are those who say that some things are certain and others uncertain. I disagree with them: I would say that some things are probable and others improbable.

8.　　Is there anything, then, to prevent me from pursuing what seems probable and rejecting the reverse? Surely by avoiding over-bold assertion one reduces the risk of being irrational, which is the very negation of philosophy. The very reason why we Academics question the certainty of everything is that the very probability which I have mentioned could not come to light except from a comparative analysis of the arguments on both sides. But I feel that all this has been adequately explained in my 'Academica'.[a] You, my son, are engaged in the study of a very fine and ancient school of philosophy—and under Cratippus[b] too, who deserves to be classed with its most distinguished founders; none the less, I would not wish you to be ignorant of our doctrines which differ little from those of your sect. But I must now return to my subject.

[a] *Academica*, II, 20, *et seqq.*
[b] For Cratippus, *Vd.* Note 1.

Chapter 3

9.   Five principles have already been expounded for the performance of duty. Two of them related to what is right and fitting, two
to things advantageous to living, such as wealth, power and opportunity, and the fifth to a method of choosing between the four
already mentioned when they seem to conflict with one another. I
have already dealt with the first two and want you to be particularly familiar with them. The next one I propose to deal with is
what is generally called expediency. As a result of general usage
the word has gradually changed its sense, resulting in a distinction
between right and expedient, so that one may now consider one
thing to be right but not expedient, and another to be expedient but
not right. This is the most pernicious error which has ever crept
into men's minds.

10.   Although philosophers of the highest authority make a theoretical distinction between these three ideas, they admit that they are
essentially interrelated, and do so on strict and honest principles;
for whatever is just they consider expedient, and what is morally
good is also just; thus it follows that what is morally good is also
expedient. Men are slow to realize this and so are often seduced by
the sophistic distinctions of charlatans and accept chicanery in the
place of wisdom. It is our duty to expose their error and every
opinion is to be directed to such an end that they realize that they
can attain their goal not by trickery and deceit, but by honourable
plans and just action.

11.   Of the things that enrich human life some are inanimate, like
gold, silver and other similar products of the earth, others are
animate and are endowed with natural impulses and appetites.
Some of these are rational creatures, others are not: the former
include gods and men; the latter include horses, oxen and other
cattle, and bees, all of which contribute something to the comforts
of human life. The favour of the gods can be won by living a dutiful
and devout life. Next to the gods men themselves can make the
greatest contribution to human well-being.

12.   The same distinction can be made between the things which can

102

cause harm and frustration to men. However in this case the gods are ruled out, as harm is considered incompatible with their divine nature; but men remain and they are often thought to be the greatest barrier to human progress. The things that we have classed as inanimate are mostly the products of human effort, which we would not possess were it not for his aptitude in handling them. Indeed without man's efforts we would not enjoy the benefits of medicine, navigation, agriculture or the production and preservation of cereal and other crops.

13.　　Moreover we would not be able to export the products we produce in great quantities or import the things that we need, unless men performed these functions. Similarly stone, which is such a necessary human requirement would not be quarried, neither would 'iron, bronze, gold and silver' be mined 'from the bowels of the earth'[a] without manual effort on the part of men.

Chapter 4

It is natural for men to live together in communities, for only in this way have they learned the advantages of mutual help and interdependence. How otherwise than by human co-operation could houses have originally been acquired to protect us from the extremities of heat and cold? How otherwise could they subsequently have been repaired when they collapsed as a result of storms, earthquakes or the decay of old age?

14.　　We should also take into account aqueducts, canals, irrigation schemes, breakwaters and harbours. How could we have had any of these without human effort? I could cite many other examples to show that every product and advantage which we derive from inanimate things is the direct result of man's physical efforts. To pass on to the animal kingdom, what product or advantage would be gained from them were it not for man's co-operation? He first of all discovered the uses to which each beast could be put; and without those efforts we would not now be able to keep animals, train them, look after them or accept what they produce in due

[a] Probably from the *Prometheus* of Accius. The line is a translation of Aeschylus, *Prometheus Vinctus*, 502.

season. Men have also practised the art of killing dangerous animals and capturing useful ones.

15.   Why should I mention all the other skills without which civilized life as we know it could not be lived? Would there be any comfort for the sick or pleasure for the healthy? Would we have either food or clothing if we had not so many skills at our disposal? This is the measure of superiority of human civilization over the way of life enjoyed by animals. Were it not for the communal efforts of mankind, cities would neither be built nor inhabited; there would be none of the laws and customs, none of the rules of justice or accepted conventions of life, to which cities give rise. These factors have combined to produce men of civilized and modest character, and the overall result is that life is more secure; moreover, by mutual giving and accepting of benefits, by exchange of commodities and opportunities, all our needs are supplied.

Chapter 5

16.   I will labour the point no more. For everyone can appreciate that point which Panaetius stresses at such length, that neither a general on a foreign campaign, nor a statesman at home could ever have achieved anything great or beneficial without the support of his fellow-men. As examples of this he cites Themistocles, Pericles, Cyrus, Agesilaus, Alexander, and says that none of them could have achieved what they did single-handed. His point is, in fact, so obvious that such a number of examples is quite unnecessary. Not only is it true that some of our greatest advantages are the fruits of human co-operation, but also that there are no calamities so great as those which men bring upon one another. That learned and prolific Peripatetic, Dicaearchus, who wrote a whole book on the ways in which men die, enumerated all the other causes such as floods, pestilence, barrenness and even the sudden attacks of wild beasts, by which he assures us that whole nations have been annihilated; then by contrast he points out how many more men have been destroyed by human violence, for example in wars and revolutions, than by all natural calamities combined.[30]

II

17. I take this point, then, as established, that men are capable of doing each other the greatest harm as well as the greatest good. It is therefore a cardinal virtue to be able to win men's hearts and ally them to one's cause. All the advantages which can accrue to human life from inanimate things and animals are the product of the more menial tasks: but to gain men's goodwill so that it is ready and willing to work for our advantage is a task for the wisdom and virtue of outstanding men.

18. Virtue may be said to consist of three factors: the first is perception of what is true and honest in any given matter, what is suited to each man's character, and what may be the motive or consequence of any given action; the second is to keep the more violent emotions (which the Greeks call πάθη) and the appetites (ὁρμαί) in check by making them subject to reason; the third is to treat those with whom we come into contact reasonably and with understanding; thus, by their efforts we shall have all the things that human nature requires in abundance, and shall be able to repel any danger that threatens us as well as taking vengeance on those who have tried to injure us, by inflicting such penalties as are compatible with the principles of justice and humanity.

Chapter 6

19. To enjoy the support of our fellow-men is a great advantage, and I shall shortly explain how we are to acquire it—but first a brief observation. Everyone recognizes the important role played by fortune in success or failure. Aided by its fair breezes we reach our destined goal; but when they veer against us we find ourselves in distress. Now some of the misfortunes which occur are comparatively rare, and can be divided into two categories: first there are those which arise from inanimate causes, such as storms, tempests, shipwrecks, the collapse of buildings and fires; secondly those resulting from the attacks of beasts, such as kicks, bites and charges.

20. These, as I have said, are comparatively rare. Much commoner are those events, which, although influenced by fortune, could not happen except by human intervention. They include military dis-

asters (of which we have had three recent examples as well as many others from time to time), deaths of generals (here again a distinguished example is still fresh in our minds),[31] the banishment, flight or downfall often of those who have performed distinguished service to the state, but have fallen from popular favour; on the other hand the same factors determine success in the form of high office, whether civil or military, and in conquest. Having made this observation let us go on to consider how we can best attract and stimulate men's enthusiasm to our own advantage. If I seem to dwell on this too long, consider the enormous advantage to be gained from such an argument, and it may well seem to have been too short.

21.   To my theme then. Whatever men do to promote the fortune or career of another is done for one of six reasons: the first is kindness, often motivated by pure affection; the second, respect, because they look up to a man because of his qualities and think him worthy of promotion to the highest sphere; the third is trust, when they think that a man will look after their interests; the fourth is fear of a man's power and influence; the fifth is hope of some return for their goodwill, a common motive of patrons and demagogues who are notorious for their largess; and the sixth is the inducement of pay or a reward, which is the lowest and most unworthy motive for those who are taken in by it as well as those who have recourse to it.

22.   It is indeed a bad state of affairs when men try to procure by bribes the things which ought to be the rewards of virtue. But since this is sometimes the only course of action, I shall explain the rules which govern its use when I have first said something about the things which are more closely related to the good life. There are even more reasons why men submit to the direction and authority of another. It is through goodwill, or gratitude for many favours received, respect for his great worth, or the hope of gain, fear that they may be forced into obedience anyway, or bribes either promised or expected, or, finally, as we have so often seen in Rome itself, the practice of hiring for a fee.

II

Chapter 7

23. Of all the factors which lead to the maintenance and preservation of our interests popularity is the most important. Fear, on the other hand, can do them most harm. Ennius puts it well when he says:

'Whom they fear, they also hate; and whom they hate they seek to kill.'[a]

We have recently become aware, if we did not know it before, that no power of resources, however great, can counter mass unpopularity. We have recently seen in the death of a tyrant, Julius Caesar, who not only crushed the state with military force in his lifetime, but now continues his domination more than ever after his death, an example of the catastrophic effects of such mass unpopularity; nor is this the only example: in the case of tyrants death by violence is the rule rather than the exception. Fear is a poor guarantee of permanence, whereas goodwill is a reliable presage of lasting rule.

24. The use of force is quite legitimate in the case of those who have to keep an empire under control, just as it is right for masters to beat their slaves, if they cannot command obedience in any other way. But for those who hold office in a free state to behave in such a way as to inspire fear is the height of madness. For although laws have been overruled by the power of the individual, although the spirit of freedom has been cowed, both freedom and the law sooner or later rise to the surface and find expression in the silent judgement of the people or in their secret votes cast for the highest offices of state. Liberty shows its teeth more when violated than when maintained. Let us accept, then, the rule that it is better to govern by love than by fear, for it is one that may be applied over a wide field, as it is not merely relevant to safety, but to power and wealth as well. Adherence to this rule, then, will ensure easy success in both public and private life; for those who inspire fear in others inevitably have reason to fear their reaction.

25. What are we to think of the elder Dionysius who was constantly racked by such agonies of fear for the barber's razor, that he used

[a] Probably from Ennius's *Thyestes*.

to singe his beard with a glowing coal?[32] What are we to think of Alexander of Pherae who, we read, lived in such fear that even when he just wanted to make love to his wife Thebe, ordered a barbarian and a branded Thracian at that, to precede him with a drawn sword as he made his way from the banquet to his bedroom; it is even said that he sent some of his bodyguard on in front to examine the women's clothes and caskets in case any weapons were hidden in them.[33] What an unhappy state of affairs when a man finds that a barbarian branded slave is more to be trusted than his own wife! His fears were not without foundation; for it was his wife herself who later killed him on suspicion of keeping a mistress. No power, then, which depends on fear can ever be lasting.

26.   Yet another example is Phalaris,[34] who was particularly notorious for his ruthlessness; he was not, like Alexander of Pherae, the victim of a domestic plot, nor was he, like Caesar, the target of a group of conspirators, but found himself in the midst of a general uprising of the people of Agrigentum. If these examples were not enough, I could quote the case of Demetrius[35] who was abandoned by the Macedonians when they seceded to Pyrrhus, or that of the Spartans, who because of their arrogant demands were suddenly almost entirely deserted by their allies who took upon themselves the role of passive spectators of their tragic defeat at Leuctra.

Chapter 8

I much prefer to illustrate my point with foreign examples than with those from our own state; but I would observe that as long as the Roman empire was held together by goodwill rather than injustice, wars were waged to protect its allies or its interests, resulting in reasonable treatment for the subject except when necessity demanded otherwise. The senate was then a haven of refuge for kings and whole peoples, and our civil and military leaders particularly sought to distinguish themselves by defending their pro-

27. vinces and allies fairly and loyally. Rome might well have won the title 'Protectress of the World' rather than 'Empress'. But such a tradition of self-discipline was already on the wane before Sulla's

108

rule and broke down entirely after his death; for amid the ruthless climate of the civil war any unjust treatment of allies went unnoticed. Sulla's cause was honourable but his victory brutal; he even had the temerity to say, while holding in the forum an auction of the possessions of men who were citizens and whose only crime was that they were rich, that he was selling his own booty. And yet he was followed by a man,[a] the injustice of whose cause scarcely matched the brutality of his victory, who not only confiscated the goods of individual citizens but embroiled all the provinces and lands of the Roman empire in one common disaster.

28.   Thus with the attack and destruction of foreign nations we have seen the city of Massilia carried along in a triumph to be as it were a symbol of our lost empire.[36] To think that we should triumph over a city without whose aid our generals would never have returned triumphant from across the Alps! I could mention many other acts of disloyalty to our allies, but I doubt whether the sun has ever looked down upon a more treacherous betrayal than this. Our disasters have been richly deserved; for if we had not let so many crimes go unpunished, we should never have seen such great abandonment of principle in one man. His legacy in terms of estate has affected but a few, but in terms of ambition many, including all the most unscrupulous.

29.   The seeds of civil war will always be present as long as that wicked sale of P. Sulla remains in the memory of wicked men and kindles their hopes. This was the man who had presided at the sale held by his uncle, the dictator, and who, thirty-six years later, did not shrink from an even more ruthless auction.[37] There was another Sulla too, who had been one of L. Sulla's secretaries, and who later became Caesar's city treasurer. Hence it is clear that there will always be civil wars as long as such great rewards are in the offing. As it is, the republic is utterly destroyed; of the city only the walls remain standing, and even they seem hardly safe from attack. But to return to the subject from which this digression emerged: this disaster has come upon us because we preferred to rule by fear than by love. And if it can happen to our whole people because of their tyrannical rule, what lessons should individuals learn from it? It is abundantly clear, then, that goodwill has a powerful influence for good and fear a weak one, and it follows from this that we should now consider how we may most easily

[a] Julius Caesar.

achieve that love based on loyalty and honour which is our goal.
30.   We do not all need love in equal measure; each man should esti-
mate, according to the sort of life he leads, whether he needs mass
popularity or the devotion of a few friends. We can surely lay
down here as a basic requirement the loyal friendship of those on
whose affection and esteem we can rely. As far as this is concerned,
there is not much difference between those of the highest rank and
those of the lowest, for both are almost equally anxious to secure
31. it. Rank, prestige and general popularity are perhaps not equally
requisite for all; but where they do exist they are a great advantage
in many ways, not least for procuring friendships.

Chapter 9

I have already discussed friendship in another work, entitled
'Laelius'.[a] Let us go on to consider glory. I have written two whole
books on the subject,[b] but I shall touch upon it again because it
is one of the main ingredients of success in the highest affairs of
state. True glory consists of three elements: general popularity,
confidence and the kind of admiration which leads to high honour.
To put it briefly and simply, these can be acquired from the people
as a whole on broadly the same lines as from individuals; but in
the case of the former there is another line of approach which enables us to find a place in their very hearts.
32.   Let us consider the first of the three elements which I mentioned
and discuss under that heading the rules for obtaining goodwill. It
may be won either by actual benefits conferred or by a willingness
to confer them, if a man's resources are not equal to the task; for
popularity is greatly influenced by a man's reputation, or at any
rate a popular impression of generosity, goodwill, justice, loyalty
and all the virtues which are the mark of a gentle and kind character. The reason is that right and proper conduct is in itself commendable and stirs the hearts of all by the very beauty of its nature.
It is particularly apparent in those virtues which I have mentioned,
and therefore our affection for those in whom those virtues are

---

[a] *De Amicitia.*
[b] *De Gloria*—known to Petrarch—is now lost.

thought to exist is demanded by nature itself. These are the most important causes of popularity; there may be others, but they are not so significant.

33.   Confidence is based on two factors: good judgement and just dealing. We have confidence in those whom we think understand matters better than we do ourselves, as well as foreseeing future events and finding solutions when matters come to a crisis by planning according to the needs of circumstance. This is what men consider to be true and really profitable wisdom. Such is men's trust in just men, by which I mean good men, that their actions are never clouded by any suspicion of falsehood or injustice. Thus we believe that our safety, wealth and children are best entrusted to them.

34.   Of these two factors justice is the more important, because justice without good judgement inspires confidence, whereas the reverse does not. The more shrewd and cunning a man is, the more his reputation for integrity suffers and he becomes suspected and hated. But justice intelligently applied, can inspire all the confidence that a man could wish. Justice without judgement will still have immense influence, but judgement without justice will achieve nothing.

Chapter 10

35.   All philosophers are agreed and I myself have often argued that the possession of one virtue means the possession of all. It may seem surprising, then, that I now separate them, as if anyone could be just without at the same time being wise. The answer is that the subtle distinctions we make when analysing abstract truth are one thing, and the language we use when commending our views to popular opinion is another. Therefore as I write this with the latter in view, I use popular language and speak of one man being brave, another good and another wise. For Panaetius has shown that when dealing with a subject which concerns the people, we must use the kind of argument which they understand and with which they are familiar. But let me return to my subject.

36.   The third of the three elements of which glory is comprised is

that admiration which leads to high honour. People generally admire an action which is great beyond all that they would expect, and particularly an action which is better than they would expect of a particular individual. Thus they respect and greatly applaud those men in whom they claim to see outstanding and exceptional qualities, while they scorn and deride those in whom they detect neither ability, courage or vigour. Not that they make all those of whom they disapprove victims of their derision: they would not by any means, for example, include among the derided those whom they consider unscrupulous, slanderous or deceitful, but they disapprove of them none the less. Therefore, as I said before, the objects of their derision are those who, as we say, 'are good to neither man nor beast' and who neither work for, nor aim at, nor care for anything.

37.   We admire on the other hand those who are thought to surpass others in virtue and not only refrain from things that are unfitting but from those vices which others find it difficult to avoid. It is the pleasures, those most alluring mistresses, which for the most part seduce men's minds from virtue; pain too, when it strikes, terrifies most people beyond all reason: life and death, riches and poverty fill all humanity with extremes of desire or horror. It is only when a man can look down on all these things with high-minded indifference and become entirely converted to and absorbed in some great and honourable task which is set before him, that we begin to admire his virtue in all its shining beauty.

Chapter 11

38.   We shall be greatly admired, then, if we show contempt for the things that most preoccupy men's minds. But justice is above all the criterion of the good man and the thing which most commends him to the mass of the people. No man can be truly just, if he is afraid of death, pain, exile or poverty, or if he puts the opposites of these before fair dealing. Contempt for riches is a most admirable quality, and the man in whom it is apparent shines out like gold tried in the fire. All the three elements of glory are the products of justice: first goodwill, because it confers the most widespread benefits, second confidence for the same reason, and third

admiration, because the just man disregards and scorns the very things which most men are spurred on by greed to pursue.

39.   I believe that no man, whatever his way of life, can do without the help of his fellow-men; in particular, he needs the sort of dialogue which can only exist between friends; this is difficult to achieve unless his integrity is apparent to others. Thus it is also essential for men who have withdrawn from public life to the country to be known for their justice. In fact, in their case it is all the more important, because if they have a reputation for injustice they will find no one to come to their aid when they themselves are the victims of injustice.

40.   Then there are those who buy and sell, who let and hire things, and who engage in business transactions generally; for them justice is a necessary prerequisite of success. In fact its influence is all-pervading, for even those who live on criminal earnings could not survive without observing some canons of justice among themselves. If, for example, one member of a gang of robbers were to steal from another, he would not even be considered fit to be a member of a society such as that, and if the robber-chief did not give the others a fair share of the loot, he would be abandoned or even killed by his comrades. Hence the rule 'honour among thieves' which they are all obliged to observe. Theopompus tells us of a certain Illyrian robber, called Bardylis, who won great influence because of his justice in the division of spoils. As an even better example one might quote Viriathus the Lusitanian, who even had some of our armies and generals in his pay until Caius Laelius, surnamed 'The Wise', when praetor, broke his grip, undermined his influence and the terror which he inspired, to such an extent that his successors found him quite easy to deal with.[38] If, then, the influence of justice is so great that it even cements and extends the power of thieves, how great must its influence be in a well-ordered and law-abiding state.

Chapter 12

41.   It was because of this concern for justice that the Persians (if we are to believe Herodotus,[a] as well as our own ancestors, con-

[a] I, 96.

fined their quest for rulers to those of the highest character. Originally the great mass of the people were ruled by those who possessed greater wealth, until they sought the protection of some man of great integrity to guard the weaker members of the community from injustice; he would restore the balance by establishing equal rights for rich and poor alike. The motives which governed their establishment of laws were the same as those governing their choice of rulers.

42.   Men have always wanted the same basic rights, for without them they have no rights at all. If they could get them from one just and good man, they were satisfied; but when they could not, they invented laws to ensure that their treatment should at all times be disinterested and impartial. It is clear, then, that only those whose integrity commanded the confidence of the great mass of the people were chosen to rule. If it also happened that they were considered men of judgement, there was nothing which men thought that they could not achieve under their leadership. Justice therefore is to be cultivated and maintained by every possible means, both for its own sake (for it would not be justice otherwise) as well as for the contribution it makes to our honour and reputation.

43.   Just as riches are not only to be amassed, but to be used generously as well as to meet recurrent expenditure, so glory should be sought and used with discretion. Socrates is quite right when he says[a] that the shortest and most direct way to glory is to be the sort of man that one would wish to be reputed to be. It is a great mistake to believe that lasting glory can be attained by vain show and pretence or by affectations of speech and expression. True glory takes root and reproduces, whereas affectation soon withers like a cut flower. Nothing that is false can last. I could give many examples of both kinds, but in the interests of brevity I shall confine myself to one family: Tiberius Gracchus, the son of Publius, will be for ever honoured in the annals of the Roman state, whereas his sons did not commend themselves to men of good judgement during their lifetime, and on their death were numbered among those justly killed.[39] True glory, then, is the fruit of the fulfilment of just obligations, for which I refer you to my former book.

[a] Xenophon, *Memorabilia Socratis*, II, 6, 39.

Chapter 13

44. Ensuring that our public image tallies with our real character brings us back to Socrates' dictum that we should be the sort of men we wish to be reputed to be. A few words of advice are necessary here: when a man at the beginning of his career finds that he is the bearer of a famous name, either because of his father's reputation (which I think has happened in your case) or through some other stroke of fortune, he is the object of everyone's gaze and speculation about his life and conduct. In fact, he is so much in the limelight, that no single word or deed of his can pass unnoticed.

45. Those, however, who have been unknown in their younger years because of their obscure or humble origins, should, when they reach years of discretion, aim for the heights and strive after them with unswerving efforts. They will do so with all the greater confidence because at their age they do not inspire jealousy, but enencouragement. A young man's first step to glory is very likely to be made in the military field. Certainly many have emerged in this way in the past, for there have been few years in our history when wars have not been going on. It has been your lot, however, to live through the Civil War in which one side bore the guilt and the other the ill luck. Nevertheless in that war Pompey saw fit to put you in charge of a cavalry detachment, and you won high praise both from the army and the great man himself for your riding, javelin-throwing and endurance of all the toils of war. Your distinction fell with the fall of the republic; but I have undertaken this work not just for you, but for the whole of your generation, and therefore your particular misfortunes will not divert me from my general purpose.

46. Just as in other matters the things of the mind rank above those of the body, so it is with attainments; those which are born of reason and natural ability are of more account than those which are the product of brute force. Particularly to be commended is the sort of good behaviour which combines filial affection with goodwill towards one's own family. Good reputation can also be at-

tained by seeking the company of the wise and distinguished men whose concern is the country's good; for, if constantly seen in such company they create the impression that they will be like those whom they have chosen for their models.

47.   Thus Publius Rutilius[a] as a young man gained a reputation for integrity and ability as a lawyer through being a frequent visitor at the house of Publius Mucius.[b] Lucius Crassus on the other hand did not adopt any model in his youth, but acquired a distinction all his own by his famous prosecution of Caius Carbo—and that at an age[c] when most orators win praise for their success at mere rhetorical exercises. A similar achievement is recorded in the case of Demosthenes.[d] Even at such a tender age Crassus showed himself capable of the sort of performance in public which he might well have been praised for practising in private.

Chapter 14

48.   I have already divided speech into two kinds, private conversation and public debate; it is the latter with its scope for eloquence which makes the greater contribution to glory, and yet it is difficult to assess how far men's affections can be won by friendly and affable conversation. Letters from Philip to Alexander, from Antipater to Cassander, and from Antigonus to Philip—all men whose wisdom is well testified—survive,[40] in which they advise their sons to win the goodwill of the masses and temper the rebelliousness of their troops by kind words and coaxing speeches. But it is the debating speech before a large audience which often arouses universal support; for people have an enormous admiration for anyone who speaks with such skill and fluency that his hearers become convinced that he has greater understanding and wisdom than the rest. Above all, if his speech contains a blend of dignity and reasonableness, nothing more excites the admiration, especially if the speaker is a young man.

[a] Publius Rutilius Rufus; *Vd.* Note 48.
[b] Publius Mucius Scaevola (consul 133 B.C.).
[c] He was twenty-one; *Vd. De Oratore*, III, 20, 74.
[d] Demosthenes brought an action against his guardians at the age of eighteen.

II

49.   The occasions for eloquence are many, and there are a large number of young men in the state who have won a reputation for themselves in both the legal and political fields as a result of their oratory. It is legal speeches that arouse the highest admiration. These can be divided into two categories, those for the defence and those for the prosecution; the former most deserve praise, but the latter generally get it. The example of Crassus I have just mentioned; Marcus Antonius as a young man did the same,[a] Publius Sulpicius[b] too established his reputation as a speaker by his prosecution of that subversive good-for-nothing Caius Norbanus.

50.   Prosecutions should seldom, if at all, be undertaken except on behalf of the state, as they were in the cases which I have just mentioned, or to redress an injustice, as in the case of the two Luculli, or in the interests of those who need protection, as in the case of my own prosecution of Verres[c] on behalf of the Sicilians or Julius'[d] prosecution of Albucius on behalf of the Sardinians. The efforts of Lucius Fufius in accusing Manius Aquilius are well known. A single prosecution is to be commended, but it should certainly not become a regular practice: and if a man is called on to prosecute more often, he should do his duty to the state, for there is no disgrace in repeatedly taking vengeance on her enemies, provided that it is done with moderation. For the man who is constantly bringing capital charges will seem unduly harsh even to the point of becoming inhuman. Moreover it will not only put him in a dangerous position, but he will also acquire the unenviable reputation of one whose sole business is to accuse others. This was the lot of Marcus Brutus, a man of distinguished birth and the son of the famous Brutus, who was particularly famed for his mastery of jurisprudence.

51.   There is one rule of duty to be particularly observed, never to jeopardize the safety of an innocent man; for to do so must always be a criminal act. In fact it would be difficult to imagine any more inhuman act than to abuse the powers of speech with which the orator is endowed by nature for the defence and protection of his fellow-men and turn them to the ruin and destruction of the inno-

---

[a] Marcus Antonius the Orator; *Vd.* III, 16, 67.
[b] Publius Sulpicius Rufus accused Norbanus of *maiestas*; he was defended by Marcus Antonius and acquitted. *Vd. De Oratore*, III, 20, 74.
[c] *In Verrem*, 70 B.C.
[d] Caius Julius Caesar Strabo Vopiscus (aedile 90 B.C.).

cent. This must always be avoided; on the other hand we need have no scruples about occasionally defending the guilty, provided that they are not utterly depraved. This is in fact a course of action commended by popular opinion, sanctified by tradition, and compelled by all decent human feeling. It is the duty of a judge always to seek the truth, but an advocate may sometimes defend that which is less true, provided that it bears some resemblance to truth. This advice I should not dare to include, particularly in work of philosophy, had not Panaetius, the greatest of the Stoics, come to the same conclusion. Defence brings the greatest measure of both glory and gratitude, especially when it means helping someone who is under attack from a man of great power and resources; thus it fell to my lot on numerous occasions; for example, when, as a young man I opposed the great might of the tyrant Sulla on behalf of Sextus Roscius of Ameria,[a] I am sure you know the speech I made on that occasion, as it still survives.

Chapter 15

52.   Having expounded the duties which young men are to perform for the attainment of glory, I must now say something about generosity and the benefits it produces. These are of two kinds: for those in need can be helped either by our money or by our efforts. The former is comparatively simple, especially for a rich man, but the latter is to be preferred in terms of credit and good repute as well as being more the mark of a man of courage and distinction. For whereas both show a genuine desire to help, in the former case the help is merely the product of the pocket, while in the latter it is a reflection of the man's moral quality. Moreover the sort of kindness which depends on a man's material resources dries up the very source of his generosity, so that his goodwill brings about its own destruction, since the more he has benefited in the past, the fewer he will be able to benefit in the future.

53.   But those who benefit others by their efforts, which to be effective require a mixture of moral fibre and hard work, gain a twofold advantage for themselves: first, the more they help, the more

[a] *Pro Roscio Amerino*, 80 B.C.

II

allies they will have in their good works; second, by acquiring a habit of good works they will become better prepared, and, as it were, more in training for service on a wider scale. I am reminded of a letter in which Alexander is admirably reproached by his father, Philip, for trying to court popularity among the Macedonians by means of bribes. 'How could you be so misguided,' he says, 'as to believe in the loyalty of those whom you had corrupted with bribes? Do you want the Macedonians to look upon you not as their king, but as a mere steward or purse-bearer?' I like his use of the words 'steward and purse-bearer', for what could demean kingly status more than that? Even better is his remark about the corrupting influence of bribes, which have a bad effect upon the recipients in that they are thus induced constantly to expect them.

54.   Philip's advice to his son might well be followed by men generally. In fact there cannot be any doubt that the latter kind of generosity which is based on a man's efforts is the more honourable, has the wider influence, and can be of greater practical help. It is true that there are times when gifts of money are called for and this kind of generosity is not altogether to be disregarded; in fact it is right that one should divide one's fortune among the deserving, provided that it is done with care and moderation, for there are many who have squandered their inheritance by indiscriminate benefactions. I cannot imagine anything more foolish than to be so generous that further generosity becomes impossible. Such largess is also apt to lead to open robbery; for those who bestow all their wealth on others are forced into recouping their losses —at someone else's expense! Those who do this defeat their own purpose which is to secure the goodwill of others by their own beneficence, for the opposition caused by their extortion outweighs the popularity won by their largess.

55.   We should therefore not lock up our coffers so tight that generosity can never cause them to be opened, nor should we throw them open so freely that their contents are available to anyone. In fact we should observe a happy mean, which means taking our circumstances into account. Altogether we should remember that saying which wide currency has made almost proverbial, that 'Bounty has no bottom'. Indeed no happy mean is possible when there are only two types of people, those who have received it and those who look forward to doing so.

II

Chapter 16

Those who give can be divided into two kinds, the prodigal and the generous. The prodigal are those who spend large sums of money on feasts, public distributions of food, the provision of gladiators, and the staging of public games or contests with animals, all efforts which are never remembered for long, if at all. The generous are those who use their money to pay off kidnappers, to relieve debts incurred by their friends, to provide dowries, or to help others to acquire a private fortune, or increase it if they already have one.

56.   I am therefore surprised to find in Theophrastus' work 'On Riches'[a] lurking in the midst of much sound advice this absurd idea, that there is much to be said for ostentation in one's public giving and that in fact the opportunity for such expenditure is one of the great fruits of wealth. It seems to me quite the contrary, that the fruits of generosity, of which I have just given a few examples, are much greater and more reliable. Surely Aristo of Ceos is much nearer the mark when he criticizes us for not being shocked at the enormous expenditure on winning popular support.[41] If men under siege were forced to pay four pounds a pint for water, we should think it odd and even refuse to believe it at first; but on mature reflection we should consider it a justifiable expense in view of the extenuating circumstances; but we cannot excuse the monstrous waste and extravagant expenditure of those who are not bent on relieving any need nor even on their own advancement, but on pleasing the masses in a way which is as short-lived as it is futile; for those who enjoy it are so worthless, that their memory of it will last no longer than the actual enjoyment of the show.

57.   Aristo goes on to point out with good reason that the only people who enjoy such shows are children and empty-headed women, slaves and those of slave-like mentality, whereas men of good judgement and fixed principles cannot bring themselves to approve of them. And yet I realize that in our own state it has long

---

[a] For Theophrastus, *Vd.* Note 3. For περὶ πλούτου *Vd.* Diogenes Laertius, V, 47.

been a tradition to expect some form of ostentation even from the best men in the course of their aedileship. There have been numerous examples: Publius Crassus,[a] who was as rich as his surname suggested, entertained with great splendour during his aedileship; not long after, Lucius Crassus joined that most moderate of men Quintus Mucius in a most magnificent aedileship. They were folfollowed by Caius Claudius, Appius' son and many others, among them the Luculli, Hortensius and Silanus. In my consulship Publius Lentulus outdid all his predecessors and was later emulated by Marcus Scaurus. But the most magnificent show of all was that of my friend Pompey in his second consulship. In each case my own view will be too obvious to require any elaboration.[42]

Chapter 17

58.   All suspicion of meanness on the other hand is equally to be avoided. Look how Mamercus in spite of his wealth was unsuccessful as a consular candidate because he had not been aedile.[b] Hence, if there is a popular demand for such shows, they must be put on, and we must not allow our reluctance to stand in the way of our approval, provided that each man is as lavish as his means allow, as I myself was. In fact, additional advantage may often be gained from acts of public largess as in the case of Orestes[c] who recently won great popularity by a public banquet in the streets given as a tithe-offering to Hercules. Not even Marcus Seius was criticized for selling the people corn at a penny a measure when prices were high; in fact he finally shook off the great unpopularity which he had acquired over a period of years, at a price which, considering his position as aedile, was not very great and was certainly not outrageous. But it was my friend Milo who recently won the greatest honour by his purchase of gladiators for the protection of the state, which depended on my safety, and scotched

---

[a] Publius Crassus, surnamed *Dives*, was the father of the Triumvir.

[b] Mamercus Aemilius Lepidus Livianus. This is not a good illustration of the point Cicero is trying to make. He was in fact consul in 77 B.C. with Decius Junius Brutus.

[c] Cneius Aufidius Orestes Aurelianus (consul 71 B.C.).

the mad designs of Publius Clodius.[43] Gifts to the people, then, are justified by either necessity or expediency.

59.   But even when either of these criteria applies, moderation should still be observed. Indeed Lucius Philippus, Quintus' son, a man of great ability and distinction, used to boast that he had scaled all the accepted peaks of political ambition without spending a farthing. Cotta and Curio used to say the same, and I myself also have good reason to boast on this account; for when I consider the scale of my own honours (which were won, incidentally, by a unanimous vote, and all of them in the first year in which I was eligible—an achievement which none of the others I have mentioned can claim) my aedileship involved remarkably little expense.[44]

60.   The best kind of expense is that which is for the benefit of the community as a whole, such as the building of walls, dockyards, harbours, aqueducts and the like. It is true that gifts which are actually received at the time are more popular, but these are the things for which people are more grateful in the long run. I would hesitate to condemn theatres, porticoes and new temples out of respect for Pompey's memory, but they are generally disapproved of by philosophers, particularly Panaetius, whom I have followed fairly closely, though not actually translated, in this work, and Demetrius of Phalerum,[2] who is very scathing about the leading statesman of Greece, Pericles, for squandering such vast sums of money on that fine building, the Propylaea. But this is a subject which I have discussed exhaustively in the *De Republica*.[a] On the whole, then, the kind of largess which I have discussed is to be condemned, although on occasion it may be necessary; even then it should be adjusted to the means of the donor and tempered by moderation.

Chapter 18

61.   The other kind of giving I mentioned, which is a product of generosity, should vary according to the needs of the recipients;

[a] Probably in the non-extant Book V.

II

for financial disaster is one thing, and the desire to improve an already flourishing position quite another.

62.   We should always be more ready to help those who are in a disastrous position, except perhaps when it has been justly deserved. We should without exception be prepared to help those who want our help, not so much to save them from ruin as to improve their status; but careful judgement is needed in selecting those who most need our help. Ennius makes a good point when he says:

'Good deeds, when ill-conceived, ill deeds become.'

63.   But when a good deed is done to a man who deserves it and is grateful, his gratitude and the general goodwill are our reward. Generosity tempered by discrimination, is a most delightful quality. In fact, many would commend it all the more, because the most generous people create by their goodness a sanctuary for all the needy. We should therefore make the effort to put as many as possible under obligation by our acts of goodwill, whose memory will remain in the minds of their children and descendants so that there will be no room for ingratitude; for no one likes the man who shows no gratitude. In fact, lack of gratitude is anti-social because it discourages generosity, and therefore the ungrateful man is the enemy of all the poorer people. The generosity by which the captive is ransomed and the poorer people enriched is of great advantage to a state as a whole; we see ample evidence in a speech of Crassus[a] for this practice being widespread among senators, and I think it is greatly to be preferred to general largess. The latter is the mark of those who flatter the people and pander to their frivolous desires; the former the mark of men of diginity and character.

64.   Leniency in one's demands is just as important as generosity in one's giving. In every transaction, whether buying or selling, letting or hiring, we should treat our neighbours with fairness and courtesy, not always insisting on our rights and, above all, avoiding lawsuits as far as we reasonably can, and, if anything, a little more. There are times when not to insist on one's rights is not only a mark of generosity, but can even be profitable. But here too a man should take his estate into account, for it is disgraceful to let it fall into neglect; on the other hand he should be generous enough to avoid all suspicion of meanness and miserliness. In fact, the correct use of money may be defined as behaving generously without

[a] Lucius Licinius Crassus the Orator (consul 95 B.C.).

123

squandering one's inherited wealth. Theophrastus was also right to commend hospitality; for nothing to my mind is more fitting than that the houses of distinguished men should welcome visitors with a hospitality that befits their rank. Moreover it reflects great credit on the state, if foreign visitors too are regaled on this scale in the city. It is also a great source of advantage for those who have an honourable desire for power to gain the favour and support of foreign nations by their hospitality. Theophrastus goes one further when he tells us that Cimon of Athens even entertained his own demesmen of Lacia, and not only made it his own custom, but ordered his bailiffs to keep open house for any member of the deme of Lacia who happened to call.

Chapter 19

65.   I come now to the kind of benefits which we confer, not by making gifts, but by our services to the state as a whole as well as to individual citizens. There are few things which contribute more to our resources and popularity than protecting the interests of clients, giving helpful advice and generally putting our professional knowledge at their disposal. There are many things for which I admire our ancestors, but the most outstanding is the fact that they paid great honour to those who studied and interpreted their excellent code of civil law. Moreover up to the present period of upheaval in which we live, this remained the province of the most eminent men of state; but now the distinction of legal learning, like all other honours and marks of rank, has passed away, and its passing is all the more to be lamented because it has happened in the time of one who was not only equal in honour to all his predecessors, but easily surpassed them in knowledge.[a] Legal services, then, bring widespread popularity and confer the sort of benefit which makes men conscious of an obligation.

66.   Closely allied to legal skill is rhetoric with its added charm and embellishment of language. Indeed what more effective weapon can be found for stimulating the admiration of one's hearers or the hopes of those who need legal help or the gratitude of the acquit-

[a] Servius Sulpicius Rufus the Jurist. *Vd.* Cicero, *Brutus*, 41, 153.

ted, than eloquence? Our forebears rightly awarded it the crown
of all civil pursuits. Hence the man who is not only eloquent, but
prepared to take pains and make himself a champion of the masses,
as our forefathers did, ungrudgingly and without payment, can be
assured of widespread goodwill and a plentiful supply of clients.

67.   My subject prompts me at this point to say a few words of lament
for the decline of rhetoric, one might even say the death of it; and
I would do, were it not that I might seem to be grinding my own
axe. And yet it is apparent, now that we have lost so many good
orators, how few there remain of any promise, fewer still of real
ability, but too many whose presumption outweighs their skill.
Now one cannot expect any but a chosen few to combine legal
expertise with real eloquence. And yet it is possible to help a large
number of people, if one is prepared to take the trouble by asking
kindnesses on their behalf, commending their case to juries and
magistrates, keeping watch over their interests, or seeking the
help of those who can give legal advice or actually defend them.
Those who do this will reap their reward in terms of popularity
and a widespread readiness on the part of others to act in their
interests.

68.   There is a further piece of advice which is so obvious that it
hardly needs stating: it is to see that in our desire to help one section of the community we do not offend others. Men often injure
those whom they ought not to, or those whom it is not wise to
injure. To do it unwittingly is careless; to do it knowingly is rash.
If, however, we cannot avoid offending people, we should excuse
ourselves as best we can by showing that there was no other course
open to us, and we should try to make up for even an apparent
injustice by good turns in the future.

Chapter 20

69.   In deciding whether to help a person we generally take into
account either his character or his position. It is easy to say, as
most men do, that we are prompted by considerations of character
rather than position. A fine sentiment! But is there really any man
who would chose to help a poor but good man rather than win the

favour of a man of wealth and power? No! We are invariably more prone to serve the interests of the one from whom we can expect a prompt and sure return. We must, however, take a more careful look at the real situation: it is true that a poor man cannot repay a favour, but, if he is a good man, he will certainly acknowledge it. Someone once made an apt remark (I don't remember the author of it) to the effect that in the case of money to have is not to have repaid, and to have repaid is not to have, whereas in the case of a sense of obligation to have repaid is to have, and to have is to have repaid. But men who consider themselves blessed with both riches and marks of honour do not like to feel obliged to repay any favour; more than that, even when they have received a great favour, they give the impression that they have conferred one, and look askance if anything is demanded or expected of them; moreover, if it were suggested that they had been patronized or reduced to the status of dependents, they would consider it a fate worse than death.

70.   The poor man on the other hand supposes that any benefit received is a reflection of his own worth rather than his status, and so is eager to appear grateful not only to the man who has deserved his gratitude, but to those to whom he looks for further help—for he needs as much as he can get. Moreover, if he does anyone else a service, he adopts a modest rather than a boastful attitude. There is another factor too worth considering: if you defend a man of power and wealth, your only reward will be his gratitude and perhaps that of his children; whereas if you help a poor man, provided that he is a man of good character and behaviour (for poor character does not always go with poor estate), then all poor but honest citizens, which, after all, constitute a large section of the community, will regard you as someone who is prepared to protect their interests.

71.   It is therefore preferable, I think, that benefits should be conferred on people according to merit rather than wealth. We should of course make every attempt to help all kinds of men, but if any conflict arises, I am sure that we should follow the advice of Themistocles, who, when asked whether he would prefer his daughter to marry an honest pauper than an unscrupulous tycoon, replied, 'A man without money is infinitely preferable to money without a man.' It is true that the corruption and decadence of our morals is largely due to our admiration for riches; and yet what

real influence does anyone's riches, however great, have on any one of us? Perhaps their owner derives some advantage from them, though this is by no means always true. But, granting this, can we say that a man is better in any sense simply by virtue of having more to spend? If a man is deserving, then riches should not affect our attitude towards him for the better or the worse, for character is the real criterion; riches are irrelevant. The final rule which I would give for conferring benefits, whether in the form of gifts or services, is that nothing should be done which is either unfair or unjust; for justice and equity lie at the root of lasting repute, and without them no action can be commended.

Chapter 21

72. Now that I have dealt with benefits conferred upon individuals, I want to discuss those which help the community as a whole. They may be divided into two categories: those which help the state in general, and those which affect particular groups of people within it. It is the latter that bring the greater popularity. Attention should of course be given to both, if possible, and in equal measure; but we should be particularly careful to see that our benefits to individual groups should bring advantage to, or at any rate do nothing to harm, the state as a whole. The corn doles of Caius Gracchus were very generous, but the treasury was emptied as a result, whereas those of Marcus Octavius were moderate; they provided for people's needs, and at the same time were within the state's means, and therefore benefited both the state and its citizens.

73. Anyone who holds office in the state should take particular care to safeguard private property, and in particular to see that individuals are not robbed by the state. An example of this can be seen in the pernicious words of Philippus as tribune, when introducing his agrarian legislation; it is true that he allowed it to be rejected without a struggle, and in that he acted with great moderation; but in the midst of his great appeal for popular support he made the dangerous observation that private-property owners in the state numbered less than two thousand. Such a statement is criminal in that it is tantamount to an advocacy of communism. In fact

it is difficult to imagine anything more subversive, for the original growth of states and cities was largely due to the desire to protect private property. It is true that men are by nature gregarious, and yet it was not so much this as the desire to protect what was their own, that led them to seek the protection of cities.

74.   Property taxes should also be avoided at all costs. They have often been imposed in the past owing to the poverty of the exchequer caused by continual wars; such contingencies should be foreseen well in advance and due provision made against them. But if any state ever finds such taxes necessary—I say *any* because I do not wish to forebode such a thing for our own, and besides I am making a generalization here—efforts should be made to ensure that everyone is aware of their necessity if they are to come through the crisis. Furthermore, it is the duty of those who hold office in the state to see that there is a sufficient supply of the necessities of life. There is no need to discuss here what these ought to be or what they usually are; in fact they immediately spring to mind, and I merely thought the subject should be mentioned *en passant*.

75.   But the main thing, both in private business and in public affairs is to avoid even the slightest suspicion of self-seeking. Caius Pontius,[a] the Samnite once said, 'I wish that Fate had held me back so that I could be born in an era when the Romans would first take bribes; I would not allow their empire to remain a day longer.' He would have had to have waited a good many generations, for this particular curse has only recently descended upon the state. If indeed Pontius was as formidable as his words suggest, I am very glad that he lived when he did. Until Lucius Piso enacted his law, there was no law against bribery, and even his law has only been in force for just over a century.[44] Since then there has been a succession of laws, each more stringent than the last; large numbers of people have been put on trial and condemned; a full-scale war with our Italian allies[b] has been sparked off by fear of these very courts, and there has been widespread extortion and pillaging in defiance of all law and judicial procedure, with the result that our present strength is due less to our own qualities than to the impotence of others.

[a] Victor over the Romans at the Battle of the Caudine Forks (321 B.C.). Zumpt suggested that Pontius's remark was quoted from Cato's *Origines*.
[b] The Social War, 92–88 B.C.

II

Chapter 22

76.   Panaetius praises Scipio Africanus,[a] and rightly so, for his self-restraint; but this was not among his greatest virtues, for it was a quality not so much peculiar to him as to the times in which he lived. Aemilius Paullus[b] had all the wealth of Macedonia, which was very considerable, at his disposal, and so replenished the exchequer that the contribution of his spoils alone has secured remission of taxes up to the present day; and yet he did not embellish his own house with anything but the lasting memory of his name. His son, Africanus, followed his father's example and did not enrich himself by a penny from the destruction of Carthage. Moreover his colleague as censor, Lucius Mummius, returned not a bit the richer from destroying the richest city on earth.[c] He preferred to adorn Italy rather than his own house, though by his adornment of Italy he brought all the more lustre to his own house as well.

77.   To return to the point from which I digressed, I would say that there is no more detestable vice than avarice, particularly in those who hold positions of authority in the state. For a man to use the state for his own ends is not merely disgraceful, but criminal. Thus the reply of the Pythian oracle that only avarice could destroy Spartan power would seem to apply not only to the Spartans, but to any wealth-possessing nation. Conversely, those who hold power can gain the goodwill of the people more by controlling their lust for money than in any other way.

78.   But those who seek popularity by radical legislation, which involves dispossessing people of their land or the remission of justly-incurred debts, are undermining the very foundations on which the state rests. For there can never be unity in the state as long as some have their debts remitted and others forfeit their just dues; nor can there be equity, unless each man is secure in his own possessions. The whole point, as I mentioned before, of men gathering together

[a] Publius Cornelius Scipio Africanus Minor (12), *Vd.*, Note 18, Appendix.
[b] Lucius Aemilius Paullus Macedonicus, Victor at Pydna in 168 B.C., father (by adoption) of above.
[c] Corinth, destroyed in 146 B.C.

II

into states and cities is that each man's possession of what is his own should be secure and unassailed.

79.   Moreover, by such an action not only do they flout the purpose of a state, but they do not even secure the goodwill at which they were aiming; for they are assured of the enmity of those whom they have robbed, while those who have benefited conceal the fact that they wanted such concessions, and are particularly prone to hide their delight in remission of debts, lest they should seem to have been insolvent. The man who has been injured harbours his grudge and makes no secret of it. Nor is there any guarantee that because the number of undeserving beneficiaries exceeds that of the injured, their influence will be any greater. For it is worth and not mere numbers that counts. How can you dispossess people who have owned land for years, and perhaps even centuries, to give it to those who have never had any, and call it justice?

Chapter 23

80.   It was because of this kind of injustice that the Spartans expelled the ephor, Lysander, and condemned Agis to a death unprecedented in their history.[45] Such was the disunity that ensued that tyrants arose, aristocrats were banished, and the best-governed state in history fell into decline. It did not fall alone. The troubles which had originated at Sparta spread until their contamination infected the whole of Greece. Furthermore, was it not upheaval due to agrarian reform that led to the downfall of the Gracchi here at Rome?[a]

81.   Aratus of Sicyon on the other hand is rightly praised; for when his country had been in the grip of tyranny for fifty years, setting out from Argos, he secretly entered the city and got control.[b] Having thus taken Nicocles, the tyrant, by surprise, he recalled six hundred of the richest citizens. In this way he freed the state by his coming; but he ran into difficulties over the possession of estates: for he thought that it would be most unfair for those whom

[a] The two sons of the famous Tiberius Cracchus and grandsons of Scipio Africanus (Cicero's note).
[b] 251 B.C.

he had restored and whose estates were in other hands to be in need, and yet it did not seem any more fair for those who had possessed them for fifty years to be driven out, particularly as after such a long time many had been passed on by way of bequests, purchases and dowries, so that they were justly possessed by their present owners. Thus he came to the conclusion that he should neither dispossess the possessors or allow the dispossessed to remain discontented.

82.　Having decided, then, that money was needed to set things to rights, he declared his intention of setting out for Alexandria, and ordered the whole matter to wait until his return. He promptly went to the court of his friend Ptolemy, who was the second king to take office after the founding of the city. When he had explained to him the need for restoring unity to his country, the rich king saw the point of his case and readily granted his request for substantial financial aid. On returning to Sicyon with it, he summoned fifteen of the leading citizens to a conference at which he reviewed the position of both possessors and dispossessed, and managed by a valuation of their various estates, to persuade some of the possessors to give up their land and accept compensation, and some of the dispossessed to accept compensation in stead of the restoration of their own lands. They all went home satisfied, and so his aim of uniting the state was realized.

83.　Here was a man of greatness and true worth! If only he had been born in our own country! This is the way in which citizens should be treated; not, as we have twice[a] seen in our own country, for public auctions to be held, and people's possessions to be left to the mercy of the crier's voice! The Greek statesman proved himself a man of outstanding wisdom and stature by seeing the necessity for guarding the interests of the community as a whole. In fact every ruler who proceeds according to canons of reason and wisdom will see that no distinction is to be made between the advantage of individuals and that of the state as a whole, but that all should be treated with the same justice. 'Let them live for nothing on another's property.' To what purpose? Presumably that I should buy, build, keep in repair and spend money on a house, so that you can enjoy what is mine without my permission? Is not this just piracy or misappropriation?

---

[a] Under Sulla and Caesar, *Vd*. II, 8, 29.

What is the meaning of 'Clean Sheets',[a] unless it is that you may buy your farm with my money? Hence you get the farm, but am I never to have my money?

Chapter 24

84.   Care should be taken, therefore, that debts never reach such proportions that they become harmful to the state. This can be done in many ways, but never in such a way that the rich lose what is their own, while their debtors gain what is not their due. For there can be no firmer cement for national unity than good faith, and this can never exist unless payment of debts is enforced. My consulship saw some of the greatest efforts to secure remission of debts. They were accompanied by armed force and undertaken by every class and kind of men; so successful was my resistance to them, that the state was completely freed from the scourge. Debt has never been more rampant than it was at that time, and yet never has the problem been more easily or more satisfactorily settled; for when all hopes of evading their obligations had receded, the debtors realized that they would have to pay. I managed to defeat Caesar then, although he has since won his point now that he has no longer anything to gain from it. Such were his criminal propensities that he took pleasure from the mere action even though the motive was no longer there.

85.   To sum up then, those who have the interests of the state at heart will abstain from the kind of beneficence which robs some in order to give to others, and they will take particular care to see that each is secure in the possession of what is his own both by legislation and the administration of justice. Moreover they will see that the poor are not defrauded by virtue of their lowly position, nor are the rich prevented from holding or getting back what is theirs by the envy of others. Above all they will contribute all their efforts both at home and on the battle front to increase the territory, power and revenues of the state. These are the tasks for men of stature; these are the things that our ancestors did, and

[a] *Tabulae Novae*, as proposed by Catiline in order to win support for his conspiracies in 66 and 63 B.C. (cancellation of debts).

those who pursue such a course will not only do great service to the state, but will gain great glory and popularity for themselves.

86.　In this discussion of the canons of expediency, Antipater, the Stoic from Tyre who recently died at Athens thinks that Panaetius omitted two things, the need to look after one's health and one's resources. It is true that they are both expedient, but I think that they are omitted by this most eminent philosopher because they are so obvious. The greatest contributions to good health are a thorough knowledge of one's constitution, observation of what agrees with it and what does not, moderation in eating and in the use of the body generally by avoiding an excess of bodily pleasures, and lastly the employment of those who have the knowledge and skill to deal with physical complaints.

87.　A family fortune should be built up honestly, and preserved and increased by careful economy. This subject is amply treated by a disciple of Socrates, Xenophon, in a work called the *Oeconomicus*, which I translated into Latin when I was about your age.[a] But discussion of all these subjects, whether they concern the acquiring of money, or investing (I would add the use of money too), is better left to those astute men who sit on the Exchange than to any academic philosopher. These are the subjects with which we must become familiar. They are all relevant to expediency, which is the subject of this book.

Chapter 25

88.　The comparison between different expedients, which is my fourth main heading, was omitted by Panaetius, but is often found to be necessary. For the expedients of the body are often compared with external expedients, while both categories are compared among themselves. This is the sort of comparison which is generally made: health is preferable to wealth, but on the other hand wealth is preferable to great physical strength. Then, when the categories are compared among themselves, the following type of example emerges: first of the body, health is to be preferred to pleasure, and strength of body to speed of movement; secondly, of external

[a] Marcus was now twenty.

expedients, glory is to be preferred to riches, and estates in the city to those in the country.

89.   This last category can be well illustrated by the famous replies of Cato, who, when asked what he thought was of prime importance in the running of an estate replied,[a] 'Feeding the stock well.' Asked what came next, he replied, 'Feeding the stock well enough.' Asked his third priority, he said, 'Feeding the stock, even though barely.' The fourth, 'Cultivation.' Moreover when his questioner asked him what he thought of usury, Cato replied, 'You might just as well ask me what I think of murder.' Many more examples could be added to show just how often such comparative estimates are made, if they were required to justify the addition of his fourth

90. heading to our study of obligations. But let us proceed to our next item.

[a] From the *De Agri Cultura* of Cato the Censor.

Book III

BOOK III

Chapter 1

1. My dear Marcus,

It used to be said of Publius Scipio Africanus[46] (the first to bear that surname) by his contemporary, Cato,[47] that he was never less idle than when he was idle, and never less alone than when he was alone. Great words, indeed, and worthy of a man of wisdom and stature! They show that even in moments of idleness he could bring his mind to public affairs and in solitude he found company in his own thoughts, so that he was never really idle and at times found his own company quite sufficient. Thus two factors, idleness and solitude, which blunt the intellect of lesser men, led in his case to a sharpening of the wits. I wish that I could truly say the same of myself, but if I cannot hope to rival such strength of character by my actions, I can at least come very close to it in intent. For now that I am wrongfully precluded by force of arms from taking part in affairs of state and legal practice, I live a life of leisure, and have for that reason left the city and divide my time in solitude between my country estates.

2. Neither my idleness nor my solitude are to be compared with those of Africanus, for the leisure which he took from time to time was a rest from the highest office of state, while his periodic retirement from the madding crowd was analogous to a ship putting into harbour. My inactivity, on the other hand, is due to a lack of commitments rather than to a need for recuperation from them; for now that the senate has been dissolved and the courts wound up, I can no longer find any decent political or legal meployment.

3. And so I who was formerly so much in the public eye, now strive to avoid the gaze of those unscrupulous men with whom the state is infested, and as far as possible go into the hiding of solitude. Philosophers tell us that we should not only choose the least of all possible evils, but even extract from them what good we can. This

137

is why I am enjoying peace, even though it is not the kind of peace which is due to one who secured peace for his country. At the same time I cannot allow myself to use without profit the solitude which has been brought upon me by force of circumstances rather than my own taste.

4.   One must admit, however, that Africanus' achievement was the greater. There are no written records to testify to his genius; no work produced in moments of leisure or solitude survives. From this we may deduce that because of constant mental activity and research into those things of which he made himself master by his very depth of study, he never enjoyed the luxuries of leisure or solitude. I on the other hand do not possess such strength of mind as to be prevented from being alone by my own unexpressed thoughts, and so turn all my care and attention to the task of writing. Such has been my leisure that I have written more in the short time since the republic was overthrown than I achieved in the many years of its survival.[a]

Chapter 2

5.   Although philosophy as a whole, my son, is a fertile and fruitful field, and no part of it has been allowed to go to waste, no branch has proved more fruitful or prolific than the study of moral obligation, which bears its fruit in the form of rules for consistent and virtuous living. Therefore, although I am quite confident that you are giving your full attention to the lessons on this subject which you receive from my friend Cratippus,[1] who is the leading philosopher of our day, I think at the same time that it is right that such rules should not only claim a hearing, but should be so drummed into you that you should not be able, if that is possible, to hear anything else.

6.   This study should be undertaken by everyone who intends to live the good life, and that applies to no one more than yourself. For you will find that you are expected to follow your father in making great efforts, in reaching the highest offices of state, and perhaps even in achieving a comparable reputation. Moreover the

[a] *Vd.* appendix on the works of Cicero, p. 206.

fact that you are under Cratippus at Athens is a great responsibility; for you have gone as it were to a market of the liberal arts and to return empty would not only be disgraceful but would be an insult to the standing of both the university and your teacher. Therefore apply all the concentration and effort that you can muster, if indeed learning involves effort rather than pleasure, and never let it be said that you have failed to do yourself justice, when I have given you every opportunity. But that is enough; I have written to exhort you on many occasions; let us now proceed to the remaining category in my discourse.

7.   Panaetius' work on moral obligation was undoubtedly extremely competent, and apart from a few minor alterations I have taken him as my authority. He laid down the three categories which his successors invariably used as a basis for discussion of the subject; they were: first, the problem of right or wrong in any particular action; second, the question of expediency or inexpediency; and third, the problem of deciding between what is expedient and what is clearly right when the two are in conflict. He dealt with the first two categories in three books and expressed his intention of dealing with the third later, but never fulfilled his promise.

8.   This I find very remarkable, because his disciple, Posidonius,[29] records that he lived another thirty years after those books had been published. It is also remarkable that although he says that there is no subject more deserving of treatment in the whole field of philosophy, he should only briefly touch upon it in his commentaries.

9.   I cannot agree with those who say that Panaetius did not forget to deal with the subject, but omitted it on purpose on the grounds that it is quite impossible to deal with it, because there can never be any conflict between the expedient and the morally good. The admissibility of the third category may well be open to dispute, but there can be no doubt that Panaetius was guilty of neglect in omitting what he had pledged himself to do. For whoever proposes three categories and then deals with two of them, must recognize the need to deal with the third; besides, at the end of the third book he declares his intention of dealing with this category later.

10.   Moreover we have a reliable authority in Posidonius, who also tells us in one of his letters that Publius Rutilius Rufus,[48] a disciple of Panaetius, used to remark that no one had attempted to complete the unfinished work of Panaetius because of the un-

challengeable excellence of what he had already completed, any more than any painter would attempt to finish the famous picture of Venus at Cos which had been left unfinished by Apelles, so beautiful is the face as to thwart any attempt to recapture its beauty in the rest of the body.[49]

Chapter 3

11. Panaetius' judgement in the matter, then, is beyond all doubt: what one might question is whether he was right in adding this category to his discourse on moral obligation. For whether we take the Stoic view that moral good is the only good, or the Peripatetic that it is the greatest—so great in fact that all the rest put together cannot match it—neither of these premisses leaves any room for doubt that expediency can never rival moral good. In fact we are told that Socrates used to curse those who first introduced the artificial dichotomy between two concepts which are by nature congruent. The Stoics accepted his views so completely as to believe that whatever was morally good was expedient, and that nothing could be expedient that was not morally good.

12. If Panaetius had been one of those who maintain that moral goodness is only to be sought in so far as it is expedient, just as there are some who measure the desirability of things by the amount of pleasure[a] or absence of pain[b] that they bring, he would then have been justified in saying that there is sometimes a conflict between them; but since he thought that the highest good is moral good, and therefore whatever apparent advantage comes into conflict with it can neither make our life better by its presence or worse by its absence, he does not seem to have any reason for creating a problem out of the conflict between expediency and moral good.

13. The meaning of the Stoic definition of the greatest good, namely to live according to nature, is in my opinion this: that we should always live virtuously, and should aim at other things which are in accordance with our nature only in so far as they are compatible

[a] E.g. Aristippus of Cyrene.
[b] E.g. Hieronymus of Rhodes.

with virtuous living. This being so, there are some who think that no guidance on the subject is required since it would rest on a false dichotomy. Now the only moral goodness which is really worth the name is to be found exclusively in philosophers and can never be distinguished from virtue. Conversely, where perfect wisdom is not to be found, there is no perfect good, although there may be some semblance of it.

14.   All the obligations which I am discussing in these books come into the 'middle category' of the Stoics,[a] for they apply to the human race as a whole, many of whom attain them either by their natural goodness or the success of their efforts to learn. But the obligation which they define as right is perfect and absolute, is, as they put it, complete in all its parts and not to be attained by any but the true philosopher.

15.   Actions, however, which fall into the middle category are often popularly thought to be perfect, because the great mass of the people do not begin to understand the discrepancy between them and true perfection; the fact that they do not see what is lacking is a measure of their lack of understanding. This is to be seen in their judgement of poems, pictures and many other things, for in their ignorance they take delight in and praise things which are not praiseworthy. The reason for this, I think, is that, not being experts, they are taken in by what good there is in them and so fail to be critical of their faults. It is only when they are taught by those who know better, that they are easily induced to forsake their earlier opinions.

Chapter 4

The obligations which I am considering in these books are what the Stoics consider a kind of 'second-rate' good not peculiar to philosophers, but for mankind as a whole.

16.   In fact they are such as concern all men of good character. When the two Decii or the two Scipios[18] are hailed as 'men of courage', or when Fabricius[50] or Aristides[51] are called 'just', we are not setting them up as patterns of courage or justice, as we might in the

[a] *Vd.* Note 9.

case of the true philosopher; for none of them was a philosopher in the sense that I wish to use the word here. Even those who were considered wise and surnamed as such, like Marcus Cato,[a] Caius Laelius[20] and the Seven Wise Men,[b] were not philosophers in the true sense, but by regularly fulfilling the 'middle' class of obligations they acquired a semblance of true wisdom.

17.   Therefore true goodness should never come into conflict with expediency any more than what is commonly called good, the aim of all who wish to be considered men of integrity, should ever come into conflict with private interest. Hence we should all keep to whatever standards of goodness we understand with the same determination with which philosophers observe standards that are *truly* good. Otherwise we cannot maintain any standards, whatever progress we may make in virtuous living. So much for those who acquire a reputation for goodness by fulfilling their obligations.

18.   It is those who measure everything by the yardstick of self-interest and never allow this to be outweighed by considerations of what is morally good, who in their deliberations draw a distinction between goodness and expediency; but this is never the action of men of moral integrity. Therefore I think that when Panaetius said that men are wont to debate the conflict between them, he meant what he said when he used the words *are wont* rather than *ought*. Indeed not only is it disgraceful to place expediency above moral good, but also to accept that there is a conflict between them and to have any doubts about its solution. You might well ask at this point why this is so often a subject which gives rise to perplexity and debate. The answer is, I think, that there is sometimes real doubt about the nature of the moral good which is under consideration.

19.   For example, an action which is generally considered disgraceful may in certain circumstances often be found to be quite the reverse. Let us take a particular case which may be extended to include a good many others. Is there any greater crime imaginable than the killing not merely of a human being, but of a close friend? And yet if a man kills a tyrant, even if he is a close friend, can we possibly regard him as being guilty of a crime? Certainly the people of Rome would not agree, for of all acts of distinction they regard that as the finest. Is this an example of the victory of expediency

[a] Marcus Porcius Cato the Censor, *Vd.* Note 47.
[b] Bias, Chilo, Cleobulus, Periander, Pittacus, Solon, Thales.

over moral good? No, quite the reverse; for expediency has here followed the lead of moral good. Therefore in order to decide the issue without any possibility of error, when what we believe to be good appears to be in conflict with what appears to be expedient, we must formulate a general rule to follow in all such conflicts, so that we may never recoil from our duty.

20. Such a rule should conform as far as possible to Stoic principles and teaching which I have particularly followed in my work; for although the old Academics and your Peripatetics (who were formerly identified with the Academics) always put moral good before expediency, I prefer the higher morality of those who argue, 'Whatever is good is expedient, and nothing can be expedient which is not good,' to that of those who argue that the good can sometimes not be expedient and that the expedient can sometimes not be good. However, our Academy gives us ample freedom to defend whatever views seem to our judgement to be most probable. But now to return to the general rule.

Chapter 5

21. To rob another or to act against his interests in order to promote one's own is more contrary to nature than death, poverty, pain or anything else which can injure a man's person or his estate; for in the first place it undermines the whole basis of human society. Now nothing is more in accordance with nature than for all men to live together as one society, and this will inevitably be disrupted if each member of it is disposed to rob and injure another for his own advantage.

22. Just as if each member of our body thought that it could be strong itself by drawing on the strength of the members around it, the whole body would inevitably be weakened and die, so if each one of us were to rob another of what is to his advantage and take all that he could for his own advantage, then the bonds of human society would inevitably be destroyed. It is quite in accordance with nature for each man to be more eager to acquire the necessities of life for himself than to provide for another; but nature does not allow us to increase our own wealth, resources and opportunities by robbing anyone else.

23. And not only nature, which may be defined as international law, but also the particular laws by which individual peoples are governed similarly ordain that no one is justified in harming another for his own advantage. Thus the laws are designed and intended for the protection of human society, and those who disrupt this society are punished with a fine, imprisonment, exile or even death. But this is enforced all the more by the requirements of nature itself, which is a combination of law both human and divine. Whoever willingly obeys it, as indeed everyone will who wishes to live according to nature, will never be guilty of coveting another's property or converting to his own use what he has taken from another.

24. Moreover high-mindedness, magnanimity, courtesy, justice and generosity are much much more in accordance with nature than pleasure, riches or even life itself; to despise all these things and regard them as of no value in comparison with the common good is the mark of the highest magnanimity. But to rob another for one's own gain is more contrary to nature than death, pain or any other evil.

25. Similarly it is even more natural to undertake the most difficult and troublesome tasks for the help and preservation of all mankind if that were possible, following the example of the famous Hercules, who is reputed among men, conscious of the benefits they have received from him, to be placed in the company of the immortal gods; even more in accordance with nature, I say, than to live in solitude not only without any trouble, but even enjoying the greatest delights and blessed with every conceivable advantage, so as even to excel in beauty and strength. Hence it is only men of the highest character and ability who prefer the former life to the latter by a long way. Thus it is that the man who lives in accordance with the dictates of nature is incapable of hurting another man.

26. Hence the man who injures another for his own benefit either thinks that is not acting in any way contrary to nature, or else thinks that death, poverty, pain, even the loss of children, relatives or friends are greater evils than doing injustice to another man. And if he thinks that by doing an injustice he is in no way acting contrary to nature, how can you argue with such a man, who denies mankind the essence of its humanity? But if he admits that such an action is wrong, but thinks that death, poverty, pain and

144

the rest are greater evils, he is mistaken in that he believes that the harm which may happen to his body or estate is more serious than any moral harm.

Chapter 6

We should all therefore have the same end in view, to identify the interest of each with the interests of all; for if each man were to grab for himself, all human society would be disrupted.

27.   If, then, nature prescribes that each man should desire what is in the interests of his fellow-man, whoever he may be, simply because he is a human being, then it follows inevitably that the advantage of all is one according to nature. This being so, we are all subject to the law of nature which is one and the same and without doubt precludes any injustice to a fellow-man.

28.   Our premiss is true; so therefore must our conclusion be. It is absurd to claim, as some do, that they would never rob a parent or a brother for their own advantage, but would not be held back by any such scruples from robbing other citizens. By their very claim they deny all justice and all association with their fellow-citizens for the common good, for their view undermines all sense of national community. Others hold that they should show consideration for their fellow-citizens, but not for strangers. They undermine the sense of community which exists between members of the human race, and when this is lost, goodwill, generosity, kindness and justice are completely lost with it. Those who abandon these standards are guilty of impiety against the immortal gods; for they are disrupting the society which the gods themselves set up among men, a society whose firmest bond is the belief that for one man to rob another for his own advantage is more contrary to nature than to suffer some distress in estate, body or even in the mind itself, provided that it leaves room for*a* justice, which is the mistress and queen of all virtues.

29.   Someone may well ask, 'Is not the wise man who is suffering from extreme hunger justified in taking food from a man who is

a I have accepted the MSS. reading *quae vacent iustitia* with Facciolati & Stuerenberg. Holden's *iniustitia* makes nonsense of what follows.

good for nothing?' No. Even life itself is not dearer to me than a state of mind which makes it impossible for me to injure another for my own advantage. 'Well, then. If a good man were able to avoid dying of cold by stealing the clothes of that cruel and inhuman tyrant Phalaris;[34] would he not do so?' This is a very easy problem to solve.

30.   If you rob another man for your own ends, however useless to society he may be, you are acting in an inhuman way and contrary to the law of nature; but if you are a man who can bring great advantage to the state and human society as a whole by continuing to live, and if in order to bring about that advantage you rob another, this is quite justifiable. In all other cases, however, a man should bear what is to his disadvantage rather than rob another of what is to his good. Sickness, poverty or any similar evil is not therefore more contrary to nature than to covet or rob what belongs to another, but neglect of the common good is contrary to nature, for it brings injustice.

31.   It follows that the natural law which contains and preserves all that is necessary for the common good, decrees without any doubt that the necessities of life may be taken from an idle and useless member of the community provided that they are needed for a man of wisdom, goodness and courage, whose death would be a disaster to the community, and provided that he does not make his high esteem of himself or his concern for self-preservation a reason for doing others an injustice. Provided, then, that he always shows concern for the public good and that human society about which I have said a great deal, he will always fulfil his moral obligations.

32.   The question of Phalaris is easily answered. Tyrants have no part in human society and can rightly be considered its worst outcasts. They are men whose lives we are justified in taking, so how can it be contrary to the natural law to rob them if one has the chance? They are a poisonous and wicked breed who need to be banished from human society. For just as limbs which have become shrivelled and lifeless and only serve to infect the rest of the body, are amputated, so these monsters, who are really wild animals in human disguise, need to be cut off from the body, as it were, of human society. In fact all cases in which moral obligation depends on circumstances belong to this type.

III

Chapter 7

33.   I believe that Panaetius would have dealt with such subjects had
not some mishap or other business foiled his designs. But in solving
such difficulties you have the ample guidance of my former books
which make quite clear what is to be avoided because of its immorality, and what is not to be avoided because of its not invariably being immoral. Now I am going to roof over, as it were, an
edifice left unfinished, but needing little for its completion. I shall
follow the example of geometricians, whose custom is not to prove
everything but to require that certain basic assumptions be made,
so that they may more easily explain what they want to explain.
Therefore, Marcus, I want you to grant me this premiss, if you can,
that only that which is morally good is to be sought for its own
sake.[a] If Cratippus[1] will not allow that, then at least you will agree
that what is morally good is more desirable for its own sake than
anything else.[b] Either of these premisses will suffice for my purpose, for each of them is more probable than any other statement
to be made on ethical questions.

34.   I must first spring to Panaetius' defence in that he never pretended, as indeed he would never have been justified in pretending,
that expediency could ever come into conflict with the good; what
he said was that apparent expediency comes into conflict with the
good; for there is no expediency which is not also good, nor any
good which is not also expedient. Moreover he repeatedly claims
that there is no greater curse known to mankind than the dichotomy produced by some philosophers between the two. Hence it
was in order that we should never put expediency before moral
good, but have a correct idea of priorities whenever the conflict
arises, that he speaks of the conflict, but he means us to understand
it as an apparent and not a real one. This, then, is the gap in his
work which I intend to fill, not by calling upon outside help, but
fighting a lone battle, as we say. For of all the accounts which have
come into my hands since the time of Panaetius, there has been
nothing to which I could give my approval.

[a] The first premiss is Stoic.
[b] The second premiss is Peripatetic. Chrysippus was a Peripatetic.

Chapter 8

35.   It is impossible to be unaffected whenever any apparent advantage presents itself; but if on taking a closer look you find that the apparent advantage contains moral wrong, then your duty is not so much to reject what is expedient, but to realize that where there is wrong, there cannot be expediency. Now if it is true that there is nothing so contrary to nature as moral wrong—for nature loves what is right and proper and consistent and scorns the opposite—and if there is nothing so in accord with nature as expediency, then it follows that expediency and moral wrong are never to be found in the same action. Similarly if we are born to do what is right and that should be our only goal, as Zeno thought, or a goal which in its importance outweighs all others, as Aristotle believed, then we must consider what is right to be the only, or at any rate the highest good. Therefore since whatever is good is undoubtedly expedient, then whatever is right must be expedient.

36.   Hence it is the mistake of wicked men to seize whatever seems to be expedient without considering whether it is right or wrong. This gives rise to murder, poisoning, falsifying of wills, stealing, embezzlement, plundering and oppression of citizens and allies alike; it gives rise to a desire for excessive influence, oppressive power and, above all, tyranny, which sometimes rises even in democracies. In fact, it is impossible to imagine anything more foul or detestable. For men see their rewards in a false perspective and do not see the penalty, I will not say of the laws which they so often break, but of their own wrongdoing, which is the worst of all.

37.   Those therefore who deliberate whether to follow the course of action which they see to be right, or knowingly expose themselves to the contamination of crime, ought to be banished from our midst, for they are utterly unscrupulous. Their very doubt is a crime, even if it does not bring them to criminal action. Therefore there is to be no discussion at all of matters in which debate itself is to be deplored. Moreover whenever an action is discussed, all hopes and thoughts of concealment are to be removed; indeed, if we have made any progress in philosophy at all, we ought to be

148

convinced that even if all heaven and earth were ignorant of our actions, we should still do nothing which exemplified greed, injustice, lust or lack of self-control.

Chapter 9

38.   This is well illustrated by Plato's story of Gyges,[a] who once went down into a chasm in the ground, formed by subsidence due to heavy rains, and found there, so the story goes, a brazen horse with a door in its side. On opening it he saw an incredibly huge corpse with a gold ring on its finger. He took it off, put it on his own finger and returned to the company of the shepherds (for he was a shepherd in the king's service). Here he found that whenever he turned the setting of the ring towards the palm of his hand, he became invisible, though everything else did not become so to him; then on turning it back again he became visible once more. Taking advantage of the opportunity afforded him by the ring he seduced the queen, and then, with her help, he killed the king, his master, and removed all those who he thought might stand in his way. He remained invisible throughout the whole course of these crimes, and so it was due to the ring that he became king of Lydia with remarkable speed. Now if the possessor of the ring had been a wise man, he would have thought himself no more justified in turning to crime than if he had not had it; for good men seek to do what is right and do not even do wrong in secret.[52]

39.   There are some philosophers of great integrity, but little perception, who say that the whole story was a product of Plato's imagination—as if he would claim that it had really happened or even could happen! No! The significance of the ring story is this: if you could do anything to satisfy your desire for riches, power, supreme rule, or sex, without anyone's knowledge or even suspicion, and if you were assured that neither gods nor men would ever know about it, would you do it? You will say that the question is an impossible one. Of course it is; but whether it is possible is not the question; the question is whether you would do it, if you had the opportunity. You stubbornly refuse to accept the possi-

[a] *Republic*, 359a, *et seqq.*

bility and persist in this view because you do not really see the point of the question; for when I ask you whether you would do a wrong action if it could be concealed, I am not asking whether it could be concealed, but am, as it were, putting you on the rack to see whether by replying that you would do what suited you if you were granted immunity, you would confess your guilty intentions. But if you denied it, you would have to agree that every wrong action is to be avoided simply because it is wrong. But let us now return to our subject.

Chapter 10

40. Cases often arise which cause perplexity because of the apparent expediency of an action. I am not referring here to the question of abandoning one's integrity because the advantage is considerable, for that is just unscrupulous, but whether what is apparently expedient can be done without injustice. For example, Brutus might seem to have acted unjustly when he deposed his colleague Collatinus from office; for he had been Brutus' adviser and aide in expelling the kings. But since the leading men of state had decided that all relatives of Tarquinius Superbus, his very name and the memory of his reign were to be obliterated, in acting in the interests of his country he not only did what was expedient, but acted with such integrity that even Collatinus himself ought to have approved his action.[53] Thus expediency prevailed because the action was right, for without right there could have been no expediency.

41. I cannot say the same of the king who founded our city; for he was motivated by apparent expediency, when he killed his brother because he thought it would be more to his advantage to reign alone than in his company.[54] He flouted all the rules of brotherly affection and humanity to attain what seemed to be expedient but in fact was not; he even pleaded the affair of the wall in his defence, a specious excuse which was as inadequate as it was improbable.

42. I would say then, with his leave, that whether as Quirinus or Romulus, he did wrong. Not that we are to abandon the things
150

that bring us advantage or hand them over to others when we are in need of them ourselves. On the contrary each man should do what is to his own advantage provided that it can be done without injustice to anyone else. One of the many sayings of Chrysippus that you ought to know is this: 'Whoever runs in a race, should try his utmost to win; but he must not by any means trip up one of his fellow-runners or give him a push; so in life it is right that each man should promote his own interests, provided that he does not defraud anyone else.'[55]

43. Friendships create some of the greatest problems of obligation. For not to give to a friend what you decently can or to give him less than his due is to fall short of your obligation. There is, however, a brief and easy rule which may serve in all such cases, and it is this: never let the things which appear advantageous, such as high office, riches, pleasure and the like, come before your friendship. On the other hand the good man will never be so anxious to act in his friend's interests that he acts traitorously, perjurously or disloyally. Even if he finds himself judge of his friend's case, he should cast aside the role of friend when he puts on that of judge. His only concessions to friendship may be to wish his friend the juster case and to grant him as much time for pleading his case as the law allows.

44. But when he comes to pronounce sentence on oath, he must remember that he calls upon a god to be his witness, that is his own conscience, the most divine gift that a god has given to any man. Hence the fine tradition handed down from our forefathers (if only we kept to it) to preface our request for the judge's favour with the words 'as far as loyalty to justice will allow'. This plea ties up with what I said a short way back that a judge may concede a friend all that he may without any violation of justice; for if men were obliged to do all that their friends required, friendships would seem more akin to conspiracies.

45. I speak here only of the general run of friendships; for no such thing could happen among perfectly wise men. Such they say was the friendship between Damon and Phintias, the followers of Pythagoras,[17] that when the tyrant Dionysius[32] condemned one of them to death and the condemned man asked for a few days' respite in order to provide for his family, the other became surety for his appearance in court, so that if he did not reappear, he himself would be put to death. When he returned on the day appointed,

the tyrant was so impressed by their loyalty that he begged to be admitted as a third member of their alliance.

46. In friendship, therefore, when apparent advantage comes into conflict with what is right, the latter should always prevail. Moreover religious beliefs should always be put before friendship whenever it demands what is not right. Thus the correct choice of obligation, which is what we are seeking, will be found.

Chapter 11

It is in public affairs that men are most often led astray by what is apparently expedient, as, for example, our ancestors in the demolition of Corinth.[a] Even more ruthless were the Athenians who decreed that all the Aeginetans should have their thumbs cut off because of their prowess at sea.[b] This was considered expedient, as Aegina by virtue of its proximity was a threat to the Piraeus. No cruel action, however, can be expedient; for cruelty is the greatest enemy of human nature, whose guidance we ought to follow in all our actions.

47. It is also wrong to prevent foreigners from enjoying the advantage of cities and driving them out, as Pennus did in our fathers' time and Papius just recently. Now it is right that no man who is not a citizen should enjoy citizen rights, and a law was passed to this effect by those consuls of outstanding wisdom, Crassus and Scaevola;[56] but to exclude foreigners from the city altogether is inhuman. There is no finer action than when what appears to be to the general advantage is rejected from considerations of moral good. Our own history abounds with examples of this, particularly during the Second Punic War when after the disaster at Cannae our people showed greater spirit than it had ever done in time of success. There was not a hint of fear, not a mention of peace. So great is the power of the good that it overshadows apparent expediency.

48. When the Athenians realized their inability to withstand the

---

[a] By Lucius Mummius Achaicus in 146 B.C.
[b] No mention of this decree is made by Thucydides or Diodorus. It is mentioned by Aelian, *Varia Historia*, II, 9.

III

Persian advance, they decided to leave the city, evacuate their women and children to Troezen, embark on board their ships and defend the liberty of Greece at sea,[a] and when a certain Cyrsilus advised them to remain in their city and admit Xerxes, they stoned him. He was advocating what must have seemed expedient; but this was of no account in the face of what was right.

49. After his victory in the Persian War Themistocles stated in the assembly that he had a plan which was to the advantage of the city, but it was necessary to keep it secret; he therefore asked the people to nominate someone with whom he could discuss the matter; they chose Aristides.[51] Themistocles then told him that the Spartan fleet which was laid up at Gytheum could be burned without any warning, and thus the whole power of Sparta would inevitably be crushed. On hearing of this plan Aristides came before the expectant assembly and told them that although Themistocles' proposal was greatly to their advantage, it was not right. Consequently, the Athenians seeing that it was not right did not even think it expedient, and on the advice of Aristides rejected the proposal even though they had not learned what it was. How much greater was their concern for morality than that of ourselves who allow pirates to operate with immunity while exacting tribute from our allies![57]

Chapter 12

Let us consider it established, then, that what is wrong can never be expedient, not even when you think that you can gain some advantage from it. In fact, the conviction that advantage can be gained from wrongdoing is disastrous.

50. But there are occasions, as I mentioned above, which frequently arise when there is an apparent conflict between expediency and moral right; in such cases one must take a close look and see whether the conflict is a real one or whether it can be resolved. This category includes questions of the following kind: if, for example, an honest merchant has brought a great quantity of corn from Alexandria to Rhodes at a time when the Rhodians are suffering from great famine and the price of corn is high, and if he knows

[a] Between the battles of Thermopylae and Salamis, 480 B.C.

153

III

that more merchants have set sail from Alexandria and has seen their ships on his way sailing in the direction of Rhodes laden with corn, is he to tell the Rhodians or keep quiet and get the best price he can for his cargo? We can assume that he is a wise and honest man, and can for the purposes of our discussion take it that he would not conceal the fact from the Rhodians if he thought it dishonest, but he is in doubt about its honesty.

51.   In cases of this kind opinion is divided between Diogenes of Babylon,[58] the great and authoritative Stoic, and Antipater,[59] his disciple and a man of sharp intellect. Antipater took the view that he should tell everything, so that the buyer can be just as much in possession of the facts as the seller. Diogenes on the other hand claimed that if selling is a man's profession, he is justified in getting the best possible price for his goods, provided that he points out any faults in them, as far as he is obliged to do by civil law, and does not use any trickery in his dealings. For example he may say: 'I have imported this corn, put it on sale and ask no higher price than any other merchant, perhaps even less, since my import makes corn more plentiful; what is there wrong in that?'

52.   Antipater argues from a different principle: 'What do you say to this?' he says: 'Surely it is your duty to act in the interests of mankind as a whole. This is what you were born for and the very principles of your being, which you must obey and follow, are to identify your own interests with the interests of all. Can you therefore honestly conceal from men what is to their advantage and well-being?' Diogenes would probably reply as follows: 'It is one thing to conceal, another to keep quiet. For example, if I do not *reveal* to you at the moment the nature of the gods or give you a definition of the highest good (which would be more useful information than that about the price of corn) it cannot be said that I am *concealing* it from you. It is simply that I am under no obligation to tell you all that it would be to your advantage to hear.'

53.   'It is indeed your duty,' Antipater would reply, 'if you will remember the bonds of social unity which nature has ordained among men.' 'I am aware of that,' Diogenes would say, 'but these bonds are not such that a man may not have anything to call his own. If that is so, there is not even any selling to be done, only giving.'

154

Chapter 13

You will observe that in the whole argument neither side advocates a wrong action on the grounds of expediency; Diogenes only advocates expediency in so far as it is not morally wrong, while Antipater urges that an action should not be performed because it is morally wrong.

54. To take another example, suppose that a good man were to sell a house because of certain faults of which he is aware, but others are not. Let us suppose that its state is thought to be hygienic, but is in fact quite the reverse; all the rooms are infested with snakes, or it is poorly constructed and about to collapse, facts of which no one but its owner is aware; now if he did not tell the purchaser of these faults and sold the house for much more than he could reasonably expect to get for it, would he not be acting completely without principle? Antipater is wholly in agreement here.

55. 'What is the difference', he asks, 'between refusing to direct a man who has lost his way (for which a man could be publicly cursed in Athens) and allowing a buyer to be carried away into most costly deception because of his own lack of knowledge? In fact the latter is worse because it involves wilfully leading another man into error.' Diogenes replies, 'Surely you couldn't claim that he forced you to buy, when he didn't even give you any encouragement? He put the house up for sale because he didn't want it, whereas you bought it because you did. Moreover if those who advertise "a sound well-built house" are not thought guilty of deception, even if the house is neither sound nor well-built, much less guilty are those who do not even commend it. For how can there be any fraud on the part of the seller, when the purchase entirely depends on the judgement of the buyer? Moreover if we accept that not all that is said about an article for sale is to be made good, are you going to claim that what is not said should be made good too? In short what could be more foolish than for a seller to advertise the faults of the article he is selling? What could be more absurd than for the owner to instruct his auctioneer to announce "a thoroughly undesirable residence for sale"?'

56. Thus doubtful cases do exist in which there are those on the one side who advocate what is morally right, while on the other there are those who advocate what is expedient so far as to show that what is expedient is not only the right course, but that to neglect it would be quite wrong. Thus we have the apparent conflict of expediency and morality of which I have spoken. We must decide between them; for I have not expounded these cases just to pose the problem, but to solve it.

57. I do not believe that the corn merchant ought to have concealed anything from the Rhodians, or the man selling his house from the purchasers. I concede that to say nothing about a fault is not the same as actively concealing it, but I think that when you know something that it is in the interests of others to know and keep them in ignorance for your own advantage, this is the same. Surely no one is under any illusions about this kind of deceit and the sort of people who practise it. It is certainly not the action of an open, sincere, ingenuous, just or good man, but rather of a shifty, sly, cunning, deceitful, malicious, inveterate trickster. Can it be to any man's advantage to acquire these and many other bad names?

Chapter 14

58. If those who have kept quiet about the faults of their goods are to be blamed, what are we to think of those who have added falsehood to their crimes? Caius Canius, a Roman knight and a man of wit and learning, retired to Syracuse to indulge, as he used to say, in *retiring* rather than *tiring* pursuits, and made it known that he wanted to buy a country estate where he could invite his friends and enjoy himself free from troublesome callers. When the word got around, a certain Pythius, a Syracusan banker, informed him that his estate was not for sale, but that Canius could, if he wished, treat it as his own, and at the same time invited him to have dinner at his house the next day. When he had accepted, Pythius, who being a banker had influence among all sections of the community, summoned some fishermen and asked them to fish the following day just off the coast by his estate. This done, he gave them their instructions. Canius came to dinner at the appointed time. Pythius

156

had prepared a banquet to match his means and had ensured that a large number of boats were visible; then each of the fishermen brought what he had caught and laid the fish at Pythius' feet.

59.　　Thereupon Canius was heard to ask, 'Tell me, Pythius, what is the meaning of all these fish and boats?' To which Pythius replied, 'It's not surprising; this is the only place where there are any fish or where there is a water supply. The people of Syracuse could not live without my estate.' Maddened with envy Canius begged Pythius to sell him the estate. Pythius was reluctant at first, or so it seemed; but in the end he agreed. Canius, because he wanted it badly and was rich, paid as much as Pythius chose to ask for the estate and all its accessories. The whole bargain was signed and sealed. Next day Canius invited some friends there, and arriving himself a little early found no trace of a single boat. He inquired of a neighbour whether the fishermen were on holiday, for he did not see any about. 'There's no holiday,' came the reply, 'but then there aren't any fishermen here normally; in fact I wondered yesterday what had happened.'

60.　　Canius was furious, but what could he do? Aquilius, my great friend and colleague, had not yet published his Criminal Fraud Laws, in which, on being asked what he meant by criminal fraud, replied that it is to do one thing while pretending to do another. A very lucid explanation, as one would expect from a man noted for his capacity for fine distinctions.[60] Pythius, then, and all others whose actions do not match their pretensions are deceitful, wicked tricksters. None of their deeds therefore can be expedient, since it will bear the stain of so many faults.

Chapter 15

61.　　If Aquilius' definition is true, then our whole life should be free from concealment and pretence, and no one should use either to improve his terms of sale or purchase. Criminal fraud has always been punishable by law, witness a breach of trusteeship made punishable by the Twelve Tables[68] or acts of fraud against minors as laid down by the Lex Plaetoria,[a] or cases not covered by the law

___

[a] The *Lex Plaetoria* first established in law the distinction between majors (over twenty-five years old) and minors.

that were covered by individual judgements which contained the provision 'that an act be done in good faith'. In other cases the following words are particularly noticeable: judgements relating to the disposal of a divorced woman's property contain the words 'better and more equitably'; in cases of loan or mortgage we find the words 'honest action amongst honest men'. Can we imagine then that any fraud was allowed by the words 'better and more equitably' or that a law which lays down the principle 'honest action amongst honest men' should leave any scope for trickery and deceit? Aquilius makes it quite clear that pretence involves criminal fraud. Deceit therefore is to be avoided in all our transactions. Sellers are not justified in hiring sham bidders, nor are buyers in any attempt to keep prices artificially low. Each should come to declare his price and not declare it more than once.

62. Quintus Scaevola, the son of Publius, once asked the seller of a farm he wanted to buy to declare his price once and for all; when he had done this, Scaevola said that he thought it was worth more and gave him an extra 100,000 sesterces. No one would deny that this was the action of an honest man, although one might question whether it was the action of a wise man, just as one would if he had sold it for less than he could have got for it. This illustrates the danger of thinking some honest and others wise, which reminds me of a saying of Ennius: 'What is the point of wisdom, if not to be wise to your advantage?'[a] I should be prepared to accept this, if I could agree with Ennius on a definition of the word *advantage*.

63. I find that Hecato of Rhodes,[61] a disciple of Panaetius, wrote in his books on moral obligations which he addressed to Quintus Tubero, 'The duty of a wise man is to look after his own estate and not contravene the laws, customs or traditions of his country. Moreover, we should seek riches not only for ourselves, but for our children, relations, friends and, above all, the state; for it is the wealth and resources of individual citizens that constitute the riches of the state.' Hecato could not possibly approve of the action of Scaevola, about whom I have just spoken; for he says that the only actions for his own gain from which he will refrain are those which are contrary to the law. Thus he will win no great favour or approval on our part.

64. However, if both pretence and concealment are to be classed as

[a] From Ennius's *Medea*. *Cf*. Euripides, *Fragment*, 905; Cicero, *Ad Familiares*, VII, 6.

criminal fraud, then few actions can be free from it; and if the good man is the one who helps as many as he can and harms no one, he is not going to be easy to find. To commit a crime can never be expedient, because it is always wrong; moreover because goodness is always right, it is always expedient.

Chapter 16

65.   As far as estates are concerned, it is laid down in our civil law that all faults known to the seller be declared at the time of the sale. For the Twelve Tables laid down that all faults expressly mentioned should be made good and that any man who denied there were faults, when there were, should pay double the penalty. There was even a statutory penalty for not mentioning faults, which laid down that if a seller knew of any defect in his estate and did not specifically mention it, he could be liable for the cost of making it good.

66.   For example, the augurs were once intending to conduct their augury from the Capitol and had ordered Tiberius Claudius Centumalus, the owner of a house on the Mons Caelius, to demolish those parts of his house which by their height obstructed their observations. Claudius, however, put the house up for sale and sold it to a certain Publius Calpurnius Lanarius. Calpurnius received a similar demolition order from the augurs, and it was only when he had carried it out that he discovered that Claudius had put the house up for sale after he had received the demolition order from the augurs. He therefore brought an action against him for 'such compensation as he was bound in good faith to make him'. Marcus Cato, the father of our contemporary,[a] was judge in the case. (Usually men are named by reference to their fathers but in this case the son is so eminent that I adopt the reverse procedure.) His sentence was couched in the following terms: 'In view of the fact that he knew of the fault when selling the estate and did not declare it, he must make good the loss to the purchaser.'

67.   His judgement meant that good faith involves any fault known to the seller being made known to the buyer. If his judgement is

[a] For the father of Cato Uticensis, *Vd.* Aulus Gellius, *Noctes Atticae*, XIII, 20.

right, then neither the corn merchant nor the seller of the condemned house was right in neglecting to make the facts known. Not all such cases of neglect, however, can be covered by the civil law, although those that can are carefully provided for. Marcus Marius Gratidianus, a relative of mine, had sold Caius Sergius Orata a house which he had bought from him a few years previously; the estate was subject to a liability which Marius had not mentioned in the contract. The case was brought to court. Orata's counsel was Crassus,[a] Gratidianus' Antonius.[b] Crassus pleaded that 'the seller be liable for any fault that he knew but refused to declare'; Antonius on the other hand pleaded that the contract had been a fair one 'since the fault could not have been unknown to Sergius, as he had sold the house; there was therefore no need to mention it, and he could not have been misled, since he knew the terms on which the purchase had been made'.[62]

68.   I quote these instances so that you may realize the distaste our forebears had for such tricksters.

Chapter 17

The attitude of the laws to such trickery is quite different from that of philosophers: laws only condemn trickery in so far as it results in an illegal act, whereas philosophers condemn the motive and intention. Reason demands that nothing be done by means of a trap, pretence or deceit. Is it not treacherous to lay a trap even if you have no intention of beating up animals or driving them into it? For animals will often fall into it without being driven. Similarly, when you advertise a house with the intention of selling it because of its faults, your bill of sale is just like a trap into which some unwary person may fall.

69.   And yet I am aware that because of our declining moral standards such an action is not considered immoral or to be condemned from the point of view of the law or of civil liberties. None the less it is contrary to the law of nature; for human society, as I have said many times before and must say many times more, ex-

[a] Lucius Licinius Crassus the Orator (consul 95 B.C.).
[b] Marcus Antonius the Orator (consul 99 B.C.).

tends its bonds to the whole human race; but although its bonds are universal, there are closer links between people of the same race and closer still between those of the same state. Thus our ancestors distinguished between universal law and the law of a particular state. Every state code should include all universal law, although it may well exceed it. We have in fact no precise and tangible picture of genuine law and justice. All we have are rough sketches. If only we used those! For they are derived from the best examples of nature and truth.

70.   Consider the value of that phrase: 'that I should neither be taken in or defrauded because of you or my faith in you.' Similarly that golden phrase: 'that honest men should be honest in their dealings and that there should be no fraud.' But what is meant by 'honest men' and 'honest dealing' is a formidable question. Quintus Mucius Scaevola, the chief priest, attached great importance to all cases in which the clause 'in good faith' was included; for he thought that this clause had the widest possible application, occurring as it does in cases of wardship and partnership, trusts, commissions, buying, selling, hiring and letting, in fact all transactions which make up human intercourse; all these cases require a judge of great ability to determine the extent of a man's liability, particularly when one considers the reciprocal actions to which they are apt to give rise.

71.   Trickery, then, must be banished from our dealings, so must that particular brand of chicanery that masquerades as cleverness, but is really the depth of stupidity; for the clever man will always be able to distinguish between good and bad, whereas the function of chicanery (if we accept that everything that is wrong is *ipso facto* bad) is to prefer the bad to the good. It is not only in the sphere of real estate that civil law, which is based on the natural law, condemns trickery and fraud, but also in the case of slave-purchase the buyer is protected by law against deception. Indeed an edict of the aediles lays down that if the seller knows that the slave is a weakling, a runaway or a thief, he must (except in the case of an inherited slave) declare it.

72.   From this it is clear that since nature is the fountain-head of law, it is contrary to nature for any man to swindle another by taking advantage of his ignorance. There is no greater curse to be found in life than sharp-practice masquerading as intelligence; for it is from this that countless apparent conflicts arise between

L

expediency and moral good. In fact there are few people who would refrain from doing wrong, if they were assured that no punishment or even knowledge of the deed would result.

Chapter 18

73.   We can put that principle to the test, if you wish, by applying it to the kind of action which public opinion does not condemn. There is no need at this point to discuss assassins, poisoners, will-forgers, thieves or embezzlers, for they are not to be quelled by philosophical arguments or disputes, but by imprisonment. Let us rather consider those who have a reputation for honesty. Consider for example those people who arrived in Rome from Greece with a document purporting to be the will of that rich man, Lucius Minucius Basilus. To strengthen their case, they chose as co-heirs two of the most influential of their contemporaries, Marcus Crassus[a] and Quintus Hortensius.[b] Although the latter suspected that the will was a forgery, they did not have any feelings of personal guilt and were quite prepared to accept this squalid gift, procured as it was by an act of fraud carried out by others. Can their action be justified by the fact that they were not directly concerned in perpetrating the forgery? I think not. I say this in spite of the fact that one was a friend while alive and the other not an enemy now that he is dead.

74.   Now Basilus' wish had been that his sister's son, Marcus Satrius (I refer to the patron of Picenum and the Sabine district—the title itself is a slur on the times), should succeed to his title and had appointed him heir. It was scandalous that the estate should go to two leading citizens and Satrius receive nothing but a title. Hence, if, as I argued in my first book, the man who does not protect another from injustice when he can is doing a positive injustice, what are we to think of the man who not only refuses to protect someone, but is actually an accomplice of those who are doing him wrong? I would go further and say that even genuine bequests are not morally justified if procured by means of acts of

<hr>

[a] Marcus Licinius Crassus the triumvir.
[b] Quintus Hortensius, consul 69 B.C., *Vd.* Note 42.

flattery with an ulterior motive and attentions which are forced rather than genuine. One must admit, however, that in such cases it sometimes happens that one thing seems expedient and another right.

75.   This is not so; for the criteria of expediency and right are one and the same. If a man fails to see that, then there is no fraud, no crime to which he will not stoop. If he argues the rights of one action against the expediency of another, he is heedlessly and wrongly tearing apart what nature has joined together; and this is the source of all fraud, crime and evil.

Chapter 19

Now suppose that a good man had the power to insert his name in rich men's wills at a snap of the fingers; he would not use it, even if he were absolutely certain that no one would ever suspect him. But if Marcus Crassus had been given this power, he would, believe me, have been prepared to dance in the forum! But the just man, or, in other words, the honest man, would under no circumstances rob a man for his own benefit. In fact if any man can respect such an action, he had better confess that he does not know what an honest man is.

76.   Indeed if a man gets his thoughts clear on this matter, he will see that the good man is he who does whatever good he can to others and never injures anyone except when provoked by injustice. Surely then, a man who used some kind of magic spell to remove the true heirs and take their place himself, would be injuring others! 'What!' someone may say, 'Is he not justified in doing what is to his own advantage and profit?' Yes indeed; but he should realise that nothing can be to his advantage or profit, if it be unjust. If he has not learned this, he cannot become a good man.

77.   I remember my father telling me when I was a boy about Fimbria,[a] a former consul, the judge in a case concerning Marcus Lutatius Pinthia, a Roman knight of great integrity, who had laid out some money as a deposit which he was prepared to forfeit, 'if

[a] Caius Flavius Fimbria, consul 104 B.C.

he did not prove his moral goodness'. Fimbria refused to pronounce judgement in the case; for he was not prepared either to ruin the reputation of a highly esteemed man by giving judgement against him, or to presume to dogmatize about a man's moral goodness, since this depends on countless good services and qualities. The fact that Fimbria saw this clearly shows that you do not have to be a Socrates to realize that no good man can ever consider anything to be to his advantage if it is wrong. Such a man, then, would not commit himself to any thought, much less any action, which he would not be prepared to declare openly. Is it not wrong therefore for philosophers to find any dilemma where even a peasant would find none? For it was among peasants that that time-honoured proverb derived its origin: 'You could play *la moure* with him in the dark,'[63] they say, when they want to pay tribute to a man's honesty and integrity. If this means anything, it means that no action can be advantageous if it is not fitting; whether anyone can prove it against you or not is irrelevant.

78.   This proverb makes it clear that neither Gyges nor the man we imagined to be able to clear up everyone's legacies at a snap of the fingers can be excused. For just as what is wrong can never be considered right, however much it is concealed, so what is not right can never be considered advantageous because it is contrary to the law of nature.

Chapter 20

79.   'But', you may say, 'there is reason for wrongdoing when the rewards are very great. For example, Caius Marius seemed to have no hope of becoming consul. For he had remained in obscurity for almost seven years after his praetorship and it looked as though he would never stand for the consulship, when he was sent to Rome by Quintus Metellus, a man of the highest distinction and loyalty to the state, who was his chief of staff. Marius attacked him before the Roman people on the grounds that he was prolonging the war unnecessarily, whereas if they made him consul, he promised to capture Jugurtha without delay and hand him over, dead or alive, to the Roman people.' He won his consulship, but

only at the cost of justice and good faith; for by his false accusation he had brought disgrace upon a noble and revered citizen who was his commander and responsible for his mission.[64]

80.   Even a relative of mine,[a] Gratidianus, failed to do his duty as an honest man during his praetorship. It was when the tribunes had consulted the college of praetors in order to reach a joint decision on the currency question; for at that time the currency was in such a state of flux that no one knew the true value of his holding. A joint edict was drafted, legal action and appropriate penalties were laid down for those who defied it, and they decided to announce it jointly from the rostrum that afternoon. The meeting was adjourned; but Gratidianus went straight from the tribunes' benches to the rostrum and announced by himself the substance of the joint agreement. I regret to say that he was greatly honoured for his action; his statue was erected in every street and incense and candles were burnt before them. But I will not labour the point: his popularity was quite unprecedented.

81.   This is the sort of case which is apt to confuse the issue; for the violation of justice involved is small compared with the resultant gain. Gratidianus did not think it very wrong to rob his colleagues and the tribunes of popularity, whereas his election to the consulship, which was what he then had in mind, seemed to be a great advantage. But in all these cases there is one rule with which I want you to be thoroughly conversant. Make sure that what appears to be advantageous is not wrong, and if it is wrong, do not consider it advantageous. In conclusion can we really consider either Marius or Gratidianus an honest man? Ponder the problem and examine your thoughts to see what concept or ideal of honesty is contained in these examples. Is it the action of an honest man to lie, rob, cheat or slander for his own gain? Of course not!

82.   Surely there is no acquisition so valuable or any gain so desirable that it is worth the sacrifice of a reputation for honesty. Can that alleged advantage contribute anything to compensate for the loss of a reputation for honesty and the abandonment of justice and good faith? For if a man is only human on the outside while within there is nothing but bestial savagery, why should we not regard him as a beast rather than a man?

---

[a] For Gratidianus, *Vd.* Note 62. He was praetor in 86 B.C. He never became consul.

Chapter 21

Furthermore, those who disregard all that is right and honourable for the sake of their own advancement are surely no different from the man who wanted to marry another man's daughter so that he might rise to power on the other's ruthlessness.[a] He thought that it would be to his advantage to build his power on the unpopularity of the other. What he did not see was that it involved harm to this country and was therefore wrong. Caesar was always quoting those lines from the *Phoenissae*[b] of Euripides (I shall translate them as well as I can, giving attention to intelligibility rather than elegance):

> 'If right be contravened, let it for rule
>
> be contravened; or else pursue the good.'

Eteocles, or rather Euripides, deserved to be put to death for making such an utterly unscrupulous exception.

83.   Why then concern ourselves with lesser crimes such as forged legacies, fraudulent buying and selling? For here you have the supreme example of a man whose ambition was to be absolute ruler of Rome and master of the world, and achieved it! Anyone who says that this is an honourable goal is mad: for he not only assents to the abandonment of law and liberty, but glories in the foul and detestable act of their subjection. But what of the man who admits that it is wrong to establish absolute rule in a state which has a tradition of freedom which it deserves to maintain, and yet considers that it can be to a man's advantage to gain such rule? Is he not to be deterred from such a wrong idea by every conceivable condemnation and reproach? What advantage, in Heaven's name, could be derived from that most foul and disgusting murder of the state? And yet the man who perpetrated it was given the title of 'Father' by the very people he had enslaved.[c]

[a] Pompey had married Caesar's daughter, Julia, in 60 B.C.

[b] ll. 524–5.

[c] Caesar had had the title *Pater Patriae* conferred upon him after the battle of Munda in 45 B.C. It must have been particularly galling for Cicero thus to share the title he had won for his suppression of the Catilinarian conspiracy of 63 B.C.

III

Expediency, then, must always be subject to moral good. In fact, in spite of the apparent discrepancy between the two terms, they are synonymous.

84. Considering the matter from the standpoint of public opinion, I cannot imagine anything which brings more advantage than absolute rule, but from the standpoint of truth I find that the man who has achieved such an end unjustly could scarcely do anything less advantageous to himself. Consider the disadvantages: the anxiety, the worries, the constant fears brought by night and day alike and the perpetual intrigue and danger to life. To quote the words of Accius:

'The throne has many enemies and traitors,
and few there are that wish it well.'[a]

The kingly power to which he referred was that legitimately bequeathed by Tantalus and Pelops.[b] But there were far more who were hostile to that dictator who had actually enslaved the Roman people with their own armies, a people who had not only been free itself, but the mistress of other nations.

85. What stains of conscience and what wounds can you imagine that he bore in his heart? Could any man consider his life profitable, when his position is such that popularity and glory in abundance await the man who takes it? If then these greatest of all apparent advantages are mere illusions because of the dishonour and disgrace that they contain, can there be any further room for doubt that no action can be expedient unless it is right?

Chapter 22

86. I could give many examples to support my conclusion: one is to be found in the war against Pyrrhus fought by Caius Fabricius (in his second consulship) and the Senate. Now King Pyrrhus had, completely unprovoked, declared war on Rome. It was a struggle for power. We were faced with a king as powerful as he was noble. During the campaign a deserter from Pyrrhus' army arrived at Fabricius' camp. He promised on condition of a reward to return

[a] Probably from the *Atreus* of Accius.
[b] Atreus was the son of Pelops and grandson of Tantalus.

167

to Pyrrhus' camp as secretly as he had come and poison the king. Fabricius, however, saw that he was returned to Pyrrhus, an action which won the approval of the Senate.[65] Now if we accept the popular criterion of apparent advantage in this case, we would agree on the right course of action: a costly war and a dangerous rival to our imperial ambitions could have been eliminated by the efforts of a single deserter; on the other hand to beat one's opponent in a struggle for prestige by crime rather than courage would have brought undying dishonour and disgrace upon us.

87.   Fabricius[50] was to Rome what Aristides[51] had been to Athens, and the Senate never drew any distinction between expediency and principle: was it not therefore more expedient to fight with arms than with poison? There can be no glory in crime; therefore there is no place for crime in any contest, such as a contest for power, where glory is at stake. In fact, in whatever way power is sought, it cannot bring advantage if acquired by disgraceful methods. We cannot therefore accept the decision of Lucius Philippus, the son of Quintus. Lucius Sulla had, with the agreement of the Senate, exempted certain cities from taxation on payment of a cash sum;[a] Philippus subsequently proposed the reimposition of taxation without any rebate of the cash sum they had paid for their exemption; the Senate accepted it. What a blot on our government's record! One would expect better faith among pirates! 'If our revenue is increased, it is to our advantage,' was the plea. How long will men have the temerity to think something to their advantage if it is wrong?

88.   Government must be based on its own prestige and the goodwill of its allies. How then can disgrace and disfavour ever be to its advantage? I have even had frequent disagreements with my friend Cato on this topic. His defence of the treasury and the taxation system as a whole seemed to me somewhat over-zealous; for he never made any concessions to the *publicani*, and rarely helped the allies, whereas our attitude to the former should be the same as that towards our own bailiffs and our attitude to the latter ought to have been one of generosity. For harmony between the various sections of the community was important to the well-being of the state. Curio[b] too was wrong; for although he admitted that the

---

[a] After the First Mithridatic War (84 B.C.).

[b] Caius Scribonius Curio, the father of Caesar's tribune, refused, as consul in 76 B.C., the demands of the Transpadani for full citizenship, eventually granted by Caesar in 49 B.C.

Transpadani had a good case, he constantly added, 'Let expediency prevail.' Rather than admitting the strength of their case but declaring that it was not expedient, he should have said that it was not strong simply because it was not expedient.[66]

Chapter 23

89.   The sixth book of Hecato's work[61] on moral obligation is full of questions like this: 'Is a good man justified in not feeding his slaves during a period of great scarcity?' He states the arguments for both sides, but finally comes to the conclusion that we should be guided in our duty by what he imagines to be our advantage rather than human feeling. Another question is: 'If something has to be jettisoned during a storm at sea, should it be a valuable horse or a valueless slave?' Here self-interest and human feeling pull in different directions. Another is: 'Supposing a ship is sinking and a foolish man has grabbed a plank; is a wise man justified in taking it away from him if he can?' 'No,' says Hecato, 'that would be wrong.' 'What about the owner of the ship then? May he take what is his own?' 'No, he may not, any more than he would be justified in throwing a passenger overboard well out at sea on the grounds that it is his ship; for until they arrive at the contracted destination, the ship is not deemed to belong to its owner but to its passengers.'

90.   'Well, then, what if there were only one plank and two shipwrecked men, both of them wise; should each try to grab it for himself, or should each give way to the other?' 'The man whose life is less valuable to himself or to his country should give way to the other.' 'But what if their lives are of equal value?' 'Then there should be no contest, but one should yield to the other, as though the matter had been decided by lot or by a game of *la moure*.'[63] 'Again, what if a man discovered that his father was robbing the temples or building a tunnel to the treasury, should he inform the magistrates?' 'No. That would be very wrong. On the contrary it would be his duty to defend his father if he were brought before the court.' 'You don't think, then, that patriotism should have priority over all other obligations?' 'Yes, indeed. But patriotism demands that children be loyal to their parents.' 'So if a man at-

tempts to betray his country or stage a *coup d'etat*, you think his son should say nothing?' 'No, of course not. He should first plead with his father not to do it. If that achieves nothing, he should rebuke and even threaten him. Finally, if the safety of the nation seems in jeopardy he will put the safety of his country before that of his father.'

91.   A further question is this: 'If a wise man inadvertently receives a forged coin, should he on discovering the fault pass it on, as though it were genuine, when paying a debt?' Diogenes says he should. Antipater says no, and I agree with him. Again. 'Suppose a man is selling wine which he knows is going off; should he mention the fact?' 'Why should he?' says Diogenes. 'An honest man would,' replies Antipater. These are the controversial points of law that the Stoics like to discuss. Again, when you are selling a slave, should you mention his faults? I do not mean just those which if not mentioned render the contract null and void, but faults of character: for example, he may be a liar, a gambler, a thief or a drunkard. Antipater thinks that you ought to declare them; Diogenes does not.

92.   What if a man is selling gold imagining that he is selling brass? Is it the duty of an honest man to tell him that it is gold, or should he buy for a penny an amount that is worth a thousand pennies? By now it is clear enough where the philosophers I have mentioned disagree and what my own views are.

Chapter 24

Agreements and promises must always be kept, provided, in the words of the praetors, they 'were not elicited by force or criminal fraud'. Supposing a doctor prescribes a cure for dropsy with the proviso that if the patient recovers as a result he should never use the same cure again; suppose the patient does recover, but a few years later is again afflicted with the same illness and fails to persuade the man with whom he made the agreement to let him use the cure again; what is he to do? Surely he is justified in looking after his life and health; for the doctor is inhuman to refuse what it would not in any way harm him to grant.

170

93.   Consider now the case of a wise man who has been bequeathed a hundred million sesterces. Suppose the man who proposes to leave him the money to have repeatedly asked him to perform a dance, publicly and in broad daylight, in the forum before he can receive his legacy. Moreover he has promised to do this, since it was a condition of his inclusion in the legacy. Should he keep his promise or not? In the first place I wish he had not promised and think he was thoroughly frivolous in doing so. But the promise was given, and therefore if he thinks it wrong to make such an exhibition in the forum, he would do better to break his promise and lose his legacy than to keep a promise (and a fortune!) which involves moral wrong. The only other way out is to contribute the money to the state in some hour of need; for even dancing in the forum is justified, if it is in the interests of his country.

Chapter 25

94.   There is however no obligation to keep promises which are not to the advantage of those to whom they were given. To give an example from mythology, it was the Sun-god who promised his son Phaeton anything he chose to ask for; he asked to be allowed to ride in his father's chariot; the wish was granted, but he was struck by a thunderbolt and burned to ashes while still in mid-air.[a] How much better it would have been in this case if his father had not kept his promise! And what about Neptune's promise to Theseus which the latter insisted was to be kept? Neptune had granted Theseus the fulfilment of three wishes. Theseus wished for the death of his son Hippolytus as a punishment for his suspected misconduct with Phaedra, his stepmother. His wish was fulfilled, but plunged him into the most bitter grief.[14]

95.   To give another example, Agamemnon had promised to sacrifice to Diana the most beautiful creature born in his kingdom that year; this turned out to be his daughter Iphigenia, who was duly sacrificed. It would clearly have been better to break his promise than commit such a hideous crime. Thus there are occasions when promises should be broken and even trusts betrayed. For example,

[a] Vd. Ovid, *Metamorphoses*, XI.

if a man entrusts you with the care of his sword when sane, but later asks for it back when he has gone mad, it would be quite wrong to return it; in fact it would be your duty not to. Again, if someone entrusts you with some money and is later found to be plotting rebellion, should you return it? I think not; for your country should be dearer to you than anything else, and therefore you should not abet any action against it.

96.   Thus there are occasions when actions which are normally by their very nature right, will be seen to be wrong, and so the fulfilment of a promise, adherence to an agreement or trust may become wrong, if the advantage which prompted the contract is reversed. I think I have now adequately dealt with those cases which seem advantageous and prompted by wisdom, and yet turn out to be the antithesis of justice.

In my first book I argued the basis of moral obligation from four basic criteria of good action.[a] Let us now consider them again in order to point out the conflict between what is right and what masquerades as expedient. I have already discussed wisdom and its counterfeit, cunning. I have also discussed justice and explained its unvarying expediency. The two remaining criteria of goodness are great courage, as seen only in those of the highest moral character, and the moulding and regulation of the personality by restraint and self-control.

Chapter 26

97.   Ulysses thought it was to his advantage to evade military service by pretending to be mad.[67] At least, this is what the tragedians tell us, although Homer, our best authority on Ulysses, does not give us a hint of it. Such a stratagem cannot be considered as morally justified, but one could perhaps argue that it was to his advantage to continue living and reigning in peace with his parents, wife and son at Ithaca. Could any amount of glory, won by day after day fraught with danger and hardship, be compared with such a peaceful existence? My own view is that that sort of peace is to be

[a] For the four cardinal virtues, *Vd.* I, 5, 15.

scorned and rejected, because it is wrong and therefore cannot be advantageous.

98.　What do you think people would have said, had Ulysses persisted in his pretended madness? Indeed, in spite of his great achievements in the war, he was criticized by Ajax in these terms:

> 'He was the man who first proposed the oath,
> and, as ye know, alone neglected it
> by feigning madness to avoid the war;
> and had not Palamede, that shrewd old sage,
> exposed the rascal's cunning trickery,
> he ne'er would have fulfilled his sacred trust.'[a]

99.　His battles, whether with enemies or waves, brought him more credit than his desertion of Greece in its moment of unity against the barbarian hordes. But let us now turn from myths and foreign lands and come to history and our own country. Marcus Atilius Regulus, while serving in Africa during his second consulship, fell into a trap laid by some Carthaginians under the leadership of the Spartan general, Xanthippus, a subordinate of Hannibal's father Hamilcar.[b] Regulus was dispatched to Rome, but not before he had sworn to return to Carthage if he failed in his mission to the senate, which was to secure the return of certain members of the Carthaginian aristocracy who had been taken prisoner.[c] On arriving in Rome, Regulus saw clearly enough the apparent advantage to which his position could be exploited, but he realized the snare which was to be borne out by future events. It was this: what was to prevent him from staying in his country, being reunited with his wife and children in his own home, considering his defeat as the sort of thing anyone might suffer in war, and retaining the high office of consul? What, I ask, was to deny the advantage of such courses of action? Only one thing—his great spirit of fortitude!

[a] From Pacuvius's lost *Armorum Iudicium.*

[b] There appears to be no good reason why Holden and others should have regarded this as a mistake. Regulus's mission to Rome took place in 249 B.C. Hamilcar is known to have been commander of the Punic fleet two years later.

[c] For the story *Vd.* Polybius, I, 32; Livy, XXII, 60; Horace, *Odes*, III, 5. For its doubtful authenticity *Vd.* Niebuhr, *History of Rome*, Vol. III, p. 598.

Chapter 27

100. Can you imagine any more authoritative guidance? The main
properties of this great virtue are total rejection of fear, utter
scorn of all dangers to human life, and the conviction that there
is nothing that can happen to a man which cannot be borne. What
then did Regulus do? He came before the senate and explained
his mission; but he refused to cast his vote on the issue, as he did
not regard himself as a senator as long as he was under oath to
the enemy. He advised the senate that it was not to their advantage
to return the prisoners, as they were young men and able leaders
whereas he was worn out by advancing years. At this point I can
almost hear the cries of 'folly' and criticisms of acting against his
own advantage; but his advice won the day and the prisoners were
detained. He himself returned to Carthage in spite of the pull of
his country and his family. He was well aware of the ruthless
enemy and the sophisticated methods of torture which awaited
him; but his only thought was to be true to his oath. Even when he
was being put to death by lack of sleep, his state was preferable to
what it would have been at home, an old man, no longer consul,
and with the stains of captivity and perjury upon his character.
101. On the other hand, it could be argued that he was foolish in
directly advocating their detention when he could merely have
refrained from voting against it. But in what way was his action
foolish? Was it foolish to promote the interest of the state? Could
a course of action which was harmful to the state be to the advantage of any individual citizen?

Chapter 28

Those who draw a distinction between what is expedient and
what is right are undermining the very foundations of natural law.
Indeed we all pursue what is to our advantage. In fact we are
174

III

irresistibly drawn towards it and are incapable of acting in any other way. Is there anyone who avoids what is to his advantage? Or rather is there anyone who fails to pursue it with great zeal? But since expediency is only to be found in actions that are laudable, right and fitting, we should give them the highest priority. In fact the very idea of expediency should be thought of not so much as a glorious goal, but as something implicit in such actions.

102.   'Of what consequence is an oath?' you may ask. 'Surely we are not afraid of Jupiter's anger!' No. This is common ground for agreement among all philosophers, not only those who say that their god is free from cares and refrains from inflicting them on others,[a] but also those who stress his constant activity in the world;[b] all agree that he is never guilty of anger or physical harm. But supposing Jupiter had been angry, how could he have inflicted greater harm on Regulus than Regulus inflicted upon himself? No religious influence, then, could have outweighed the apparent advantage of the other course of action. Was he afraid of doing wrong then? There are two answers here: in the first place one should always choose the least of two evils, and surely the evil involved in breaking his oath was not as great as that in the torture that he had to suffer; secondly, we should bear in mind those famous lines of Accius:

'Broke you your faith?'
'I neither pledged nor pledge to faithless faith.'[c]

We must admire the sentiment here, however much we disapprove of the character of the king who spoke those words.

103.   A further objection is this: just as we claim that there are some things which seem expedient but are in fact not so, so they claim that there are some things which seem right but are not. The action of going back to Carthage to be tortured in order to be true to an oath may seem right, but surely the fulfilment of an oath exacted by an enemy under compulsion is not obligatory. Finally there is the objection that what is outstandingly expedient may prove to be right even if it did not seem to be in the first place. These are the main objections to Regulus' course of action; let us now deal with them one by one.

[a] The Epicureans.
[b] The Stoics.
[c] Lines from the *Atreus* of Accius, spoken by Atreus himself.

III

Chapter 29

104. The first objection was that there was no need to fear any anger or physical harm from Jupiter because these are not attributes of Jupiter. This argument is no more valid in the case of Regulus' oath than in the case of any other oath. But in the taking of an oath we ought to bear in mind not so much the consequences of breaking it as the obligations we have brought upon ourselves: for an oath is a sacred declaration. A solemn promise should be considered as being made before a god as witness and is therefore to be kept. Its fulfilment should be considered not in the light of non-existent divine anger, but of justice and good faith. Ennius puts it well when he speaks of:

'O gracious winged Faith and oath that's sworn by Jove.'[a]
Therefore the man who breaks his oath is guilty of a breach of Faith, that deity to which, as a speech of Cato[b] puts it, 'Our ancestors assigned a temple on the Capitol next to that of Jupiter the Greatest and Best.'

105. Next the objection that even if Jupiter had been angry, he could not have inflicted greater harm upon Regulus than Regulus inflicted upon himself. This would be true if pain were the only evil. But philosophers of the highest authority[c] not only deny that pain is the greatest evil, but that it is an evil at all. Regulus is no mean witness to this truth; on the contrary, he is probably the best we have, and so we should not impugn his authority. What more convincing example could we look for than that of a leader of the Roman people who chose to accept torture as the cost of doing his duty?

Then there was the 'least of all evils' objection. This implies that doing wrong is to be preferred to personal disaster. But is there any worse evil than wrongdoing? For if we find even physical deformity repellent, surely we should see in the corruption and degradation of the soul something far worse.

[a] Probably from Ennius's *Thyestes*. Cf. I, 8, 26; II, 7, 23.
[b] Marcus Porcius Cato the Censor.
[c] The Stoics.

106.   This is why the more rigorous philosophers[a] even claim that wrongdoing is the only evil, and even the more lax Peripatetics have no hesitation in calling it the greatest of all evils. As for those words of Accius: 'I neither pledged nor pledge to faithless faith,' they were designed to suit the character of Atreus and were therefore correctly used in that context. The danger of using the argument that there is no obligation to honour a pledge given to the faithless is that it provides a pretext for perjury.

107.   Even in warfare there is a code to be observed, and situations often arise in which an oath sworn to an enemy must be honoured. If an oath has been sworn in such a way as to create a concept of obligation in the mind of the one who swore it, then it must be kept; if on the other hand there is no such concept, there can be no perjury. Suppose, for example, that you agree to pay pirates a ransom for your life, and then do not pay it; in such a case you cannot be considered guilty of fraud, even though you defaulted while under oath. For a pirate is not classified as a normal enemy, as he is an enemy common to all, and so there can be no question of good faith or oaths in our dealings with him.

108.   For perjury is not simply swearing an oath which you do not keep; it is the failure to perform an action promised, according to the traditional formula, 'as a matter of conscience'. Euripides expressed it well in the line: 'With tongue I swore it, but my mind's unsworn.'[b] Regulus, on the other hand, would not have been justified in violating the conditions of an agreement made with an enemy. For we were dealing with a normal declared enemy and were therefore bound by our Code of War as well as many other international laws. Had this not been so, the senate would never have surrendered the distinguished men that it did in chains to our enemies.

Chapter 30

109.   Titus Veturius and Spurius Postumius during their second consulships were defeated at the battle of the Caudine Forks[c] and

[a] The Stoics.   [b] Euripides, *Hippolytus*, 612.
[c] The Roman defeat was at the hands of Caius Pontius in the Second Samnite War (321 B.C.).

their legions compelled to pass under the yoke; but because they made peace without the authority of either Senate or people they were handed over to the enemy. So at the same time were Tiberius Numicius and Quintus Maelius,[a] the then tribunes of the people, since they had supported the peace treaty. Their handing-over signified the repudiation of the treaty. Moreover the action was actually instigated by Postumius himself, although it included him. Caius Mancinus was similarly punished many years later.[b] For having made a treaty with the people of Numantia without the authority of the senate, he supported the proposal for his own extradition brought before the senate by Lucius Furius and Sextus Atilius. It was passed, and he was duly handed over to the enemy. His action was more honourable than that of Quintus Pompeius, who spoke against a similar proposal and secured its defeat.[c] In this case apparent advantage rather than honour prevailed, while in the previous examples we see the temptation of evil masquerading as advantage rejected by the power of right.

110.   A further argument was there can be no obligation to honour an oath extracted by force. As if any man of spirit would be influenced by force! Further, there is the objection that if Regulus intended to advise against the return of the prisoners, there was little point in him coming to Rome. This is a criticism of the most creditable feature of his action! For he did not act on his own judgement, but merely put his case and left the decision to the senate. Had he not advocated the course of action that he did, the prisoners would of course have been returned to the Carthaginians and he would have remained safe in his own country. But he did not consider this to his country's advantage and therefore felt obliged to propose otherwise—and take the consequences. Finally, the objection that what is outstandingly advantageous may prove to be right, which presumably means that it *is* right; for nothing can be advantageous unless it is right. It cannot become right because it is advantageous, but only be advantageous because it is right. Hence, of all the great actions of the past one could hardly choose a more praiseworthy or outstanding example than this act of Regulus.

---

[a] According to Livy, IX, 8, Maelius' colleague was Lucius Livius.
[b] 137 B.C.
[c] Quintus Pompeius Rufus (consul 140 B.C.) concluded a treaty with Numantia which he subsequently disowned.

Chapter 31

111. But the most laudable aspect of Regulus' conduct was his proposal that the captives should not be released. For although we now admire him for returning, at that time he could hardly have done otherwise; so the merits of his return are those of his times rather than of Regulus himself. For our ancestors believed that there was no stronger guarantee of good faith than an oath. Our evidence for this is the laws contained in the Twelve Tables, the Sacred Laws, the treaties which make good faith, even with an enemy, mandatory, and the investigations and penalties ordered by the censors, who judged cases concerning oaths far more strictly than any others.[68]

112. Take for example the action of Marcus Pomponius, who as tribune brought an action against Lucius Manlius, the son of Aulus, who was then dictator, for continuing his dictatorship a few days beyond the statutory limit. He also accused him of banishing his own son, Titus (later known as Titus Manlius Torquatus) and ordering him to live in seclusion in the country. When the young Manlius heard of his father's treatment, he is said to have rushed to Rome and arrived at Pomponius house early one morning. When his presence was announced, Pomponius, thinking that he was intending in his anger to bring him some support for his prosecution, rose from his bed, removed all witnesses from the room, and ordered the young man to be admitted. Titus entered, immediately drew his sword, and promised to kill him on the spot unless he gave him his oath that he would drop the case against his father. Pomponius, terrified, had no alternative. He gave his oath, and later, reporting the matter to the popular assembly, he explained why he was obliged to abandon his case against Manlius. Such was the respect commanded by the oath in those times! Incidentally it was the same Titus Manlius who was challenged to fight by a Gaul in the battle of the River Anien. He killed the Gaul and stripped him of his collar (*torques*), whereafter he became known as *Torquatus*. He was also the Manlius who in his third consulship routed the Latins near Veseris,[a] a great man, whose

---

[a] Commonly called the Battle of Mount Vesuvius (340 B.C.). *Vd.* Livy, VIII.

III

concern for his father was only matched by his ruthless treatment of his own son.[a]

Chapter 32

113.   We should be just as lavish in our praise of Regulus for keeping his oath as we should in our criticism of the ten men whom Hannibal dispatched to the senate after the battle of Cannae. They were bound by oath to return to their camp, which had been captured by the Carthaginians, unless they could secure a return of prisoners. There are however different accounts of the episode. Polybius, a particularly reliable source,[69] tells us that of the ten aristocrats who went on this mission nine returned, having failed to achieve their objective. The remaining one stayed in Rome. His excuse was that shortly after leaving the camp he had returned on the pretext that he had forgotten something, and so considered himself justified in claiming that he had by this action discharged the obligation of his oath. In fact he had not; for such deceitful conduct exacerbates rather than exculpates an act of perjury. Such an action, then, though perversely wearing the mask of cleverness, is the product of misguided dishonesty. The senate therefore decreed that this hardened criminal should be returned to Hannibal in chains.[b]

114.   But the most important part of the story was this: Hannibal held eight thousand prisoners who had neither been captured in battle nor had they fled for their lives, but had been abandoned in the camp by the consuls Paullus and Varro. Although they could have been ransomed very cheaply, the senate chose not to do this in order to instil into our soldiers the principle that they should conquer or die. Polybius describes Hannibal's reaction to this news as one of utter despondency that the senate and people of Rome were capable of such spirit in adversity. Yet another example of apparent advantage yielding to right.

[a] A famous example of the sternness of the Roman paterfamilias. He ordered his son to be beheaded for fighting contrary to orders, even though he fought with great success. *Vd.* Livy, VIII, 7, *et seqq.*

[b] The story is also told in Book I (13, 40), but there seems to be no good reason for regarding either passage as spurious.

III

115. The historian Acilius, however, who wrote in Greek,[70] tells us that more than one played the trick of returning to the camp so as to be technically absolved from their oath, and that they were severely denounced by the censors.[a] Let us not labour the point; for it is clear that any example which is lacking the courage (as Regulus would have been, had he been motivated by his own advantage rather than that of the state and stayed at home), cannot be advantageous, because such conduct is unlawful, distasteful and wrong.

Chapter 33

116. There still remains our fourth heading which includes 'decorum', restraint, moderation, temperance and self-control. Can anything ever be to our advantage, if it runs counter to such a host of virtues? And yet the philosophical schools of Aristippus of Cyrene[26] and Anniceris[71] considered pleasure the source of all good, and virtue only to be praised in so far as it produces pleasure. Their views have now given place to those of Epicurus, which are, however, strikingly similar and are widely accepted. But if we are to guard and defend what is right, we must resist them with might and main.

117. If we are to accept Metrodorus'[72] definition of supreme advantage, and in fact of happiness in life as a whole, as having a good bodily constitution and good reasons to hope that it will last, then there will be an inevitable conflict between such a concept and what is right. For how can such beliefs be reconciled with our pursuit of the four great virtues? Take wisdom first: presumably its sole duty will be the search for pleasure; but what more distressing servitude could be imagined than for such a virtue to be subject to pleasure? To what task will it be assigned? No doubt that of intelligent discrimination between different pleasures? I agree that this may have its attractions, but could one imagine anything more despicable? Secondly courage: how can those who think pain the

[a] The Censors were Marcus Atilius Regulus and Publius Furius Phlius. *Vd.* Livy, XXII, 61, 9.

greatest evil understand that contempt for pain and hardship which is the mark of the courageous man? I am aware that Epicurus frequently recognizes the place of courage in resistance to pain; but this is beside the point. What we need to consider are the logical implications of a creed which identifies good with pleasure and evil with pain. Thirdly temperance and self-control: he has a great deal to say about these virtues too, but becomes bogged down, so to speak, with contradictions. For how can singing the praises of temperance be reconciled with the belief that pleasure is the highest good? For pleasure finds its allies in the passions, but temperance is their deadliest foe.

118.   The Epicureans' answer, then, to these great virtues is one of ingenius special-pleading: wisdom is explained as the knowledge by which pleasures are produced and pains banished; courage is somehow made to square with their ideas inasmuch as it enables men to endure pain and face death with equanimity; even temperance is found a place—not, admittedly, a very comfortable one, but the best that can be found—by defining the highest pleasure as exemption from pain. The fourth virtue, justice, totters, or rather, collapses completely under the strain. So do all the other virtues which are relevant to human relationships and social intercourse; for there can be no goodness, or generosity, no kindness or friendship, if they are sought, not as an end in themselves, but simply to promote pleasure or personal advantage.

119.   To sum up, just as I have shown that nothing can ever be to our advantage if not right, so I insist that all pleasure comes into this category. This is why I think that Calliphon and Dinomarchus[a] are particularly to be criticized for imagining that they would solve the problem by identifying pleasure with right—which is as bad as identifying a man with an animal. True goodness cannot admit such identification; it can only scorn and reject it. Ultimate good is essentially uncompounded and therefore cannot be an amalgam of contradictory qualities.

120.   But this is a big question and I have dealt with it elsewhere.[b] Let me return to what concerns us here. I think I have adequately dealt with the problem of settling the conflict between apparent advan-

---

[a] Calliphon and Dinomachus (3rd century B.C.) tried to find common ground between Stoicism and Epicureanism through the union of virtue with pleasure. *Vd.* Clement of Alexandria, *Stromateis*, II, 128.

[b] *De Finibus*, II.

III

tage and what is right. While it is true that pleasure may sometimes masquerade as advantage, it cannot in any way be reconciled with right. The most that can be said of pleasure is that it is sauce to the dish; it can certainly never be said to be to our advantage.

121. Well, this is your father's present, Marcus. I think it is a considerable one, but that will depend on the use you make of it. However, I want you to welcome these three books as guests among your normal company—Cratippus' lecture notes. I should certainly have come to Athens myself had not my country's interests unequivocally demanded my return.[73] Had I come; you would have been called to hear my advice from my own lips, but as it is, my voice comes to you in these volumes. Do give them as much time as you can—that is to say as much time as you are prepared to give them. And when I hear that you are enjoying your philosophical studies, I hope that we shall soon be discussing them face to face. Meanwhile, in your absence I can only address you from a distance. Farewell, my son! Be assured of my great affection for you—which will grow in proportion to your delight in my books and the precepts which they contain.

NOTES

1. *Cratippus* (I, 1, 1)

Cratippus was a leading Peripatetic philosopher, born at Mytilene in Lesbos. Cicero seems to have had a high regard for him as he refers to him in more than one place in *De Officiis* as 'the leading philosopher of the age'. *Vd.* I, 1, 3; III, 2, 5, etc. His son seems to have been very attached to him, as can be seen from a letter he wrote to Cicero's secretary, Tiro (*Epistulae ad Familiares*, XVI, 21). He also seems to have visited the province of Asia with him (Ibid. XII, 16).

2. *Demetrius of Phalerum* (I, 1, 3)

Demetrius, surnamed after the Attic deme of Phalerum where he was born in 345 B.C., was the son of the Athenian statesman Phanostratus. He studied under the Peripatetic Theophrastus, and, according to Diogenes Laertius (39, 52), enabled him to buy the school which the latter, being an alien, was not permitted to do. He was appointed *strategos* at Athens by Cassander in 317 and the ten years of his rule were a period of peaceful consolidation of which Cicero speaks with approval (*De Re Publica*, II, 1). When Athens fell to Demetrius Poliorcetes (*q.v.* Note 26) in 307, he fled first to Thebes and later to the court of Ptolemy Lagus at Alexandria, where he became librarian and devoted himself to literary pursuits. Diogenes Laertius (5, 80) gives us a voluminous list of writings, which included philosophy, history, literary criticism and speeches. He was regarded by Quintilian (*Institutio Oratoria*, X, 1, 80) as the last of the great Attic orators, his speeches being characterized more by their charm than their rhetorical force. Cicero confirms this: 'His style', he writes (*Brutus*, 9, 17), 'delighted rather than inspired his hearers.' He does not appear to have been an original thinker of any depth, but rather a popular exponent of Theophrastus' views. (*Vd.* Cicero, *De Legibus*, III, 6).

3. *Theophrastus* (I, 1, 3)

Theophrastus (369–285 B.C.) was the most loyal pupil of Aristotle whom he succeeded as president of the *Peripatos* in 323–2 B.C. He wrote voluminously; Diogenes Laertius gives a list of his writings (V, 42). They included the classification and physiology of plants, metaphysics, character sketches, law, physics, medicine, mineralogy and meteorology. His elegance of style is contrasted by Cicero with the vigour of Aristotle (*Vd. Brutus* 31, 131; *Orator*, 19, 62). Quintilian (*Institutio Oratoria*, X, 1, 83) remarked that, true to his name, he spoke with the voice of the gods.

4. *Demosthenes* (I, 1, 3)
Demosthenes, the orator (384–322 B.C.), studied law under Isaeus and from an early age practised as a *logographos*. He soon graduated to private cases, and his success in these led to the public briefs which paved the way for his political speeches, which date from 354. According to Cicero (*Brutus*, 31, 121), he read Plato avidly and was influenced by his style. Cicero also tells us (*Orator*, 4, 21) that his early leanings were towards philosophy, which he gave up for oratory on the advice of Isocrates.

5. *Isocrates* (I, 1, 4)
Isocrates, the Orator (436–338 B.C.), studied rhetoric under Prodicus, Protagoras and Gorgias, and was very much influenced by the sophists in his use of words and cultivation of elaborate prose rhythms. Apart from his political speeches he wrote a pamphlet on education, in which he attacked the sophists, and a number of political tracts. Cicero's criticism of his scorn for philosophy is therefore probably overstated.

6. *Aristo of Chios* (I, 2, 6)
Aristo lived about the middle of the third century B.C. He was a pupil of Zeno of Citium (*q.v.* Note 51), from whom he differed radically in rejecting all branches of philosophy except ethics. Even this he circumscribed by denying the right of the philosopher to outline any particular duties, but asserted as his sole function the discovery of the *summum bonum*. 'Aristo's one conviction', writes Cicero in *De Finibus* (V, 25, 73), 'was that, apart from virtue and vice, there exists nothing to be sought or avoided.' He rejected Zeno's distinction between the preferable and the non-preferable in external things; this led him to the doctrine of *adiaphoria*, or indifference to every thing non-moral. Cicero, in a fragment of a lost philosophical work (*Vd.*, p. 481 in Orelli's edition) refers to him as 'an austere thinker who considered moral good to be the only good.' *Vd.* also *De Finibus*, II, 13, 43; III, 3, 11; IV, 16, 43; IV, 17, 47; and *Academica*, II, 42, 130.

7. *Herillus of Carthage* (I, 2, 6)
Herillus was a contemporary of Aristo, and like him differed radically from Zeno of Citium of whom he had also been a pupil. To him knowledge was the only virtue, since it alone is stable and consistent, whereas standards of moral goodness vary for different men in different circumstances. Like Aristo, he taught indifference to all external conditions of life and was similarly criticized by Cicero on the grounds that if we do not regard poverty, suffering, etc., as evils, we can be under no obligation to combat them when we see men oppressed by them. In fact, such beliefs leave little or no basis for moral obligation. *Vd.* Cicero, *De Finibus*, II, 13, 43; V, 8, 23; V, 25, 73; and *Academica*, II, 42, 129.

8. *Pyrrho of Elis* (I, 2, 6)
Pyrrho (*c.* 360–*c.* 270) was the founder of scepticism. Born of a poor family, he studied under Bryso of Heraclea Pontica and Anaxarchus of Abdera, a follower of Democritus the Atomist. According to Diogenes Laertius,

186

he later made a living by painting. He left no written record of his teaching, which was handed down by his pupil, Timo of Phlius, of whom a few fragments have been preserved. Pyrrho denied all bases for ascertaining truth and consequently the point of any attempt to teach the desirability or undesirability of anything external. The only aim of life thus becomes *aphasia*—a rejection of any attempt to assert what we do not and cannot know about; this leads to *ataraxia*—imperturbability, which alone can free us from the passions by which we might otherwise be governed. His ethical scepticism, developed into a logical scepticism by Arcesilaus of Pitane, the founder of the Middle Academy, had a great influence on later philosophy. Cicero in *De Finibus* (IV, 16, 43) regards Pyrrho as the most misleading of all the philosophers he criticizes because his restriction of virtue to *aphasia* leaves no real moral goal for human life. *Vd.* also *De Finibus*, II, 13, 43; V, 8, 23; *Tusculanae Disputationes*, V, 30, 85; *Academica*, II, 42, 130.

9. *The Greeks* (I, 3, 8)

Cicero is referring here to the Stoic division into *absolute* and *secondary* obligations. Absolute obligations (κατορθώματα) implied a moral imperative, and only a philosopher, who by definition understood the moral imperative could perform them. Secondary obligations(τὰ μέσα καθήκοντα) were those whose performance was neither good or bad in itself, but only in so far as it implied good or bad intentions; and they could be performed by the general mass of the people. As Cicero is concerned in this work with a guide to the good life for all mankind, it is the latter with which he is primarily concerned, and it is to this that the term *officium* generally applies. This distinction coincides exactly with that made in the preceding section (I, 3, 7) and is repeated in Book III (3, 14) and in *De Finibus* (III, 17, 58).

10. *Caius Sulpicius Gallus* (I, 6, 19)

Sulpicius was praetor in 169 B.C. and consul in 166. While serving as a military tribune under Lucius Aemilius Paullus in the Third Macedonian War, he predicted an eclipse of the moon on the eve of the battle of Pydna (168 B.C.) and so prevented the alarm which its unheralded appearance would have caused. Cicero refers to him in *De Re Publica* (I, 14, 21) as 'a most learned man and a skilled astronomer'. *Vd.* also *De Senectute*, 14, 49; *De Amicitia*, 27, 101; Livy XLIV, 37; Pliny the Elder, *Naturalis Historia*, II, 12, 9.

11. *Sextus Pompeius* (I, 6, 19)

Sextus was the brother of Gnaeus Pompeius Strabo and uncle of Pompey the Great. In *Brutus* (47, 175) Cicero pays tribute to his great work on civil law as well as his deep knowledge of geometry and Stoic thought.

12. *Quintus Ennius* (I, 8, 26)

Ennius (239–169 B.C.) was born in Calabria and brought up with a knowledge of Greek, Latin and Oscan. After service in the Roman army he settled in Rome where he taught Cato the Censor (*q.v.* Note 47) Greek and

187

became an intimate friend of Scipio Africanus Major (*q.v.*, Note 46). He is regarded as the 'father of Latin poetry'. He was the first to introduce the Greek epic hexameter into Latin and his epic poem, the *Annales*, portrayed in eighteen books of rugged but often expressive verse the history of Rome down to 171 B.C. No complete book is extant, but about 550 lines survive, mostly in quotation. He also wrote twenty-one tragedies, mostly on Greek models, of which some 400 lines survive. No doubt his example influenced his nephew Pacuvius (*q.v.*, Note 24). This quotation is from an unknown work, probably a tragedy. *Vd.* also I, 16, 51; I, 24, 84; II, 7, 23; III, 29, 104.

13. *Publius Terentius Afer* (I, 9, 30)
According to Suetonius Terence was born in Carthage and brought to Rome as a slave. His master, Terentius Lucanus, from whom he took his name, gave him a good education, set him free and launched him into a Roman literary circle. Terence followed the example of Plautus (*q.v.*, Note 23) in writing Latin comedies based on the Greek *New Comedy*. He was accused of plagiarism, against which he frequently defends himself in his prologues. Borrowings from Menander are apparent in the *Adelphi* and the *Eunuchus* and the *Heautontimorumenos* is almost entirely derivative, but the six surviving comedies show a distinctly Terentian ethos of elegance and humanity (the line quoted here—*Heautontimorumenos*, I, 1, 25—is an often-quoted example of the latter) which is in sharp contrast to the rumbustious coarseness of Plautus. *Vd.* also II, 2, 26.

14. *Theseus and Hippolytus* (I, 10, 32)
Theseus had a son, Hippolytus, by the Amazon Hippolyta. Hippolyta died and Theseus married Phaedra. During Theseus' journey to the Underworld Phaedra fell passionately in love with Hippolytus, who was a devotee of Artemis and refused to submit to the dictates of Aphrodite. Since Phaedra could not win Hippolytus she resolved to destroy him, and after writing a note accusing Hippolytus of rape, hanged herself. It was because Theseus believed her note (in spite of all his son's protestations) that he used the third of three wishes granted him by Neptune (Poseidon), only to learn the truth from Artemis after his son's death. This is the subject of Euripides' play *Hippolytus* (*Vd.* III, 25, 94; 29, 108). The substance of Theseus' three wishes is given in the scholiast's note on Euripides' *Hippolytus* 1349 as, first, the return from Hades, secondly, the escape from the labyrinth, and thirdly, the death of Hippolytus.

15. *Tusculans, Aequians etc.* (I, 11, 35)
Tusculum, the oldest *municipium* in Italy, was admitted to *civitas Romana* in 381 B.C. (*Vd.* Livy VI, 26). The Aequians, according to Livy (IX, 45), were almost annihilated in 304 B.C. A very small remnant must have been admitted. A proportion of the Volscians (Livy, X, 1) were admitted to non-voting rights (*civitas sine suffragio*) in 303 B.C. and full citizenship in 188. The Sabines received non-voting rights after their defeat by Manius Curius Dentatus in 290 B.C. and full citizenship in 268 (*Vd.* Livy, *Perioche*,

11; Velleius Paterculus, I, 14, 6). The Hernicians had had a defensive alliance with Rome as early as 486 B.C. and fought side by side with her against the Aequians and Volscians, but in 306 with the exception of three cities they came in on the side of Anagnia, were defeated, granted non-voting rights and later full citizenship (*Vd.* Livy, IX, 43).

Carthage was utterly destroyed after the Third Punic War (146 B.C.) by Publius Cornelius Scipio Aemilianus at the instigation of Marcus Porcius Cato, whose famous cry 'Delenda est Carthago' had inspired the renewed conflict. Numantia, a fortress of the Celtiberian tribe in Spain, was also utterly destroyed by Scipio in 134 (*Vd.* I, 22, 76). Corinth was razed to the ground by Lucius Mummius Achaicus in 146, an act condemned by Florus (II, 16) as *facinus indignum.* (*Vol.* also III, 11, 46).

16. *Hesiod* (I, 15, 48)
Born at Cyme probably in the eighth century B.C., Hesiod migrated to Greece and settled at Ascra. He is generally regarded as the founder of didactic poetry and Vergil acknowledges his debt to him in the *Georgics* (II, 176). Only two works are now generally attributed to him, the *Theogony* [Hesiodic authorship denied by Pausanias (IX, 31), but strongly asserted by Herodotus (II, 53)], a genealogy of the gods, and the *Works and Days*, which is a blend of homely morality (*e.g.* the need for every man to work for his living) and practical hints on agriculture and navigation. Cicero is here referring to II. 349 et seqq., the gist of which is: 'Give your neighbour, good measure and better than that if you can, so that you can be sure of finding help later when you need it.'

17. *Pythagoras* (I, 17, 56)
Pythagoras (*floruit* late sixth century B.C.) was born at Samos, but later emigrated to Croton in Southern Italy where he established a semi-philosophical, semi-mystical school of thought. His main beliefs were the transmigration of souls and an interpretation of the world in terms of numbers based on the ratios inherent in the musical scale. No original writings have survived, and because of his enormous prestige in the Greek world as a mystic, a great many ideas were later attributed to him. The 'unity in plurality' concept is later to be found in Aristotle (*Nicomachean Ethics*, IX, 9) and in Stoic philosophy (*Vd.* Diogenes Laertius, VII, 23).

18. *Horatius, the Decii, the Scipios and Marcellus* (I, 18, 61)
Horatius Cocles is famous for his defence of the Tiber bridge against the army of Lars Porsena (*Vd.* Livy, II, 10).

Publius Decius Mus and his son of the same name won fame by sacrificing themselves for their country, the former in a battle against the Latins in 340 B.C., the latter in the battle of Sentinum in 295. (*Vd.* Livy VIII, 9; X, 38).

The Scipios here mentioned (cf. III, 16) were the sons of Lucius Cornelius Scipio (2). Cnaeus (3), as consul in 222 B.C., defeated the Insubres at Mediolanum; later with his brother Publius (4) he utterly defeated Has-

189

drubal near Ibera in 215 and captured Saguntum in 212. They were both killed in Spain in the following year. For the Scipio family *Vd.* below.

Marcus Claudius Marcellus was the third and last general to win the *spolia opima* (spoils offered by a Roman general who had killed an enemy leader in single combat) in his campaign against the Insubres in 222 B.C. He also beat off Hannibal's attack on Nola in 216 and captured Syracuse in 211.

Appendix to Note 18: The Scipio Family

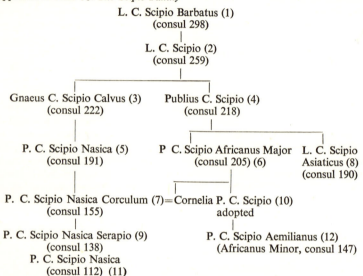

L. C. Scipio Barbatus (1)
(consul 298)

L. C. Scipio (2)
(consul 259)

Gnaeus C. Scipio Calvus (3)   Publius C. Scipio (4)
(consul 222)   (consul 218)

P. C. Scipio Nasica (5)   P C. Scipio Africanus Major   L. C. Scipio
(consul 191)   (consul 205) (6)   Asiaticus (8)
                                                            (consul 190)

P. C. Scipio Nasica Corculum (7)=Cornelia P. C. Scipio (10)
(consul 155)   adopted

P. C. Scipio Nasica Serapio (9)   P. C. Scipio Aemilianus (12)
(consul 138)   (Africanus Minor, consul 147)
P. C. Scipio Nasica
(consul 112) (11)

C. here stands for the name of the gens (Cornelius), not normally abbreviated.
For Publius Cornelius Scipio Africanus Major (6) *Vd.* Note 46.
For Publius Cornelius Scipio Nasica Corculum (7) *Vd.* Note 47.
For Publius Cornelius Scipio Nasica Serapio (9) *Vd.* Note 39.
For Publius Cornelius Scipio Africanus Minor (12) *Vd.* Notes 15 and 21.

19. *Callicratidas, Cleombrotus and Quintus Fabius Maximus* (I, 24, 84)
Arginusae saw the defeat of Callicratidas by the Athenians under Thrasybulus in 406 B.C. Cicero here tries to strengthen his argument by deliberately exaggerating the words of Callicratidas as recorded by Xenophon (*Hellenica*, I, 6, 32).

Cleombrotus commanded the Spartans against the Thebans at Leuctra in 371 B.C. His rashness in engaging battle was prompted by taunts about his sympathy for the Theban cause. *Vd.* Xenophon, *Hellenica*, VI, 4, 4.

Q. Fabius Maximus Verrucosus Ovicula was elected dictator by the Romans after their defeat by Hannibal at Lake Trasimene in 217 B.C. He preached the folly of pitched battles, a policy confirmed when the Romans, disregarding his advice, engaged Hannibal at Cannae and were utterly

190

defeated. The title *Cunctator* (the delayer), at first a taunt, thus became honorific. Ennius' claims to lasting fame for Fabius were justified; Vergil preserved the celebrated line about the *Delayer* in *Aeneid*, VI, 846.

20. *Caius Laelius* (I, 26, 90)
Caius Laelius the Younger (consul 140) was an intimate friend of Scipio Aemilianus (12—*Vd.* Appendix to Note 18) and shared with him the leadership of the influential 'Scipionic Circle'. Their friendship has its memorial in Cicero's *De Amicitia*. Laelius was a distinguished philosopher (like Cicero, a follower of Panaetius; he was surnamed 'Sapiens' for his Stoic erudition) and a fine orator who delivered the *laudatio* on Scipio. With Scipio he did much to promulgate Greek ideas and literature, and their circle numbered among its members Polybius the historian (*q.v.*, Note 69), Lucilius the satirist and Terence the comedist (*q.v.*, Note 13).

21. *Philip and Alexander* (I, 26, 90)
Philip of Macedon (ruled 359–336 B.C.) unified Macedonia, created a professional army, extended his power eastwards to Amphipolis, and by a series of diplomatic *coups* outwitted his opponents in Thrace, Thessaly and Athens. His son Alexander (ruled 336–323) built on this foundation and extended the Macedonian empire as far as India. His rule displayed superbly versatile generalship, courage and vision, but he could be ruthless and vengeful. Justin (IX, 8) refers to him as being greater than his father in both virtue and vice. Livy (IX, 18) speaks of Alexander's excessive love of praise, his cruelty and lack of self-control.

22. *Aeacus, Minos and Atreus* (I, 28, 97)
Aeacus and Minos were two sons of Jupiter who were so distinguished for their justice and integrity during their lifetime, that after their deaths they were made judges in Hades. *Vd.* Plato *Gorgias* 524a et seqq. Atreus was the son of Pelops and father of Agamemnon. As a result of a quarrel with his brother Thyestes he bore a grudge against him, and served up the flesh of his (Thyestes') children at a banquet. *Vd.* Aeschylus *Agamemnon* 1583 et seqq.

23. *Plautus and Greek Comedy* (I, 29, 104)
Titus Maccius Plautus (*c.* 250–184 B.C.) wr otein Latin plays modelled on the Greek New Comedy of Menander and others. His plays contain similar elements of love-intrigue, recognition scenes and stock characters, such as parasites, gluttons, choleric old men, etc. That his plays were not mere translations can be seen from the number of topical allusions and Latin puns. His popularity can be measured by the number of plays falsely attributed to him, about 130 (*Vd.* Aulus Gellius, *Noctes Atticae*, III, 3, 11). The twenty-one which Varro regarded as undoubtedly Plautine are the ones which are now extant. Cicero's compliments are not universally echoed: *Vd.* Horace, *Ars Poetica*, 270–2: 'Your ancestors praised Plautus for his poetry and wit, but their admiration was over-tolerant to the point of folly.' The principal exponents of Old Comedy were Eupolis, Cratinus

191

and Aristophanes (*Vd.* Horace, *Satires*, I, 4). Only plays of Aristophanes (11 in number) are extant. Their main characteristics were a formal plan, complete with choral odes, and biting satire on contemporary public figures, often set against a highly imaginative or mythological background.

Cicero speaks approvingly of the ironic wit which is a feature of the 'Socratic' dialogues of Plato, Xenophon and Aeschines, in *Brutus*, 85, 292, Examples of Catonic ἀποφθέγματα are to be found in Cicero *De Oratore*, II, 67, 271.

24. *Latin Tragedies and Tragic Actors* (I, 31, 114)

The *Epigoni* was a tragedy of Lucius Accius (170–*c.* 85 B.C.), which dealt with the vengeance of the sons of the Seven Champions who fell at the gates of Thebes with Polynices, and was possibly based on a play from the *Septem* trilogy of Aeschylus. Accius also wrote the *Melanippe* and the *Clytemnestra*. The *Medus* was a tragedy of Marcus Pacuvius (220–*c.* 130 B.C. *Vd.* Note 12), dealing with Medus, the son of Aegeus and Medea, whom Perses, his great-uncle, threatened to kill, a fate from which he was saved only by the timely arrival of his mother. Pacuvius also wrote the *Antiope*, which was based on a play of Euripides of the same name.

Rupilius, noted for his passionate acting, was well suited to the part of a Euripidean heroine; Aesopus on the other hand was a grave, dignified actor unsuited to the role of madness. Cicero says of him in the *Tusculanae Disputationes* (IV, 55), 'Can we imagine Aesopus ever acting in anger?'

25. *The Cynics* (I, 35, 128)

The most famous member of this school was Diogenes of Sinope, whose philosophy led him to reject all human conventions and live like a dog (κύων). He was probably not the founder of the school, as his ideas have been traced back to Antisthenes, a pupil of Socrates. Stoicism was an off-shoot of Cynicism (Zeno of Citium, its founder, [*q.v.*, Note 51] being a disciple of the Cynic philosopher Crates), and was close to it in many ways. *Vd.* Diogenes Laertius, VII, 121; Juvenal, *Satires*, XIII, 121–2; Cicero, *De Finibus*, III, 20, 68; *De Officiis*, I, 45, 148.

26. *Aristippus of Cyrene* (I, 41, 148)

Aristippus the Elder (*floruit* early fourth century B.C.) was a pupil of Socrates, a self-indulgent teacher of rhetoric, who, according to Diogenes Laertius, II, 66, took a pride in being able to control all circumstances for his own pleasure. It was his grandson, Aristippus the Younger, who first taught the ideas (e.g. that immediate pleasure is the *summum bonum*) which subsequently became known as *Cyrenaic*, and it is not certain how many of them can correctly be attributed to his grandfather. The Cyrenaic philosophy was essentially amoral, since actions were seen as neither good or bad *per se*, but only in so far as they contributed to momentary pleasure or pain. Nor are the Cyrenaics to be equated with the Epicureans, who saw pleasure in totality, and not as a series of isolated delights. *Vd.*, Note 71 (Anniceris); Horace, *Epistles*, I, 1, 18; I, 17, 23.

192

27. *Epaminondas and Lysis* (I, 44, 155)

Epaminondas was educated by Lysis, a follower of Pythagoras, who had emigrated from Tarentum to Achaea and later to Thebes. Lysis has been credited with some of the verses which are extant under the name of Pythagoras (*Vd*. Diels, *Fragmente der Vorsokratiker*, I, 420) but this is by no means certain. The most notable achievements of Epaminondas were as commander of the Theban army in its victories over the Spartans at Leuctra in 371 B.C. and at Mantinea in 362, in which battle he was killed. According to Cornelius Nepos (*Epaminondas*, III), he was particularly noted for his wide culture, his courage, truthfulness and frugality. *Vd*. also Diogenes Laertius, VIII, 42; Cicero, *De Oratore*, III, 139.

28. *Dion of Syracuse and Plato* (I, 44, 155)

Dion, the uncle of Dionysius II of Syracuse, was an adherent of the Pythagorean school, until he was completely captivated by Plato when the latter visited Syracuse in 389 B.C. Dion, with the support of Plato, tried to realize in Dionysius Plato's ideal of a 'philosopher-king'. They failed miserably and were dismissed in 366. Dion returned in force and seized Syracuse in 355. His attempt to rule the city according to a constitution based on Plato's *Republic* failed, largely because intrigues against him forced him to become a tyrant in spite of his lofty ideals.

29. *Posidonius of Apamea* (I, 45, 159)

Posidonius (*c*. 135–*c*. 50 B.C.) was a disciple of Panaetius and a man of many interests; among them are numbered poetry, rhetoric, geography, geometry and lexicography in addition to the work on history and philosophy for which he is most famous. There are many testimonies to his distinction: Strabo refers to him as 'the most learned of our philosophers'; Cicero attended his school in Rhodes in 78 B.C., and refers to him as 'the greatest even of all the Stoics' (*De Finibus*, I, 1, 2); and Pompey went to Rhodes on his way back from the east in 63 to hear him lecture. Only fragments of his work remain, collected by Athenaeus. For his philosophy *Vd*. Introduction.

30. *Dicaearchus* (II, 5, 16)

Dicaearchus was born at Messana in Sicily, but emigrated to Greece, where he became a pupil of Aristotle. His works were numerous and covered many topics, philosophical, political, biographical, literary and geographical. Only fragments survive. Cicero, in the *Tusculanae Disputationes* (I, 31, 77), refers to his attempt to prove the corporeal nature, and hence the mortality, of the soul. No doubt this led him to consider the ways in which men die in the περὶ φθορᾶς ἀνθρώπων. Cicero mentions him several times in his letters (*Vd. Ad Atticum*, VI, 2, 3; XIII, 31, 2), and appears to have admired him as an exponent of the practical life in contrast to his contemporary Theophrastus, the exponent of the contemplative life.

31. *Military Disasters* (II, 6, 20)
Cicero is referring to the defeats by Caesar of Pompey at Pharsalus (48 B.C.), of Pompey's sons at Munda (45 B.C.), and of Scipio at Thapsus (46 B.C.). Pompey, defeated at Pharsalus, fled to Egypt where he was stabbed to death. *Vd.* Suetonius, *Divus Julius*, 35; 36.

32. *Dionysius I of Syracuse* (II, 7, 25–6)
Dionysius I ruled Syracuse from 406 to 367 B.C. He was a *strategos autokrator*—a constitutional tyrant, who greatly fortified Syracuse and built elaborate war-machines and a large fleet. His aim—to free Sicily from Carthaginian domination—achieved some short-lived successes and his influence extended beyond the island. He concluded alliances with Locri Epizephyrii, Alcas and possibly Taras. He destroyed Rhegium and may possibly have planted colonies well up the Adriatic coast and entered into relations with Rome, but there is no certain evidence of this. What is established is the alliance with Sparta, whose intervention to drive out the Carthaginian Himilco in 397 was later repaid with military help against Athens and Thebes. His undoubted unpopularity at home was due to his extravagence and oppression. The anecdote related by Cicero here is also recorded in *Tusculanae Disputationes* (V, 20, 58) and, with some variations, by Valerius Maximus (IX, 13, 4).

33. *Alexander of Pherae* (II, 7, 25–6)
Alexander succeeded his uncle Jason (*Vd.* I, 30, 108) as tyrant of Pherae in 369 B.C. His cruelty stood out in contrast to Jason's good diplomacy in his dealings with the cities of Thessaly. Cicero's facts are inaccurate here: his murder, according to Xenophon (*Hellenica*, VI, 4, 35) was planned by his wife, but carried out by her three brothers. Plutarch tells us that his wife's motive was one not so much of personal suspicion as of a general hatred of his cruelties, but he is the heir of a tradition which glorified Pelopidas at the expense of Alexander. *Vd.* Plutarch, *Pelopidas*, 26–35.

34. *Phalaris of Agrigentum* (II, 7, 26)
Phalaris (again referred to at III, 6, 29 as 'a cruel and inhuman tyrant') ruled Agrigentum from 570 to 554 B.C. His victims are said to have been imprisoned and roasted alive in a brazen bull. He was deposed by Telemachus, the grandfather of Theron. The letters attributed to him, which were the subject of a famous controversy between Bentley and Boyle, were proved by the former to have been written by a sophist, possibly in the second century A.D.

35. *Demetrius Poliorcetes* (II, 7, 26)
Demetrius (336–283 B.C.) was the son of Antigonus I, king of Macedonia. His army deserted to Pyrrhus (*q.v.* Note 65) because of their disapproval of his campaign against Lysimachus in 288 B.C. He was left in Cilicia with only a small force of mercenaries and forced to surrender to Seleucus, with whose encouragement, according to Plutarch (*Demetrius*, 52), he drank himself to death.

194

36. *Massilia* (Marseilles) (II, 8, 28)
Massilia had been for many years a staunch ally of Rome, supplying naval crews in the Second Punic War. In return Rome allowed her a considerable degree of independence within the Gallic *provincia*. Massilia supported Pompey in the civil war and was besieged and captured by Caesar (49 B.C.). Caesar had a model of the town constructed and carried in his triumphal procession in 44. The event is again referred to by Cicero with horror (*Philippic*, VIII, 6, 18); nor was it unique: *Vd.* Tacitus, *Annales*, II, 41; Persius, *Satires*, VI, 47.

37. *Sullae* (II, 8, 29)
Publius Cornelius Sulla, the nephew of Lucius Cornelius Sulla the dictator, presided over the sale of property of the proscribed in 82 B.C., and again in 46. In spite of his obvious distaste for the man, Cicero defended him (successfully), when accused by Lucius Torquatus of being a party to the Second Catilinarian Conspiracy (63). The speech—*Pro Sulla*—is extant. Caesar's city treasurer (*quaestor urbanus*) was one of the many *Cornelii Sullae* who were freedmen of the dictator, and accordingly took his name.

38. *Theopompus of Chios* (II, 11, 40)
Theopompus (born *c.* 378 B.C.) was the author of a history of Greece in twelve books (*Hellenica*—a continuation of Thucydides' history from 411 B.C. to the battle of Cnidus in 394). It was followed by a history of Philip of Macedon in fifty-eight books (*Philippica*). The *epitome* of the twelfth book is preserved in Photius. He was a pupil of Isocrates (*q.v.*, Note 5), whose view of history as subordinate to politics he adopted.
    Bardylis is referred to by Diodorus Siculus (XVI, 4) as 'King of the Illyrians'. He waged war with Philip of Macedon in 359 B.C. and was the father-in-law of Pyrrhus (*q.v.* Note 65).
    Viriathus was a Lusitanian guerrilla chief who rose from humble origin to champion his people against the Romans. Between 148 and 146 B.C. he achieved remarkable victories. Caius Laelius cannot be said to have broken him, as Caius Plautius and Claudius Unimanus were heavily defeated soon after Laelius' victory (147 B.C.). Viriathus, like Jugurtha some years later (*Vd.* Note 64) proved elusive, and his death was only finally secured by treachery.

39. *The Gracchi* (II, 12, 43)
Tiberius Gracchus the Elder (born 210 B.C.) was the father (by Cornelia, daughter of Scipio Africanus Major) of the two tribunes Tiberius and Caius Gracchus. As pro-praetor he won several successes against the Celtiberians in Spain (179 B.C.), and as consul reduced Sardinia (177 B.C.). His main constitutional reform was, as censor (169 B.C.) to confine the *libertini* to one tribe (*Tribus Esquilina*), thus restricting their political influence. Cicero also speaks of him in the *De Finibus* (IV, 24, 65), where he says, 'No one would deny that Tiberius Gracchus the Elder lived a more happy life than his son (Tiberius), since the former devoted his life to defending the constitution, the latter to subverting it.' Cicero's judgement

here is unduly harsh: Tiberius' Agrarian Law of 133 B.C. was a necessary measure of social justice and had the support of a notable constitutionalist, Publius Mucius Scaevola the Jurist. If Tiberius was unconstitutional in his methods, it was because the senate left him no alternative. Tiberius was put to death by Publius Scipio Nasica (9. *Vd.*, Note 18). His task of challenging the senate's authority was continued by his brother Caius (tribune, 123 B.C.). His measures resulted in the riots of 122, in which the consul Opimius obtained the supreme powers of the *Senatus Consultum Ultimum* for the first time, and Caius was killed.

40. *Letters from Philip to Alexander, etc.* (II, 14, 48)
Cicero does not seem to doubt the authenticity of the letters, which were proved by Bentley to have been forgeries. According to the *Souda*, there were two books of *Epistles* by Antipater, whom Alexander left as his regent on his departure to Asia in 334 B.C. Antigonus was one of Alexander's generals; he had two sons, Philippus and Demetrius Poliorcetes (*q.v.* Note 35).

41. *Aristo of Ceos* (II, 16, 56)
Aristo of Ceos (not to be confused with the Stoic Aristo of Chios—*Vd.* Note 6) became head of the Peripatetic school in 230 B.C. He was more distinguished as a writer than as a philosopher. All the MSS read *Aristoteles* here, but no such idea is to be found in Aristotle; on the contrary it conflicts with the ideas expressed in *Nicomachaean Ethics*, IV, 1. Aristo is known to have written a work on vainglory, and the sentiment quoted here is consistent with that attributed to Aristo by Plutarch, *Cato Major*, 18.

42. *The Ostentation of the Aedileship* (II, 16, 57)
Publius Crassus, surnamed *Dives* (aedile 105, consul 97 B.C.), was the father of Marcus Crassus the triumvir. L. Crassus the orator and constitutionalist foreshadowed Cicero, who greatly admired him. The expense of Quintus Mucius Scaevola as aedile (103) cannot have been trifling. Pliny the Elder (*Natural History*, VIII, 16) refers to his inauguration of multiple lion fights. For his ostentation, as well as that of L. Crassus and Claudius, *Vd.* Cicero, *In Verrem*, IV, 59, 133. Caius Claudius Pulcher instituted fights between elephants (99 B.C.). The Luculli staged a fight between elephants and bulls (79). Hortensius, the famous rival of Cicero who defended Verres in 70, was aedile in 75, Decius Junius Silanus in 70, Publius Cornelius Lentulus Spinther in 63. For the latter's lavish equipment of a chorus *Vd.* Valerius Maximus, II, 4. 6. Asconius speaks of large debts contracted by Scaurus during his year as aedile (58), and Pliny the Elder (*op. cit.* XXXVI, 24) of his lavish expense on a theatre. Pompey, in his second consulship (58), inaugurated his magnificent stone theatre with an exhibition unprecedented even in Rome. Valerius Maximus (*loc. cit.*) tells of 600 lions, 410 panthers and 20 elephants imported for the occasion. Cicero himself, as aedile in 69, put on three lots of games in honour of Ceres, Liber and Libera; for the expense *Vd. In Verrem*, V, 14, 36.

43. *Clodius and Milo* (II, 17, 58)

Publius Clodius Pulcher was prosecuted in 62 B.C. for appearing in women's clothes at the festival of the *Bona Dea*, held in the house of Caesar as *Pontifex Maximus*. It was Cicero's destruction of his *alibi* that secured his conviction. Clodius retaliated by engineering Cicero's banishment in 58, on the grounds that he had put the Catilinarian Conspirators to death without trial. Milo, tribune in the following year, tried to obtain Cicero's recall, and was opposed by Clodius. Gang warfare broke out, and in 52 Milo murdered Clodius. Clodius' supporters were so angered that they set fire to the senate house as his pyre. So hostile to Milo was the climate, that Cicero did not dare defend him, although he later published the speech *Pro Milone*, which is still extant.

44. *The Lex Annalis and Leges de Repetundis* (II, 17, 59; 21, 75)

Minimum ages for each office had been laid down by the *Lex Villia Annalis*, which was later modified by Sulla. They were: quaestor 30, aedile 36, praetor 39, consul 42. Cicero (born 106 B.C.) was quaestor in 76, aedile in 69, praetor in 66, and consul in 63. The achievement of being elected to each office *suo anno* is one of which he often speaks with pride: cf. *In Catilinam*, I, 11, 27; *In Pisonem*, 1, 1. *Brutus*, 93, 321.

The *Lex Calpurnia de Repetundis* of 149 B.C. had established a permanent court to try cases of bribery and extortion. It was succeeded by the *Lex Servilia de Repetundis*, enacted by the demagogue Glaucia in 105, which restored the jury courts to the *equites*. The *Lex Cornelia* of Sulla (81) created new courts and handed back control of the existing ones to the senate. The penalties for bribery were stiffened by the *Lex Julia* of Caesar in 59.

45. *Lysander, Agis and the tyrants of Sparta* (II, 23, 80)

The famous Spartan admiral, son of Aristoclitus, was never ephor. Cicero refers to Lysander the son of Libys, who supported the land reforms of Agis IV in 242 B.C. Their aim was to cancel the mortgages under which a large part of the citizen body laboured, and redistribute the land, which existed in large estates in the hands of the few. Idealistic, but naïve, they were outwitted and punished by the more reactionary ephors (*Vd.* Plutarch, *Agis, c.* 6–13). Cleomenes III married Agis' widow, Agiatis, and on becoming king in 235 B.C. inherited Agis' ideas of social reform and decreed a return to Lycurgus' constitution, cancelling debts, redistributing land, and replenishing the citizen body with *metics* and *perioeci*. Cleomenes was banished in 222, and died in Egypt two years later. A succession of tyrants followed, Lycurgus, Machanidas and Nabis. The latter was the victim of an Aetolian *coup d'etat* in 192. Sparta was compelled to join the Achaean League and become a *civitas foederata* in the Roman province of Achaea. *Vd.* Polybius, 13, 6–8; 16, 13–17; Livy, XXIX, 31–5; XXXVIII, 34.

46. *Scipio Africanus Major* (III, 1, 1)

Publius Scipio Africanus Major (6—*Vd.* Note 18) was for ten years in

197

supreme command of the war against Hannibal (212–202 B.C.). His success came first in Spain, where he defeated Hasdrubal (at Baecula in 208), and later in Africa, where he took the war in spite of strong senatorial opposition and defeated Hannibal at Zama in 202. A profound philhellene, he took over from Alexander the Great the concept of the world unified under a single leadership, but his success as a statesman did not equal his success as a general, and he soon retired to private life after the war.

47. Cato the Censor (III, 1, 1)
Marcus Porcius Cato the Elder (234–149 B.C.) was born of peasant stock, held the offices of quaestor, aedile, praetor and consul, but reached the height of his influence as Censor in 184 B.C. His foreign policy was the destruction of Carthage, in which he was opposed by Scipio Nasica Corculum (7—*Vd.* Note 18); but he lived to see only the beginning of the Third Punic War, in which his ambition was fulfilled. At home his aim was to strengthen the traditional customs and values of the Roman agrarian society, but he was not the vigorous anti-hellenist that he has often been portrayed (as can be seen from his portrait in Cicero's *De Senectute*). He was famous as an orator (80 fragments of his speeches are extant) and as the writer of the treatise *De Agri Cultura* and a history (*Origines*) in seven books.

48. Publius Rutilius Rufus (III, 2, 10)
Rutilius (consul 105 and 95 B.C.) was a man of great integrity who so firmly crushed the extortions of the *publicani* (*q.v.*, Note 66) when legate under Scaevola in Asia, that he was impeached as a result of a conspiracy among the *equites*. He retired to Smyrna, where he devoted the rest of his life to literary pursuits.

49. Apelles (III, 2, 10)
Apelles of Colophon (late fourth century B.C.) studied painting under Ephorus of Ephesus and Pamphilus of Sicyon. His fame as a painter was due mainly to his paintings of Philip and Alexander and the *Aphrodite Anadyomene* (Venus rising from the sea, a subject which later inspired many painters, notably Botticelli), to which Cicero refers here. According to Pliny the Elder (*Natural History*, XXXV, 10, 36), Apelles started another Venus, but, like the first it was unfinished when he died, and no one could be found to complete it, even thought the outline of the finished picture had been drawn.

50. Fabricius (III, 4, 16)
Gaius Fabricius Luscinus (consul in 282 and 278 B.C., censor in 275) is notable for his part in the war against Pyrrhus (*q.v.*, Note 65), particularly because of his incorruptibility in resisting the bribes both of Pyrrhus himself and of would-be betrayers. (*Cf.* I, 13, 40; III, 22, 86; *Vd.* also Cicero, *Paradoxa Stoicorum*, 50; Livy, *Perioche*, 13; Aulus Gellius, *Noctes Atticae*, III, 8).

51. *Aristides the Just* (III, 4, 16)
Aristides, the Athenian statesman—surnamed the Just, was archon in 489
B.C. and played an active part in the battles against the Persians at Marathon (490), Salamis (480) and Plataea (479). He also commanded the
Athenian navy in the capture of Sestus in 478, and it was due to his influence that the Ionian Greeks seceded from Pausanias and turned to
Athens. He was famous for his integrity, which did a great deal to win the
confidence of the Ionians in Athens when the Delian League was formed
after the Persian Wars. *Cf.* III, 11, 49. There seems to be no good reason
for regarding his name as an interpolation here, as Baiter and several subsequent editors have done. It would be perfectly natural for Cicero to link
the outstanding examples of integrity in Greek and Roman history, as he
also did at III, 22, 87.

52. *Gyges of Lydia* (III, 9, 38)
Gyges was a Lydian shepherd who founded the dynasty of the *Mermnadae*
by murdering King Candaules and marrying his widow. For the original
story *Vd.*, Herodotus, I, 8–12. He reigned from 685 to 657 B.C. His reign
is particularly notable for the invention of coinage and the origin of the
word *tyrant* (probably Lydian). Plato uses the story of the magic ring (*Vd.*
Republic, II, 359a et seqq.) to point the same moral that Cicero does. The
Gyges story is also the subject of a fragment of a Greek tragedy of unknown authorship discovered at Oxyrrhynchus and published by Lobel in
1950: *Vd. Proceedings of the British Academy*, vol. XXXV (1950), pp. 1–12.

53. *Tarquinius Superbus* (III, 10, 40)
Tarquinius Superbus (534–510 B.C.) was the last of the Roman kings.
The legends concerning his fall are of doubtful historicity. It was said that
Tarquin's son seduced Lucretia, the wife of Lucius Tarquinius Collatinus.
She told her husband of the outrage and then committed suicide. The
result was a popular rising against the king (led by Lucius Junius Brutus)
and his explusion. Rome was henceforth ruled by two consuls, the first
pair being Brutus and Collatinus. The latter was exiled with all the Tar-
quins, as he was the grandson of Aruns, the brother of Tarquinius Priscus,
and had fortified popular support by advocating restoration of property
to the former royal family. *Vd.* Livy, II, 2. Dionysius of Halicarnassus, V,
221.

54. *Romulus and Remus* (III, 10, 41)
For the legend of the birth and survival of Romulus and Remus *Vd.*
Livy, I, 3, 10 *et seqq.* Livy also tells how Romulus founded the city of
Rome on the Palatine Hill and walled it, and how he, or possibly his
lieutenant Celer, killed Remus for his contemptuous gesture of leaping
over the wall. The story is no doubt an aetiological myth to explain the
origins of the name Rome. The idea is Greek, as is the story of Romulus'
disappearance after a reign of forty years to become the god Quirinus.

199

55. *Chrysippus of Soli* (III, 10, 42)

Chrysippus of Soli (280–207 B.C.) was a pupil of Cleanthes, whom he succeeded as head of the Stoa in 232. His introduction to philosophy had been at the feet of Arcesilaus, the head of the *Academy*. He was later won over to Stoicism by Cleanthes. He was particularly famous for his propositional logic, which he used to devastating effect against Arcesilaus and the Middle Academy. He became so identified with Stoicism that he was for for future generations the exemplar of Stoic orthodoxy. Diogenes Laertius (VII, 183) goes so far as to say that if there had been no Chrysippus, there would have been no Stoa.

56. *Pennus, Papius, Crassus and Scaevola* (III, 11, 47)

Marcus Junius Pennus (tribune 126) was the author of the *Lex Junia de Peregrinis* (revived by Gaius Papius in 65 B.C.), which made all non-citizens liable to expulsion from Rome. *Vd.* Plutarch, *Caius Gracchus*, III; Aulus Gellius, *Noctes Atticae*, XV, 12; Dio Cassius, XXXVII, 9. Lucius Licinius Crassus and Quintus Mucius Scaevola (consuls 95 B.C.) passed the *Lex Licinia Mucia de Civibus Redigundis* which expelled the Latins from Rome. It was bitterly resented by the allies and contributed to the outbreak of the Social War four years later.

57. *Treatment of Pirates and Allies* (III, 11, 49)

The pirates of Cilicia had been put down by Pompey in 67 B.C. and settled at Pompeiopolis, but they renewed their activities during the Civil Wars and are believed to have been used by Antony against Brutus and Cassius.

Allies: for the treatment of Massilia *Vd.* Note 36. King Deiotarus of Galatia and others, who had given Pompey support in the Civil War against Caesar, were made subject to Roman taxes by Caesar's supporters.

58. *Diogenes of Babylon* (III, 12, 51)

Diogenes was born in Seleucia *c.* 240 B.C. He became a pupil of Chrysippus (*q.v.*, Note 55) and later taught Antipater of Tarsus (*q.v.* Note 59) and Panaetius. He succeeded Zeno of Tarsus as head of the Stoa, and was a member of the influential legation from Athens to Rome in 156–5 B.C. (the others were Carneades of Cyrene and Critolaus the Peripatetic), which first stimulated interest in Greek philosophy. *Vd.* Cicero, *Tusculanae Disputationes*, IV, 3, 5; Aulus Gellius, *Noctes Atticae*, VIII, 14; Pliny, *Naturalis Historia*, VII, 30.

59. *Antipater of Tarsus* (III, 12, 51)

Antipater (*floruit* mid-second century B.C.) was a pupil of Diogenes of Babylon (*q.v.*, Note 58), whom he succeeded as head of the Stoa, and a teacher of Panaetius. He was a bitter opponent of the Academics, and was said to have such fear of their dialectic that he avoided any open debate with them. (*Vd.* Cicero *Academica*, II, 17 et seqq.) He confined himself to writing and thus acquired the nickname καλαμοβόας, or *pen-scratcher*. Titles of two of his works are known, and his description of the end of life is recorded by Stobaeus (*Eclogae*, II, 11).

200

60. *The Criminal Fraud Laws of Aquilius* (III, 14, 60)
Caius Aquilius Gallus was a distinguished Roman jurist of the first
century B.C. He is described by Valerius Maximus as 'a man of great
authority, distinguished for his legal knowledge'. He was a disciple of
Quintus Mucius Scaevola (*q.v.*, Notes 39 and 56) and Cicero's colleague
as praetor in 66. Cicero (*De Natura Deorum*, III, 30, 74) refers to his
iudicium de dolo malo as 'the drag-net for catching all forms of wickedness'.
He is also credited with the *Lex Aquilia de Damno*, which laid down
penalties for damage to property.

61. *Hecato of Rhodes* (III, 15, 63)
Hecato was a pupil of Panaetius, and after him possibly the most influential thinker of the Middle Stoa. His work on moral obligation is one
of eight works whose names have been preserved. Some examples of the
kind of moral questions he discussed are quoted in III, 23, 89 *et seqq.*

62. *Gratidianus and Orata* (III, 16, 67)
Marcus Marius Gratidianus was the son (or possibly the grandson) of
Marcus Gratidius of Arpinum. The sister of the latter was married to
Cicero's grandfather; hence the reference to him as a relative here and at
III, 20, 80. The name Marius indicates his adoption by Marcus Marius,
brother of Caius Marius (consul 107–101 B.C.). According to Lucan
(*Pharsalia*, II, 75), he was murdered by Catiline in the Sullan proscriptions.
  Caius Sergius Silus Orata was praetor in 97 B.C., and is mentioned by
Cicero in *De Finibus*, II, 22, 70, and by Macrobius (*Saturnalia*, III, 15, 3),
who tells us that, like the Murenae, he got his surname because of his
fondness for goldfish.
  The case is also quoted in *De Oratore*, I, 39, 178.

63. *La Moure* (III, 19, 77)
La Moure is derived from the Latin *micare*; cf. Italian *morra*. One person
quickly raises a number of fingers and another immediately has to guess
at the number. They then check the guess. It was commonly practised as a
game of chance, and also, like tossing a coin or drawing lots, as a means
of deciding issues in doubt: *Vd.* Suetonius, *Divus Augustus*, 13. In the dark,
of course, each would rely entirely on the honesty of the other.

64. *Caius Marius* (III, 20, 79)
Caius Marius (157–86 B.C.) was a provincial from Arpinum who had no
distinguished ancestors and few hopes of high office. He was tribune in 119
and praetor in 115. Quintus Metellus (consul 109) had already won a
victory over Jugurtha in Numidia and was known by the surname *Numi-
dicus*, when Marius, his legate, declared his intention of standing for the
consulship. Both Sallust (*Jugurtha*, 64) and Plutarch (*Marius*, 8) agree that
Marius left to contest the consulship with the derision of Metellus; but he
won, and held the office for seven years (107–101), adding victories over
the Cimbri (*Vd.* I, 12, 38) and Teutones to his conquest of Jugurtha. The
latter was due largely to luck, but the former owed a great deal to the

201

military reforms which were his most important and lasting contribution to Roman life.

65. *Pyrrhus* (III, 22, 86)
Pyrrhus was the most notable of the Molossian kings of Epirus. During his reign (297–272) he freed Epirus from the influence of Macedonia and established it as an independent state. He exploited the unpopularity of Demetrius Poliorcetes (*q.v.* Note 35) and as a result won half Macedonia, Thessaly and an alliance with Athens and Aetolia. His first clash with Rome came in 280, when in response to an appeal by Tarentum he came over and defeated the Romans at Heraclea (280) and Asculum (279). He almost succeeded in expelling the Carthaginians from Sicily before returning to confront the Romans at the inconclusive battle at Beneventum (275). He was a brilliant general, but could not consolidate his victories and overstrained his country's meagre resources. His influence in Italy died with him.

66. *Cato Uticensis* (III, 22, 88)
Cato the Younger (grandson of Cato the Censor—*Vd.* Note 47) was the main opponent of Caesar in Africa. He committed suicide after the battle of Thapsus in 46 B.C., an action which won approval from Cicero for being entirely in accord with the austere standards of his character (*Vd.* I, 31, 112).

The *publicani*, members of the important *ordo equestris* who bought the right to collect taxes in the provinces, frequently petitioned the Senate for a rebate when they found that they had paid more than they could recover in taxes. Cicero, himself an *eques*, had a natural sympathy for them as well as a desire for their political support. His policy was therefore one of conciliation—*Vd. Ad Atticum*, I, 179. He was strenuously opposed by Cato, who insisted that they should adhere to their bargain. This was typical of his uncompromising integrity, but short-sighted politically, since many of the equites became opposed to the senate when their demands were refused, and were thus ready support for the Caesarian party. Cato was also ungenerous in his treatment of the brother of Ptolemy Auletes, an ally of Rome, during his annexation of Cyprus in 58 B.C.

67. *Ulysses' Feigned Madness* (III, 26, 97)
The story was that Ulysses pretended to be mad by yoking an ox and an ass to a plough and sowing salt. Palamedes suspected the trick and placed Ulysses' infant son Telemachus in the path of the plough. Ulysses stopped the plough and his ruse was discovered. He was then obliged to fight because of a promise made by all the suitors of Helen to defend the possession of whoever won her. The story is not known to have been part of any tragedy, but the Scholiast on Pindar, *Isthmian* IV, refers to a play (also mentioned by Hesychius), the *Odysseus Mainomenos* of Sophocles, which might well have dealt with this theme.

68. *The Twelve Tables, Sacred Laws and the Censorship* (III, 31, 111)
The Twelve Tables are the earliest Roman code of laws, drawn up by the *Decemviri Legibus Scribundis* in 451–450 B.C. They were published in the forum on wooden tablets, which were destroyed when Rome was burned by the Gauls in 390 B.C. One hundred and twenty-eight fragments (about one-third of the whole) survive in quotation. The scope of the laws is uncertain; Livy probably exaggerates when he says (III, 34, 6) that the Twelve Tables were the source of all civil and criminal law.

For the laws known as *Sacratae Vd.* Festus, *Glossaria Latina*, p. 318. They placed the guilty person under the sanction of a god. The censors were originally established in 443 B.C. to draw up a census of citizens and keep it up to date. They were to some extent the guardians of public morals, and had power to strike any citizen off the list of equites for perjury, immoral behaviour, maladministration, etc. The *Lex Ovinia* of 312 B.C. extended their power to senators, and the censorship remained a position of influence until reduced to a virtual sinecure by Sulla.

69. *Polybius* (III, 32, 113)
Polybius was a distinguished Greek, born at Megalopolis in 204 B.C., and sent to Rome in 168 as one of a deputation of a thousand to answer for the Achaean League the charge of refusing to help Rome against Perseus in the Third Macedonian War. He found a ready patron in Lucius Aemilius Paullus and became a life-long friend of his son, Scipio Aemilianus (12— *Vd.*, Note 18). It was under the patronage of the Scipionic Circle that he wrote his *Universal History* in forty books dealing with the period from 220 B.C. down to the fall of Corinth in 146. Only the first five books are extant *in toto*, although excerpts from the rest have survived. The passage here referred to (VI, 56 et seqq.) exists in a fragment.

70. *Acilius* (III, 32, 115)
Acilius was a contemporary of Cato the Censor and wrote a history of Rome down to his own time. Livy refers (XXV, 39) to *Annales Aciliani* translated from the Greek by a certain Claudius (probably Claudius Quadrigarius, the Sullan annalist).

71. *Anniceris of Cyrene* (III, 33, 116)
Anniceris was probably a contemporary of Alexander the Great, and, although himself a Cyrenaic, differed from Aristippus (*q.v.*, Note 26) in that he believed that certain loyalties, such as friendship and patriotism, are good *per se* and not merely inasmuch as they contribute to pleasure. He also opposed the Epicureans on two points: he did not accept that all human actions have one *telos*, but that each action has its own individual *telos*; he denied that pleasure was merely the absence of pain, for, if it were, then death would be a pleasure. His philosophy was completely overshadowed by Epicureanism, and no mention of it is recorded until Clement of Alexandria (*Vd. Stromateis*, II, 498b).

72. *Metrodorus of Lampsacus* (III, 33, 116)

Metrodorus was possibly the most distinguished of the followers of Epicurus, who dedicated his *Metrodorus* and *Eurylochus* to him. He won fame as an expounder rather than as an original thinker, as can be seen from the numerous fragments of his work that remain. His philosophy centred mainly round the cult of the body, and was more sensual that that of Epicurus. *Vd. De Finibus*, II, 28, 92; *Tusculanae Disputationes*, II, 6, 17; Clement, *op. cit.*, II, 417c.

73. *Cicero's Last Journey* (III, 33, 121)

Cicero, no longer feeling secure in Italy, departed for Greece in July 44 B.C., but his ship soon put back to land because of unfavourable winds. On landing he received news of an invitation from Marcus Brutus to work for his party and returned to Rome. His remaining energies were directed towards opposing Antony, and the invective of the *Philippics* flowed unabated. His death came in December of the following year, and he never saw his son again.

Chronological List
of Cicero's Works

B.C.	Speeches	Translations	Verse
85		Xenophon, Oeconomicus	Marius
84			Pontius Glaucus
81	Pro Quinctio		(early works of
80	Pro Roscio Amerino		unknown date)
?77	Pro Roscio Comoedo		
70	In Caecilium Divinatio		
	In Verrem, I & II, 1–5		
69	Pro Caecina		
	Pro Fronteio		
68	Pro Tullio		
66	Pro Cluentio		
	Pro Lege Manilia		
63	In Catilinam, I–IV		
	Contra Rullum		
	Pro Murena		
	Pro Caio Rabirio		
62	Pro Archia		
	Pro Sulla		
?61		Aratus, Phaenomena	
60		Aratus, Prognostica	De Suo Consulatu
59	Pro Flacco		
58			
57	De Domo Sua		
	Post Reditum ad Quirites		
	Post Reditum ad Senatum		
56	De Haruspicum Responso		
	De Provinciis Consularibus		
	In Vatinium. Pro Balbo		
	Pro Caelio. Pro Sestio		
55	In Pisonem		De Temporibus Suis
54	Pro Plancio. Pro Scauro		
53	Pro Rabirio Postumo		
52	Pro Milone		
?51		⎧ Demosthenes, Pro	
		Ctesiphonte	
46	Pro Ligario	⎨ Aeschines, In	
	Pro Marcello	Ctesiphontem	
45	Pro Rege Deiotaro	⎩ Plato, Protagoras	
44	↑ Philippicae I–XIV		
43	⏐ ↓		

N.B. Works not underlined are extant. Works semi-underlined are fragmentary.

# of Cicero

B.C.	Letters	Philosophy	Rhetorica
85			De Inventione, I–III
81			
80			
77			
70			
69			
68	↑		
66			
63			
62	↑		
61	Ad Atticum, I–XVI	Ad Quintum ↑ Fratrem I–III	
60			
59			
58			
57			
56			
55	Ad Familiares, I–XVI		De Oratore, I–III
54			Oratoriae Partitiones
53		De Re Publica	
52			De Optimo Genere Oratorum
51			
46		Academica Priora (Lucullus)	Brutus (De Claris
		Academica Posteriora	Oratoribus) Orator
45	Ad Brutum, I–II III–IX ↑	De Consolatione. De Fato	
		De Divinatione. De Finibus	
		De Natura Deorum. Hortensius	
		Tusculanae Disputationes	
		Cato Major (De Senectute)	
44		Cato Minor	Topica
		De Gloria	
		De Officiis	
		Laelius (De Amicitia)	
		Paradoxa Stoicorum	
43		De Virtutibus	
		De Legibus (published postumously?)	

Works underlined are totally lost.

INDEX
of Proper Names in the Text

References are to books, chapters and section numbers

Academics, I, 2, 6; III, 4, 20
Accius, III, 21, 84; III, 28, 102;
    III, 29, 106; Note 24
Acilius, III, 32, 115; Note 70
Aeacus, I, 28, 97; Note 22
Aeacus, Sons of, I, 12, 38
Aegina, III, 10, 46
Aemilius Paullus, Marcus, II, 22,
    76; III, 32, 114
Aequians, I, 11, 35; Note 15
Aesopus, I, 31, 114; Note 24
Agamemnon, III, 25, 95
Agesilaus, II, 5, 16
Agis, II, 23, 80; Note 45
Agrigentum, II, 7, 26
Ajax, I, 31, 113-14
Alexander of Macedon, II, 5, 16;
    II, 14, 48; Note 21
Alexander of Pherae, II, 7, 25;
    Note 33
Alexandria, II, 23, 82; III, 12, 50
Anien, River, III, 31, 112
Anniceris, III, 33, 116
Antigonus, II, 14, 48; Note 40
Antipater of Macedon, II, 14, 48;
    II, 24, 86; Note 40
Antipater of Tarsus, III, 12, 51;
    III, 23, 91; Note 59
Antippe, I, 31, 114
Antonius, Marcus, the orator, II,
    14, 49; III, 16, 67
Aquilius, Caius Aquilius Gallus,
    III, 14, 60; Note 60
Aquilius, Manius, II, 14, 50
Aratus of Sicyon, II, 23, 81
Areopagites, I, 22, 75

Arginusae, battle of, I, 24, 84;
    Note 19
Argos, II, 23, 81
Aristides the Just, III, 4, 16; III,
    11, 49; III, 22, 87; Note 51
Aristippus of Cyrene, I, 41, 148;
    III, 33, 116; Note 26
Aristo of Ceos, II, 16, 56-7; Note
    41
Aristo of Chios, I, 2, 6; Note 6
Aristotle, I, 1, 4: III, 8, 35
Arpenates, I, 7, 21
Atilius, Sextus Atilius Serranus,
    III, 30, 109
Atreus, I, 28, 97

Bardylis, II, 11, 40; Note 38
Basilus, Lucius Minucius, III, 18,
    73-4
Brutus, Lucius Junius, III, 10, 40;
    Note 53
Brutus, Marcus Junius, II, 14, 50

Caesar, Caius Julius Caesar Strabo
    Vopiscus, I, 30, 108; I 37, 133;
    II, 14, 50
Caesar, Caius Julius Caesar, the
    Dictator, I, 8, 26; I, 14, 43; I,
    31, 112; II, 1, 2; II, 24, 84; III,
    21, 82-4
Calliphon, III, 33, 119
Calpurnius, Publius Calpurnius
    Lanarius, III, 16, 66
Calypso, I, 31, 113
Canius, Caius, III, 14, 58

o

Cannae, battle of, I, 13, 40; III, 11, 47; III, 32, 113
Capitol, the, III, 16, 66
Carbo, Caius, II, 13, 47
Cassander, II, 14, 48
Cato, Marcus Porcius, the Censor, I, 11, 36; I, 23, 79; I, 29, 104; II, 25, 89; III, 1, 1; III, 4, 16; III, 29, 104
Cato, Marcus Porcius, grandson of the above, III, 16, 66
Cato, Marcus Porcius of Utica, son of the above, I, 31, 112; III, 16, 66; III, 22, 88
Catulus, Quintus Lutatius (consul 102 B.C.), I, 22, 76; I, 30, 109; I, 37, 133
Catulus, Quintus Lutatius (consul 78 B.C.), I, 30, 109; I, 37, 133
Caudine Forks, battle of the, III, 30, 109
Celtiberi, the, I, 12, 38
Chrysippus, III, 10, 42
Cicero, Marcus Tullius (Cicero's son), I, 1, 1; II, 1, 1; III, 2 5 et seqq.; III, 33, 121
Cimbri, the, I, 12, 38
Cimon, II, 18, 64
Circe, I, 31, 113
Claudius, Appius Claudius Pulcher, II, 16, 57
Claudius, Caius Claudius Pulcher, son of the above, II, 16, 57
Claudius, Tiberius Claudius Centumalus, III, 16, 66
Cleombrotus, I, 24, 84; Note 19
Cleomenes, II, 23, 80
Clodius, Publius Clodius Pulcher, II, 17, 58; Note 43
Clytemnestra, tragedy of Accius, I, 31, 114
Cocles, Horatius, I, 18, 61; Note 18
Collatinus, Lucius Tarquinius, III, 10, 40
Comedy, Old Attic, I, 29, 104; Note 23

Conon, I, 32, 116
Corinth, Destruction of, I, 11, 35; III, 11, 46
Cotta, Caius Aurelius, II, 17, 59
Crassus, Lucius Licinius, the Orator (consul 95 B.C.), I, 37, 133; II, 13, 47; I, 30, 108; II, 16, 57; III, 11, 47; III, 16, 57
Crassus, Marcus Licinius, the Triumvir (consul 70 B.C.), I, 8, 25; I, 30, 109; III, 18, 73; III, 19, 76
Crassus, Publius Licinius (consul 131 B.C.), II, 16, 57; Note 42
Cratippus, I, 1, 1; II, 2, 7; III, 2, 5; III, 7, 33; III, 33, 121; Note 1
Curio, Caius Scribonius, II, 17, 59; III, 22, 88
Cynics, the, I, 35, 128; I, 41, 148; Note 25
Cyrsilus, III, 11, 48
Cyrus, II, 5, 16

Damon, III, 10, 44
Decii, the, I, 18, 61; III, 4, 16; Note 18
Demetrius of Phalerum, I, 1, 3; II, 17, 60; Note 2
Demetrius Poliorcetes, II, 7, 26; Note 35
Demosthenes, I, 1, 4; II, 13, 47; Note 4
Diana, III, 25, 95
Dicaearchus, II, 5, 16; Note 30
Dinomachus, III, 33, 119
Diogenes of Babylon, III, 12, 51; III, 23, 91; Note 58
Dionysius the Elder, II, 7, 25; III, 10, 44; Note 32
Dio of Syracuse, I, 44, 155; Note 28
Drusus, Marcus Livius the Elder, I 30, 108

Ennius, Quintus, I, 8, 25; I, 16, 51; I, 24, 84; II, 7, 23; III, 29, 104; Note 12

Epaminondas, I, 24, 84; I, 44, 155; Note 27
Epicurus and Epicureans, III, 33, 116–18
Epigoni, tragedy of Accius, I, 31, 114
Eteocles, III, 21, 81
Euripides, I, 10, 32; III, 21, 81

Fabius, Quintus Fabius Labeo, I, 10, 33
Fabius, Quintus Fabius Maximus, I, 24, 84; I, 30, 108; Note 19
Fabricius, Gaius Fabricius Luscinus, I, 13, 40; III, 4, 16; III, 4, 16; III, 22, 86; Note 50
Faith (Fides, the cult of), III, 29, 104
Fetial Laws, the, I, 11, 36
Fimbria, Caius Flavius, III, 19, 77
Fufius, Lucius, II, 14, 50
Furius, Lucius Furius Phlius, III, 30, 109

Gracchus, Caius, II, 21, 72; Note 39
Gracchus, Tiberius the Elder, II, 12, 43; Note 39
Gracchus, Tiberius the Younger, I, 22, 76; I, 30, 109; II, 12, 43; Note 39
Gratidianus, Marcus Marius, III, 16, 67; III, 20, 80; Note 62
Gyges, III, 9, 38; II, 19, 78; Note 52
Gytheum, III, 11, 49

Hamilcar, III, 26, 99
Hannibal, I, 12, 38; I, 30, 108; III, 26, 99; III, 32, 113–14
Hecato of Rhodes, III, 15, 63; III, 23, 89; Note 61
Hercules, I, 32, 118; II, 17, 58; III, 5, 25
Herillus, I, 2, 6; Note 7
Hernicians, the, I, 11, 35; Note 15
Herodotus, II, 12, 41

Hesiod, I, 15, 48; Note 16
Hippolytus, I, 10, 32; III, 25, 94; Note 14
Homer, III, 26, 97
Horatius Cocles I, 18, 61, Note 18
Hortensius, Quintus, II, 16, 57; III, 18, 73; Note 42

Iphigenia, III, 25, 94
Isocrates, I, 1, 4; Note 5
Ithaca, III, 26, 97

Jason of Pherae, I, 30, 108; Note 33
Jugurtha, III, 20, 79; Note 64
Jupiter, III, 28, 102–5

Labeo, Quintus Fabius, I, 10, 33
Lacia, deme of, II, 18, 64
Laelius, Gaius Laelius Sapiens, I, 26, 90; I, 30, 108; II, 9, 31; II, 11, 40; III, 4, 16; Note 20
Lanarius, *Vd.* Calpurnius
Latins, I, 12, 38
Lentulus, Publius Cornelius Lentulus Spinther, II, 16, 57; Note 42
Leuctra, I, 18, 61; II, 7, 26; Note 27
Laws, *Vd. seqq.*
Lex Aquilia de Damno, III, 14, 60; Note 60
Lex Calpurnia de Repetundis, II, 17, 59; Note 44
Lex Junia de Peregrinis, III, 11, 47; Note 56
Lex Licinia Mucia de Rebus Repetundis, III, 11, 47; Note 56
Lex Ovinia, III, 31, 111; Note 68
Lex Plaetoria, III, 15, 61
Lex Villia Annalis, II, 17, 59; Note 44
Lucullus, Lucius Licinius Lucullus, I, 39, 140; II, 14, 50; II, 16, 57; Note 42

Lucullus, Marcus Licinius Lucullus, II, 14, 50; II, 16, 57
Lycurgus, I, 22, 76
Lydia, Gyges, king of, III, 9, 38; III, 19, 78; Note 52
Lysander, son of Aristoclitus, Spartan admiral, I, 22, 76; I, 30, 109
Lysander, son of Libys, Spartan ephor, II, 23, 80; Note 45
Lysis, I, 44, 155

Maelius, Quintus, III, 30, 109
Mamercus Aemilius Lepidus Livianus, II, 17, 58
Mancinus, Caius, III, 30, 109
Manlius, Lucius, III, 31, 112
Manlius, Titus Manlius Torquatus, III, 31, 112
Marathon, I, 18, 61
Marcellus, Marcus Claudius, I, 18, 61; Note 18
Marius, Caius, I, 22, 76; III, 20, 79; Note 64
Massilia (Marseilles), II, 8, 28; Note 36
Maximus, Quintus Fabius Maximus Cuncator, I, 24, 84; I, 30, 108; Note 19
Medus, tragedy of Pacuvius, I, 31, 114
Melanippe, tragedy of Accius, I, 31, 114
Metellus, Quintus, I, 25, 87; III, 20, 79
Metrodorus of Lampsacus, III, 33, 117; Note 72
Milo, Titus Annius, II, 17, 58; Note 43
Minos, I, 28, 97; Note 22
Mons Caelius, III, 16, 66
Mourre, La, III, 19, 77; III, 23, 90; Note 63
Mucius Manda, Quintus, I, 30, 109
Mucius Scaevola, Publius, II, 13, 47; Notes 39 & 56

Mucius Scaevola, Quintus, I, 32, 116; II, 16, 57; III, 11, 47; III, 15, 62; III, 17, 70; Note 42

Nasica, Publius Scipio, *Vd.* Scipio
Neapolis, I, 10, 33
Neptune, I, 10, 32; III, 25, 94; Note 14
Nicocles, II, 23, 81
Nola, I, 10, 33
Norbanus, Caius, II, 14, 49
Numantia, I, 11, 35; I, 22, 76; III, 30, 109; Note 15
Numicius, Titus, III, 30, 109

Octavius, Cnaeus, I, 39, 138
Octavius, Marcus, II, 21, 72
Odysseus, *Vd.* Ulysses
Oeconomicus of Xenophon, II, 24, 87
Oracle at Delphi, the, II, 22, 76
Orata, Caius Sergius, III, 16, 67; Note 62
Orestes, Cnaeus Aufidius Orestes Livianus, II, 17, 58

Pacuvius, Marcus, I, 31, 114; Notes 12 & 24
Palamedes, III, 26, 98; Note 67
Palatium (Palatine Hill), the, I, 39, 138
Panaetius, I, 2, 7; I, 3, 9; I, 26, 90; I, 43, 152; I, 45, 159; II, 5, 16; II, 10, 35; II, 14, 51; II, 17, 60; II, 22, 76; II, 24, 86; II, 25, 88; III, 2, 7 *et seqq.*
Papius, Caius, III, 11, 47; Note 56
Paullus, *Vd.* Aemilius
Pausanias, I, 22, 76
Pelops, III, 21, 84
Pennus, Marcus Junius, III, 11, 47; Note 56
Pericles, I, 30, 108; I, 40, 144; II, 5, 16; II 17, 60
Peripatetics, I, 1, 2; I, 2, 6; I, 25, 89; II, 5, 16; III, 4, 20; III, 29, 106

Phaedra, III, 25, 94; Note 14
Phaethon, III, 25, 94
Phalaris, II, 7, 26, III, 6, 29–32;
Note 34
Philip of Macedon, I, 26, 90; II,
14, 48; Note 21
Philip, son of Antigonus, II, 14, 48
Philippus, Lucius, I, 30, 108; II,
17, 58; II, 21, 73; III, 22, 87
Phintias, III, 10, 44
Phoenissae of Euripides, the, III,
21, 81
Picenum, III, 18, 74
Pinthia, Marcus Lutatius, III, 19,
77
Piraeus, III, 10, 46
Pirates, III, 11, 49; Note 57
Piso, Lucius Calpurnius, II, 21, 75
Plaetoria, Lex, III, 15, 61
Plataea, I, 18, 61
Plato, I, 1, 4; I, 5, 15; I, 7, 22; I, 9,
28; I, 19, 63–4; I, 25, 85–7; I,
44, 155; III, 9, 38–9; Notes 28
& 52
Plato, followers of, I, 1, 2
Plautus, I, 29, 104; Note 23
Polybius, III, 32, 113; Note 69
Pompeius, Cnaeus (Pompey the
Great), I, 22, 76–8; II, 6, 20; II,
13, 45; II, 16, 57; II, 17, 60;
Note 31
Pompeius, Quintus Pompeius
Rufus, III, 30, 109
Pompeius, Sextus, I, 6, 19
Pomponius, Marcus, III, 31, 112
Pontius, Caius Pontius Heren-
nius, II, 21, 75
Popilius, Marcus Popilius Laenas,
I, 11, 36
Posedon, *Vd.* Neptune
Posidonius, I, 45, 159; III, 2, 8–10;
Note 29
Postumius, Spurius, III, 30, 109
Prodicus, I, 32, 118
Propylaea, the, II, 17, 60
Ptolemy Philadelphus, II, 23, 82
Punic War, the First, I, 13, 39

Punic War, the Second, I, 12, 38;
I, 13, 40; I, 18, 61; I, 24, 84;
III, 11, 47; III, 32, 113; Notes
18 & 19
Punic War, the Third, I, 11, 35;
I, 23, 79; III, 26, 99; Note 15
Pyrrho, I, 2, 6; Note 8
Pyrrhus, I, 12, 38; II, 7, 26; III,
22, 86; Note 65
Pythagoras, I, 17, 56; I, 30, 108;
III, 10, 44; Note 17
Pythian Oracle, the, *Vd.* Oracle
Pythius, III, 14, 58

Quirinus (Romulus), III, 10, 41–2;
Note 54

Regulus, I, 13, 39; III, 26, 99–32,
115
Remus, III, 10, 41–2; Note 54
Rhodes, III, 12, 50
Romulus, III, 10, 41–2; Note 54
Roscius, Lucius of Ameria, II, 14,
51
Rufus, Publius Sulpicius, *Vd.*
Sulpicius
Rupilius the actor, I, 31, 114;
Note 24
Rutilius, Publius Rutilius Rufus,
II, 13, 47; III, 2, 10; Note 48

Sabine country, III, 18, 74
Sabines, the, I, 11, 35; I, 12, 38;
Note 15
Sacred Laws, the, III, 31, 111;
Note 68
Salamis, battle of, I, 18, 61; I, 22,
75
Samnites, the, I, 12, 38
Satrius, Marcus, III, 18, 73
Scaevola, *Vd.* Mucius
Scaurus, Marcus, I, 22, 76; I, 30,
108; II, 16, 57
Scipio, the Scipionic Family, *Vd.*
Note 18
Scipio, Gnaeus Cornelius Scipio
Calvus, I, 18, 61; Note 18

Scipio, Publius Cornelius Scipio, I, 18, 61; Note 18
Scipio, Publius Cornelius Scipio Africanus Major, II, 23, 80; III, 1, 1; III, 4, 16; Note 46
Scipio, Publius Cornelius Scipio Africanus Minor (Aemilianus), I, 11, 35; I, 22, 76; I, 25, 87; I, 26, 90; I, 30, 108; I, 32, 116; I, 33, 121; II, 22, 76; III, 4, 16; Notes 15, 18 & 21
Scipio, Publius Scipio Nasica, I, 30, 109 (1)
Scipio, Publius Scipio Nasica Corculum, Note 47
Scipio, Publius Scipio Nasica Serapio, I, 30, 109; Note 39
Seius, Marcus, II, 17, 58
Sergius, Vd. Orata
Serranus, Vd. Atilius
Sicyon, II, 23, 82
Silanus, Decius Junius, II, 16, 57
Socrates, I, 26, 90; I, 30, 108; I, 41, 148; II, 12, 43; II, 24, 87; III, 3, 11; III, 19, 77
Socrates, Followers of, I, 1, 2; I, 29, 104; I, 37, 134
Socratic Dialogues, I, 29, 104
Solon, I, 22, 75; I, 30, 108
Sophocles, I, 40, 142
Spinther, Vd. Lentulus
Stoics, The, I, 2, 6; I, 7, 22; I, 35, 128; I, 40, 142; III, 3, 11–14; III, 4, 20; III, 23, 91; III, 29, 105–6; Note 9
Sulla, Lucius Cornelius Sulla the Dictator, I, 14, 43; I, 30, 109; II, 8, 27–9; II, 14, 51; III, 22, 87; Note 37
Sulla, Publius Cornelius Sulla, nephew of above, II, 8, 29; Note 37
Sulpicius, Caius Sulpicius Gallus, I, 6, 19; Note 10
Sulpicius, Publius Sulpicius Rufus, II, 14, 49
Sun-god, Helios, III, 25, 94

Syracuse, III, 14, 58

Tantalus, III, 21, 84
Tarquinius Superbus (Tarquin the Proud), III, 10, 40
Terence, I, 9, 30; I, 42, 150; Note 13
Thebe, II, 7, 25
Themistocles, I, 22, 75; I, 30, 108; II, 5, 16; II, 20, 71; III, 11, 49
Theophrastus, I, 1, 3; II, 16, 56; II, 18, 64; Note 3
Theopompus, II, 11, 40; Note 38
Thermopylae, I, 18, 61
Theseus, I, 10, 32; III, 25, 94; Note 14
Timotheus, I, 32, 116
Torquatus, Vd. Manlius
Transpadani, III, 22, 88
Troezen, III, 11, 47
Tubero, Quintus Aelius, III, 15, 63
Tusculani, the, I, 7, 21; I, 11, 35; Note 15
Twelve Tables, the, I, 12, 37; III, 15, 61; III, 16, 65; III, 31, 111; Note 68

Ulysses, I, 31, 113; III, 26, 97–8; Note 67

Varro, Caius Terentius, III, 32, 114
Venus of Apelles, the, III, 2, 10; Note 49
Verres, II, 14, 50
Veseris, battle of, III, 31, 112
Veturius, Titus, III, 30, 109
Viriathus, II, 11, 40; Note 38
Volscians, The, I, 11, 35; Note 15

Wise Men of Greece, the Seven, III, 4, 16

Xanthippus, III, 26, 99
Xenocrates, I, 30, 109
Xenophon, I, 32, 118; II, 24, 87
Xerxes, III, 11, 48

Zeno of Citium, III, 8, 35

214